WALKING IN GRACE

2024

Acknowledgments

Every attempt has been made to credit the sources of copyrighted material used in this book. If any such acknowledgment has been inadvertently omitted or miscredited, receipt of such information would be appreciated.

Scripture quotations marked (AMP) are taken from the *Amplified Bible.* Copyright © 2015 by The Lockman Foundation, La Habra, California. All rights reserved.

Scripture quotations marked (AMPC) are taken from the *Amplified Bible, Classic Edition.* Copyright © 1954, 1958, 1962, 1964, 1965, 1987 by The Lockman Foundation.

Scripture quotations marked (ASV) are taken from the *American Standard Version Bible* (public domain).

Scripture quotations marked (ESV) are taken from the *Holy Bible, English Standard Version.* Copyright © 2001 by Crossway Bibles, a division of Good News Publishers. Used by permission. All rights reserved.

Scripture quotations marked (GNT) are taken from the *Holy Bible, Good News Translation.* Copyright © 1992 by American Bible Society.

Scripture quotations marked (GW) are taken from *GOD'S WORD Translation.* Copyright © 1995 by God's Word to the Nations. Used by permission of Baker Publishing Group.

Scripture quotations marked (ICB) are taken from *The Holy Bible, International Children's Bible®.* Copyright © 1986, 1988, 1999, 2015 by Tommy Nelson™, a division of Thomas Nelson. Used by permission.

Scripture quotations marked (JPS) are taken from *Tanakh: A New Translation of the Holy Scriptures according to the Traditional Hebrew Text.* Copyright © 1985 by the Jewish Publication Society. All rights reserved.

Scripture quotations marked (KJV) are taken from the *King James Version of the Bible.*

Scripture quotations marked (MSG) are taken from *The Message.* Copyright © 1993, 1994, 1995, 1996, 2000, 2001, 2002 by Eugene H. Peterson.

Scripture quotations marked (NABRE) are taken from *The New American Bible, Revised Edition,* © 2010, 1991, 1986, 1970 by Confraternity of Christian Doctrine, Inc., Washington, DC. All rights reserved.

Scripture quotations marked (NASB and NASB1995) are taken from the *New American Standard Bible.* Copyright © 1960, 1962, 1963, 1968, 1971, 1972, 1973, 1975, 1977, 1995 by The Lockman Foundation, La Habra, California. Used by permission.

Scripture quotations marked (NET) are taken from the *NET Bible®.* Copyright © 1996–2017 by Biblical Studies Press, L.L.C.; http://netbible.com. All rights reserved.

Scripture quotations marked (NIV) are taken from *The Holy Bible, New International Version.* Copyright © 1973, 1978, 1984, 2011 by Biblica, Inc. Used by permission of Zondervan. All rights reserved worldwide. zondervan.com

Scripture quotations marked (NKJV) are taken from *The Holy Bible, New King James Version.* Copyright © 1982 by Thomas Nelson.

Scripture quotations marked (NLT) are taken from the *Holy Bible, New Living Translation.* Copyright © 1996, 2004, 2007 by Tyndale House Foundation. Used by permission of Tyndale House Publishers Inc., Carol Stream, Illinois. All rights reserved.

Scripture quotations marked (NLV) are from the *New Life Bible,* copyright © 1969 by Christian Literature International. Used by permission. All rights reserved.

Scripture quotations marked (NRSV) are taken from the *New Revised Standard Version Bible.* Copyright © 1989 by the Division of Christian Education of the National Council of the Churches of Christ in the United States of America. Used by permission. All rights reserved.

Scripture quotations market (NRSVCE) are taken from the *New Revised Standard Version Bible: Catholic Edition,* copyright © 1989, 1993 by the Division of Christian Education of the National Council of the Churches of Christ in the United States of America. Used by permission. All rights reserved.

Scripture quotations marked (NRSVUE) are taken from the *New Revised Standard Version, Updated Edition.* Copyright © 2021 by National Council of Churches of Christ in the United States of America. Used by permission. All rights reserved worldwide.

Scripture quotations marked (PHILLIPS) are taken from *The New Testament in Modern English by J. B. Phillips.* Copyright © 1960, 1972 by J. B. Phillips. Administered by The Archbishops' Council of the Church of England. Used by permission.

Scripture quotations marked (RSV) are taken from the *Revised Standard Version of the Bible.* Copyright © 1946, 1952, 1971 by the Division of Christian Education of the National Council of the Churches of Christ in the United States of America. Used by permission.

Scripture quotations marked (TLB) are taken from *The Living Bible.* Copyright © 1971 by Tyndale House Publishers, Inc., Carol Stream, Illinois. All rights reserved.

Scripture quotations marked (TPT) are taken from *The Passion Translation.* Copyright © 2016 by Broadstreet Publishing Group, Savage, Minnesota. All rights reserved.

Cover and interior design by Müllerhaus
Cover photo by Dean Fikar / Getty Images
Monthly page opener photos from Unsplash
Indexed by Kelly Allen
Typeset by Aptara, Inc.

ISBN 978-1-959634-01-0 (softcover)

Printed and bound in the United States of America
10 9 8 7 6 5 4 3 2 1

Dear Friends,

Welcome to *Walking in Grace 2024*! We're excited to share this volume filled with 366 (that's right, it's a leap year!) encouraging devotions that will help you draw close to God each day. If you're new to *Daily Guideposts/Walking in Grace*, welcome to the family. If you're a devoted reader of many years, welcome back. We're so happy you're holding this book in your hands.

This year, our theme "Called to Peace" was inspired by Colossians 3:15 (NIV), "Let the peace of Christ rule in your hearts, since as members of one body you were called to peace. And be thankful." Our world changed over the past few years—we experienced a global pandemic that changed many of our lives, and we have experienced other significant cultural and political changes. Life can be unsettling. What a balm that Jesus assures us He never changes. He offers us His solace and comfort as we focus on His words in the Bible, where He tells us, over and over again, that He is a peace-bringer. What good news to set our minds upon, to hold close.

In a changing world, we praise God for His Word and His steadfastness. Our fifty-one writers called upon Him this year in the midst of their heartbreak, their worry, their joy, their delight, their grief, their blessings, and their celebrations. This book is filled with these moments from their lives, moments when they received His blessings with delight, moments when they grieved and sensed His nearness, moments when they saw God's work and praised Him for His beauty and care.

We are privileged to be joined by so many talented writers who share vulnerable, beautiful, sorrowful, and joyful stories from their own lives and their own faith walks. These fresh insights can open up a window into your own spiritual life and relationship with God to encourage and help you as you walk daily with the Lord.

Evelyn Bence reflects on the eternal value of some of her friends, valued by God even if they are not important in the world's eyes. Rhoda Blecker discovers her late husband has been buried in the wrong grave… and she is moved by God's sovereignty and love when she discovers his new eternal resting place. Nicole Garcia shares how God provides grace and patience to her as she parents a son on the autism spectrum. Edward Grinnan's beloved golden retriever, Gracie, has taken the reins again—she makes an adorable, funny cameo as a writer, just as she did in last year's book. Mark Collins shares a special conversation he had with a minister and what it can teach all of us. Sabra Ciancanelli revels in the pure, ineffable joy that God has gifted us through this beautiful world. Erin Janoso reflects on how even difficult situations like tense school board meetings can provide moments of learning and connectedness with her daughter. Rick Hamlin focuses on the joy and gift of another new grandson in his life. Pam Kidd shares about the hurt of church rejection and subsequent healing she's experienced. Tia McCollors tells us how even sharing a coloring book with her daughter can be a moment for God to help expand her generosity. Debbie Macomber recalls the sacrifices her father made for our country, ones she didn't know about until she was an adult. Adam Ruiz remembers his own health struggles as he encourages patients as a hospital chaplain. These are only a handful of the funny, touching, and thought-provoking stories you'll encounter within these pages.

Two beloved *Walking in Grace* writers weren't able to write for us this year; we will miss Julia Attaway and Bill Giovanetti's insightful voices and are eager to welcome them back in future editions.

We are excited to introduce you to two new writers who are joining us in the 2024 volume: Nicole Garcia and Adam Ruiz. We hope you enjoy getting to know them and find inspiration in their earnest, heartfelt offerings.

This year, we have six special series for you. Carol Knapp takes a deep dive into the Bible in "Seeking Connection in the Bible's Stories" to find God's guidance for her life as she personally connects with biblical stories and characters. Gail Thorell Schilling reveals surprises from her life and her practice of focusing on one "Star Word" each year at the start of Epiphany. Carol Kuykendall shares how she has learned to recognize and dwell on God's goodness in her life—in both small and big ways—in "Celebrate!!" Roberta Messner reflects upon people who have blessed her as she is given a chance to remember each of them in "Remembering Gratitude." Shawnelle Eliasen's Advent series, "A Christmas Offering," beautifully focuses on the intangible gifts we can bring the Lord during Advent season. And Marci Alborghetti shares movingly from the heart in "Seeking Joy in a Time of Grief," a journey through both the Holy Week season and Marci's search for peace throughout her mother's dementia and death.

As you draw close to God's heart this year, we pray you will be richly blessed by the peace of Christ.

Faithfully yours,
The Editors of Guideposts

P.S. We love hearing from you! We read every letter we receive. Let us know what *Walking in Grace* means to you by emailing WIGEditors@ guideposts.org or writing to Guideposts Books & Inspirational Media, 100 Reserve Road, Suite E200, Danbury, CT 06810. You can also keep up with your *Walking in Grace* friends on facebook. com/DailyDevofromGP.

JANUARY

*And the effect of righteousness
will be peace, and the result of
righteousness, quietness and
trust forever.*

—Isaiah 32:17 (ESV)

New Year's Day, Monday, January 1

I am sure that God who began the good work within you will keep right on helping you grow in his grace. . . . —Philippians 1:6 (TLB)

This year, I am not going to get the least bit upset over the fact that I haven't thought of, planned out, or written down any New Year's resolutions. But I am going to get excited that I have 366 days (leap year) to become a better person. I can work, help, accomplish, experience, worship, create, write, exercise, visit, fix, entertain, share, ponder, read, counsel, dance, and dream of ways to be better and do better with as much gusto as I can muster.

Instead of making resolutions, I am going to look at last year's calendar and remember all the people I spent time with and prayed for, things I did, places I visited, social engagements I participated in, and work I accomplished. After my trip down memory lane, I'm going to thank God for giving me the health, energy, and means to do all that.

Then I'm going to turn back to today, happy that my calendar is clean and fresh and that opportunities are everywhere, especially when it comes to helping others. I'm going to start by offering my neighbor a ride to the grocery store. It's a grand day, today, the very first day of a new year.

Oh, I'm also going to eat some pickled herring because my ancestors said it would bestow blessings on my family at the start of a new year. Hmm. Good thing I like pickled herring.

Heavenly Father, thank You for this New Year,
a chance to start again to be the person
You designed me to be. —Patricia Lorenz

Digging Deeper: 2 Corinthians 8:10–12;
Ephesians 1:4–5; Hebrews 3:12–14

Tuesday, January 2

Your word is a lamp for my feet, a light on my path.
—Psalm 119:105 (NIV)

For over twenty years, I've asked God to give me
a word to focus on for the upcoming year. Often
people want to know how I chose the word, and the
answer is, I don't. God does. I open my heart to Him
and seek His guidance. Invariably a certain word will
appear any number of times over the next few days.
I stop, pray, ask for verification, and if I see that
word again, then I know it's the one the Lord has
given me. I then seek that word in Scripture and pay
attention to how it is used and what God is saying to
me through His Word.

As I prayed about my word for this year, the Lord
steered me toward *trust*. As I look at retirement, I
knew I was going to need to put my trust in the
Lord as I step away from what is most familiar and
comfortable in my daily routine.

This year it came to me that, since I'm adding a
word to my life, perhaps it is time I start to eliminate
one as well. It didn't take me long to discover what
that word would be: *clutter*. This was God's first

assignment to me as I retire. It's time to clean out my closets, my kitchen drawers, and pantry. And, yes, hard as it is to surrender a single skein, even my yarn room.

Perhaps there's a word in your life that needs to be eliminated. Words like *doubt* or *fear*. Words like *hurry* or *distrust*. All you need to do is ask, and He will answer.

Father, help me to listen for Your words of wisdom, Your words of guidance. —Debbie Macomber

Digging Deeper: Proverbs 15:23, 25:11; Isaiah 55:11; Jeremiah 15:16; James 3:5–6

Wednesday, January 3

For I know the thoughts that I think toward you, saith the Lord, thoughts of peace....
—Jeremiah 29:11 (KJV)

I sat down for morning devotion, my thoughts racing. Some of them were pleasing, some mundane—too many of them downright disturbed by what I *hadn't* done for the Lord.

Given His promises to forgive my trespasses, why was I lingering overlong about my shortcomings? *I should be rejoicing about God's endless kindness,* I thought—His lavishly given mercies. Yet like a child the day after Christmas, staring at a pile of gifts and still unsatisfied, I felt incomplete. My failure to "take hold of that [list of perfect accomplishments] for which Christ Jesus took hold of me" (Philippians 3:12, NIV) had upended my quiet time.

The one day I was listening to an audio meditation that suggested I ask God what *He* thought about me. I was moved toward Jeremiah's beloved passage, as quoted above: "I know the thoughts that I think toward you..." New hope bloomed. "In the final analysis," I whispered to my heart, "these thoughts of inadequacy are from the 'accuser,' not from God."

Too often we draw a grim picture of what Christ thinks of us. In reality, it's not about how we see ourselves; it's about what the forgiving Lord sees in us. The potential. The plans He has for us. The small but godly things we do but forget we've done. Only He knows what's in our hearts to do for Him and how to help us do it.

Holy Spirit, thank You for showing me that my peace does not always rest upon my self-assessment but on how You see my heart. —Jacqueline F. Wheelock

Digging Deeper: Psalm 139:23–24; Revelation 12:10

Thursday, January 4

Be still, and know that I am God....—Psalm 46:10 (KJV)

Winter sunsets dazzle me most evenings as I watch them from my back porch.

Compared with their red and yellow brilliance other months of the year, the winter range of colors leans toward softer hues like peach, rose, and French vanilla. More than likely a scientific explanation exists for the color differences, but I prefer to think the change is intentional. With shorter daylight hours and cooler temperatures, the soothing shades encourage me to slow down, relax, and enjoy quieter times. Sipping a cup of hot tea and reading a good book by the fire on a cold night come to mind.

Maybe God thought the same when He painted the winter sky with such pleasing and peaceful colors at sunset. Perhaps He created the mellow tones to make us pause and appreciate His artwork. Or possibly He knew from the beginning of time we would develop hundreds of ways to run ourselves ragged, as my grandmother used to say about folks never stopping to enjoy their blessings.

Whatever the reason, I'm grateful for God's calming touch as night approaches—reminding me of a parent tucking a blanket around a sleeping child, kissing their cheek, and whispering, "sweet dreams." How blessed I am to have a Heavenly Father who wraps me in His everlasting arms day and night so I can rest in Him.

Lord, thank You for providing our weary souls refuge, rest, and renewal. May we wake up refreshed each morning, choose the blessed path You offer us, and walk it daily. —Jenny Lynn Keller

Digging Deeper: 2 Samuel 22:31–33; Psalm 23:1–3; Matthew 11:28–29

And Jesus grew in wisdom and stature, and in favor with God and man. —Luke 2:52 (NIV)

The January wind stung my face as I walked along the sidewalk. My dog, Old Sport, picked his way around frozen patches of ice.

"We're almost home, boy," I said.

I was eager to get out of the cold. But I was not looking forward to finishing my repetitive routine. Pack briefcase. Eat breakfast. Drive to office. Work until five.

Sport and I had recently spent Christmas with my family. I had enjoyed the change of pace—the freedom and flexibility to spend time how I wished. Sport had enjoyed the energy of the holiday season. But normal life had resumed. Sport and I passed a curbside Christmas tree. Its branches looked thin and brittle. Sport sniffed them.

"It's just a tree now, Sport," I said. "The magic is gone."

Sport paused, still looking at the Christmas tree. He tilted his head. I wondered how Joseph felt when he and Mary returned home from the first Christmas in Bethlehem. Joseph had spoken with angels and seen prophecies fulfilled. And then—back to the carpenter's bench. Revelation exchanged for repetition.

There must have been so many ordinary days between the first chapters of Luke. But didn't those ordinary days hold their own importance? Those were the days when the Christ-child learned and stretched and grew into the man who would one day carry a cross.

Today might be an ordinary day. But it was also an opportunity to grow and draw closer to the Lord.

"Sport," I said. "Time to go. I have important things to do."

And together, we finished our route home.

Jesus, help me to use each day to become more like You. —Logan Eliasen

Digging Deeper: 1 Samuel 2:26; 2 Peter 3:18

Feast of the Epiphany, Saturday, January 6

You, LORD, keep my lamp burning; my God turns my darkness into light. With your help I can advance against a troop; with my God I can scale a wall. —Psalm 18:28–29 (NIV)

Our family room is lit by two fake Tiffany-style table lamps—cheap knockoffs we bought as temporary lighting until the kids were gone and we could afford new ones. (New lamps, I mean, not new kids.)

The kids are now gone; the lamps remain. One lamp had a nice bend in the shade. I balanced that out by knocking its mate to the floor while taking out the Christmas tree. Now they match.

I don't know why we keep the off-brand, off-kilter lamps—probably because they still work, albeit a bit mangled. As I age, my night vision worsens; without a simple light from a simple lamp, I would've stubbed my simple toes a countless number of times.

That's all the Magi had: a simple, faint light in the East. But they were following more than a star. They were following some gut-level faith that said, *Yes, this is where our journey takes us*. No doubt there were a few stubbed toes along the way, yet they persisted.

I would love to have that kind of resolute conviction: to believe that my journey was guided by a distant light. Truth is, my guiding light has taken several spills, most of them caused by me. I do my best—through my imperfect vision—to sidestep the shadows and follow the lit path before me. Despite many falls, I'm still here. To paraphrase the old country song attributed to Martha Ellis, I ain't broke, though I may be badly bent.

Lord, in our darkness, keep our pathways lit.
—Mark Collins

Digging Deeper: Exodus 10:23; Nehemiah 9:19

Sunday, January 7

STAR WORDS: Surprise

…and the star they had seen when it rose went ahead of them until it stopped over the place where the child was. When they saw the star, they were overjoyed. —Matthew 2:9–10 (NIV)

Until I learned about the spiritual practice of star words, Epiphany most reminded me of the year that Curate Herb processed down the church aisle dangling a glass star above his head. Close behind, a tall parishioner beamed a flashlight through the star to dramatic effect. Behind both shuffled three pint-sized magi in nativity play regalia. Curate Herb intoned: "Follow the star! Be people of the star!" A memorable service.

These days, I follow the star all year using my star word. Each Epiphany, a member of the clergy chooses words at random for parishioners who request them. The word guides meditation, prayer, and reflection, much like the star guided the magi. The star word also helps us to discern God's presence in past events as well as in the coming year. Many denominations participate in this spiritual practice.

This year my word is *surprise*. Already I'm primed for the unexpected, whether joyful or not. I started by looking up the origins of my word in both dictionary and concordance and was *surprised* to learn that it's often used in a context of battle, as in surprising the enemy. (I hope I am not to be surprised this way!) Already I'm focused on unpredictable places where I may discern God on my faith journey. Already I'm following His example. No flashlight needed.

All-knowing Father, secure in Your love,
no surprise can shake me—at least, not for long.
—Gail Thorell Schilling

Digging Deeper: Luke 21:25; 1 Corinthians 15:41;
2 Peter 1:19

...Rejoice with me; I have found my lost coin.
—Luke 15:9 (NIV)

When I see a penny on the ground, I pick it up and throw it into my purse. Some of the coins are shiny. Some of them, to use an old phrase, "have been through the wringer"—maybe like Tracey, who's been on dialysis for years; like Robert, losing his way through an emotional maze; like Ted, who can't beat his drug addiction. Last week, I tried to give correct change to my friendly gas station guy. But he pushed back the mangled pennies. "I don't want these," he said. "Customers won't take them."

"But—" I stifled my protest that they were legal tender, coins of the realm. I closed my palm around the nicked, dirty pennies and took them home.

This evening, from the corner of my eye, I catch a glimpse of the coins that have landed in a jar on my dresser. But this, I know, is not their final resting place. Feeling drawn toward a mundane activity, I dump out the cache and set aside fifty pennies to line up and roll into a paper tube. As I nudge and poke at the coins, I place hardly recognizable pennies alongside shiny new Lincoln heads. Fifty accounted for, safe and secure, I close the ends and set the roll aside, ready to hand in at the bank.

And now, as I pray for friends Tracey and Robert and Ted, I envision them as coins of an otherworldly realm—battered down, beaten up—but accepted at face value where it counts.

Lord, just as I am, I turn to You for redemption.
—Evelyn Bence

Digging Deeper: 2 Samuel 9:1–13

Tuesday, January 9

As iron sharpens iron, so one person sharpens
another. —Proverbs 27:17 (NIV)

The gym held the mid-morning regulars. The ultrafit
early birds had flown. The lunch-hour fits hadn't
arrived. I'd found my place in the center, where
middle-aged folks fight hard when numbers on the
scale threatened to rise like our years.

"Morning," said my friend on the elliptical. He
smiled and glanced at the clock. "You're right on time."

"Yep!" I said. "And you're doing great!"

I climbed on the stationary bike. "Morning,
Joanie," I said to the woman next to me. We chatted
as we pushed pedals. She shared a fitness setback, and
I listened with empathy because I'd been there too.

I love this gathering of people. Most of us are
recovering from surgeries and started at the gym after
physical therapy. There's a commonality. A desire to
encourage. An openness with struggles. A willingness to
be a balm to others—and to allow others to be a balm
to us. Transparency is key.

It was easy to draw a parallel between the physical
and the spiritual. Recently, a young mama I mentor
shared a sin struggle she'd been trying to conquer alone.

"Why didn't you tell me sooner?" I asked.

"I didn't want you to know."

My spirit saddened. Maybe the desire to guard her struggle was her own pride. But maybe it was mine. Had I been transparent in my own struggles? Had I allowed her to see them so that she could see God's faithfulness too? What a checkpoint. I want to be as genuine as my gym friends. For my experiences to be used for the benefit of others.

"Joanie, you can get back on track," I said.

She nodded.

Iron sharpens iron, and sharing is part of the sharpening.

Lord, if my struggles can help others, let me be humble. Amen. —Shawnelle Eliasen

Digging Deeper: James 5:16

Wednesday, January 10

Rejoice always, pray without ceasing, give thanks in all circumstances, for this is the will of God in Christ Jesus for you. —1 Thessalonians 5:16–18 (NRSV)

Haven't we all scratched our heads at Paul's injunction to pray without ceasing? *How on earth am I going to do that?* I wonder. In the crux of a busy day, I figure I'm doing OK by reading a few Psalms at breakfast and carving out some meditative prayer time on the sofa. How do I squeeze in more?

One morning after a half hour on our lumpy couch, I felt wholly inadequate. Sure, I'd concentrated on a short Bible verse and mentioned the names of people who had needs that had to be addressed, but I was chagrined about how much time I had spent *not* praying, instead fretting about my own mundane concerns—a work meeting, emails to answer, bills that needed to be paid, an assignment I had taken on. They all seemed like distractions from my spiritual purpose.

Wait a minute, I thought. *Wasn't I unwittingly putting all that stuff in God's hands? The mind had wandered in prayer. Why wouldn't God be wandering with it?*

This is the key, I think, to an enriching spiritual life. Bringing God into stuff that we normally keep Him out of. Like writing those checks and typing that email and prepping for that meeting. God is with us all day long, even if we forget to acknowledge it.

I greet the morning by giving God the hours, the minutes, and all the worries that come with them. Later I might occasionally murmur "God!" quietly, but He's always here whether I address Him or not. Without ceasing.

Today, Lord, I shall not forget Your presence, whether I express myself in words or not. —Rick Hamlin

Digging Deeper: Jeremiah 33:3; Romans 8:26; Philippians 4:6

Thursday, January 11

Let your unfailing love surround us, LORD, for our hope is in you alone. —Psalm 33:22 (NLT)

What gifts has the pandemic brought? The question from a podcast offended me. Upheaval and unrest in America. A million deaths. Many more had been gravely ill or lost jobs. Healthcare workers were burned out. What could be the gift in any of that?

The long-lasting pandemic changed many things for me and my family too. Loved ones became sick and died. Shut-in relatives were sad and lonely. The gym I visited daily shut down for months. My high-school daughter was sent home for remote learning. The following year, her senior activities were curtailed. My husband, who had traveled weekly, started working from home.

Instead of going to in-person Bible study twice a week, my group met via Zoom. Our family now attended church online and worshipped from our living room couch. I ordered groceries that were loaded into the back of my SUV. No lunches with friends. I rarely saw those who didn't live in my household. *How could any of those things be gifts?*

I shrugged off the question, but it wouldn't let go of me. If God is sovereign, good, and loving all the time, which He is, then times of pain are no less blessings than times of prosperity. Gifts are wrapped in different packages, yet they still contain blessings.

What gifts has the pandemic brought me? The realization that despite my circumstances, whether good or bad, with God, I am always blessed.

Lord, help me to see Your gifts in every burden I bear.
—Stephanie Thompson

Friday, January 12

Now may the Lord of peace himself give you peace at all times and in every way. The Lord be with all of you. —2 Thessalonians 3:16 (NIV)

For years, my husband and I have been looking for a house. We love the home we bought over a decade ago, but that was before we had children and a dog, and our needs have changed.

Every few months, a house comes on the market that's a good fit. We go see it and work through the process of whether to put in an offer or not. Mostly, the answer is not.

One night, our neighbor texted us that they were selling and asked if we were interested in looking before they put it on the market. Of course we were!

The house had the bedrooms and baths we needed, plus lots of other features we hadn't dared to wish for. Then, we heard from another friend who had visited the house. And another. We were shocked to find out that the house already had six offers on it.

Brian and I prayed, visited the house again, submitted our best offer, and, in the end, did not get it. Why? Hadn't God basically walked this house right into our hands? We knew while the house might have seemed great, we couldn't force a new house for ourselves if it wasn't in God's plan right now.

Walking away from the situation, I can truly say that we felt peace. Now, when a house comes on the market, I don't stress that I'll make a bad decision; I trust that God will open the front door to our new house wide open when the timing is right.

Thank You, Lord, for the peace You give me, even amid disappointment and closed doors.
—Ashley Kappel

Digging Deeper: Philippians 4:6; 1 Peter 5:7

Saturday, January 13

For I know the plans I have for you.
—Jeremiah 29:11 (NIV)

Wait, what was I doing with my hand up?
Our rural community ambulance service posted a call for volunteer drivers. Years ago, my husband had been a first responder. He decided to sign up. Since he offered to buy dinner on the way, I went with him to the meeting. And found myself volunteering.

I left the meeting with mixed feelings. Even with my experience doctoring cattle on the ranch, I felt inadequate for the calling. I'd never remotely considered helping people in life-or-death situations on a regular basis. Could I mentally deal with human illness and trauma? Was I up for this? Was it God's will for me?

I went deep into prayer. If I volunteered like this, I would be dispatched to assist someone on the worst day of their life, when they were most vulnerable and in pain. Odds are, in this small community, I would know the patient.

But as I went to more meetings, other personnel's experiences resonated with mine. "I had zero medical experience when I started," Pam, an EMT, said. "I had no idea when I went to my first training that I would love it so much that I would still be doing it thirty years later."

Looking around the room, I saw mostly volunteers. Dairymen, hay growers, ranchers, retirees. Nobody was in it for the money. Everyone was there to help their community. And the need was great.

Lord, I hear the call. Please give me the strength to help others. —Erika Bentsen

Digging Deeper: Isaiah 41:10; Romans 8:31

Sunday, January 14

Two people are better off than one, for they can help each other succeed. —Ecclesiastes 4:9 (NLT)

Squeezing a thirty-two-inch-wide couch through a twenty-seven-inch-wide front door was not mathematically possible, so my husband, Kevin, and I maneuvered the lanky piece of old furniture through the double doors off the back deck of our cabin in northern Arizona.

To the top of twelve steps. Covered in snow.

Our dog, Mollie, danced around us as we hefted the unwieldy mass—a hide-a-bed that I swear weighed seven thousand pounds.

"A bit more to the right," I cautioned Kevin, who, at the front end, had the added burden of walking backwards. "No, to the left." Inch by inch, we lugged the couch down the steps and around the cabin, taking breaks when our muscles screamed for mercy.

After we finally hefted the old couch into the back of our truck, we eyed the new couch sitting in the driveway with reluctance.

"On the count of three, let's lift together," Kevin instructed as I got in position.

As we retraced the path we had just finished, I couldn't help but think of the different burdens we had shouldered in our forty years of marriage. Several miscarriages. A breast cancer diagnosis. Pressures in Kevin's job as a pastor and a mayor. The loss of our parents.

That night as I nestled into the new couch in front of a glowing fire in the fireplace, I sent up a prayer of thanks that I had someone to help lift the weight and share the load.

Jesus, in marriages and friendships, You provide people to share the heavy lifting. Thank You.
—Lynne Hartke

Digging Deeper: Psalm 68:19;
Ecclesiastes 4:10

Martin Luther King Jr. Day, Monday, January 15

...do not forget the things your eyes have seen or let them fade from your heart as long as you live. Teach them to your children and to their children after them. —Deuteronomy 4:9 (NIV)

This January, snowy weather shut down my community's annual MLK Day march, allowing me a day to rest and reflect on the legacy of Dr. Martin Luther King Jr. My reflections led me to a treasure my late mother had left behind—a 2014 church newsletter in which she shared a first-person account of the 1963 March on Washington led by Dr. King.

As I read my mother's words, I felt her excitement, even six decades later. She spoke of "rumors of expected trouble, low participation, and possible groups of 'bandits' intent on harming marchers." Yet she and my father "were not to be discouraged."

Her account of the march is glorious: "The day dawned hot and humid—not a cloud in the sky." Three buses that transported fellow church members from our hometown Baltimore to Washington, DC, "were filled with excited marchers in great spirit and voices as we sang freedom songs on the way."

When the group reached the Washington Monument, "the thousands, many more than predicted, who made their way from all over the country, marched, sang, cooled our feet in the Reflecting Pool, greeted strangers, shared experiences, met and listened to civil rights leaders and celebrities."

Though I was born years after this historic day, my mother's essay serves as a front-row seat to one of the most epic events in history and lives on as a legacy for me and my children.

Lord, thank You for the stories and admonishments of my ancestors; may they point me to You.
—Carla Hendricks

Digging Deeper: Deuteronomy 11:19–21; Esther 9:28

Tuesday, January 16

When times are good, be happy; but when times are bad, consider this: God has made the one as well as the other. —Ecclesiastes 7:14 (NIV)

I was chatting with a friend the other day about the last few difficult years and the toll they have taken.

"I wish we had a time machine," she said. "So things could go back to the way they were."

There are days when I wish that too, but time moves in one direction and one direction only. The one force that exists outside the bounds of time is God. He connects the past to the present to the future because He exists everywhere.

I think as we move through time, we move closer to God. Time is our path to Him, our spiritual trajectory. I don't know how many times I've wished I could go back and fix the mistakes I've made or relive the difficult times in my life with more wisdom and faith. And maybe those times were difficult precisely because I lacked sufficient faith. Yet those were also the times when I learned and grew. My faith was made stronger even when I doubted it, even when I resisted. And I have resisted God's will as often as I have accepted it.

I felt bad for my friend, so I said, "We do have a time machine. We're in it right now; we just can't go backwards, only forward. There's no reverse gear!"

That got a smile out of her, and we both felt a little better about these past few years, realizing that the temporal breeze was in our hair.

Lord, You are with us always, past, present, and future. I pray my faith grows as I move closer to You.
—Edward Grinnan

Digging Deeper: Psalm 37:18–19; Ecclesiastes 3:1–11; Mark 10:29–31

Wednesday, January 17

Now to him who is able to do immeasurably more than all we ask or imagine, according to his power...—Ephesians 3:20 (NIV)

Bumping down our long driveway in my Subaru, I glanced ruefully up at the sky. For weeks, it'd been a gray-white monotone that blended almost seamlessly with the frozen white of the world beneath it. *And with the low ebb of my spirits,* I thought with a frown. Sometimes it felt hard to be bright when the world around me wasn't. I'd been so excited that today's forecast had called for sunshine. But it looked like a few measly breaks in the clouds were all I was going to get. I sighed. It didn't feel like enough.

But then, I rounded the driveway's next bend...and brought the car to a sliding stop. The clouds had shifted overhead. Sunlight—abundant, angled, and golden—poured across the snowy landscape in front of me, painting everything it touched with deep shades of amber, pink, and orange. Birch and aspen trees, adorned in lacy cloaks of delicate hoarfrost, seemed to glow from within like blazing copper torches. And ice crystals, suspended in the air, glittered like diamond dust, causing the very air to sparkle.

I stared, mouth agape. Tears pricked my eyelids. Just seconds ago, I'd been ruing the clouds, sure I was missing out on something I needed. But, as I gazed at the light-filled masterpiece in front of me now—more brilliant than anything I could've ever known to hope or pray for—I knew. I needn't worry or grasp. God had my needs covered. And then some.

Thank You, God, for Your light. For Your limitless imagination. And for this priceless glimpse of Your glory. —Erin Janoso

Digging Deeper: Job 37:22; Matthew 6:28–31; Luke 12:22–31

Thursday, January 18

... "I do believe; help me overcome my unbelief!"
—Mark 9:24 (NIV)

I stood in line in a local department store with my cart full of items, inching slowly through the maze of shelves meant for last-minute purchases.

In the past, I had always ignored the chaotic display of random things—copper mugs, bags of pasta shaped like trains, and fuzzy socks. Yet this time, something caught my attention. It was a long, white, wooden block with gray typewriter font proclaiming "The Best Is Yet to Come."

I scoffed at those words. *The best is well behind me,* I thought.

I couldn't imagine anything in the future that I would ever identify as the best. The best was when I lived in France and traveled through Europe for a year. The best was when my kids were younger and raced toward me yelling "Mami" every time I walked through the door. The best was when I visited my parents in Florida to relax by the pool, not like my recent visit when I realized my father's dementia is getting worse.

Despite all of my skepticism and negativity, I picked up this ridiculous block and added it to my cart. I took it home and put it against my window where I could see it each day. I displayed it, not because I believed those words, but simply in hope that one day I would.

Lord, help us to hold on when we cannot see beyond our circumstances. Remind us that our hope and future is in Your loving hands. —Karen Valentin

Digging Deeper: Isaiah 40:31; Hebrews 11:1

Friday, January 19

Many designs are in a man's mind, but it's the LORD's plan that is accomplished. —Proverbs 19:21 (JPS)

"How old would you be if you didn't know how old you are?" asked my friend Janet.

The question took me by surprise. I had never before thought about age that way. I was much more accustomed to "How old do you feel?" A "feeling" way of looking at the issue made me think about the years we spend losing things we used to do: I used to be able to do a cartwheel but no longer; I used to lift a fifty-pound package as if it weighed nothing; I used to be able to hike in the Grand Canyon. Sometimes I even wondered why God had made us with "declining years"—years in which to resent the limitations of aging.

But Janet's question drew me away from what I couldn't do physically into thinking about how I had grown spiritually. It had taken me a very long time to learn I could accept help and to recognize that I was blessed with caring friends. That was a gift I might never have received back in the days when being independent was a matter of pride. I had learned to accept help graciously, and now I could accept what I had lost, too, because there were huge compensations in recognizing what God had decided was best for me.

Janet was waiting patiently for an answer.

"Well," I said, "not a teenager by any means or in my twenties. Maybe about fifty, when I'd stopped thinking about myself and started thinking more about why God put me here."

You always know better than I do, God, and I have to relearn that every single day. Thank You for Your patience. —Rhoda Blecker

Digging Deeper: Ecclesiastes 3:1; Jeremiah 12:16

Saturday, January 20

...for the kingdom of God belongs to such as these. —Luke 18:16 (NASB)

She comes to me with her big, questioning brown eyes...

"Pop Pop?"

My apologies to all other grandparents out there, but this little girl standing in front of me is the cutest, bravest, most curious creature on earth.

She holds up a little stuffed dragon and smiles. At least, it looks like a dragon to me. To her, it's a baby dinosaur. I know what to do. I take the toy, do my best Mister Rogers, and start in with Baby Dinosaur voice.

Now, a two-year-old mind is a fickle thing. You would think she'd be quickly distracted and our game would last only a minute or two. You would be wrong. This can literally go on for hours. In my granddaughter's mind, everything else fades away. It's just Baby Dino and the endless adventures this promises.

Jesus invites us to come to God like little children. Innocent, with the unwavering faith that our Heavenly Father has us in His arms. I know this precept. I've been around the block enough times to have the house numbers memorized. I've seen His miraculous hand in my life over and over again. You would think our conversation would last hours before distraction set in.

You would think, but you would be wrong.

I've found a Pop Pop's mind is a fickle thing.

But there are times, every once in a while, when I manage to keep my soul still in His presence. And when I do, the world fades. It's just me, my Beautiful Friend, and the great adventure that will never end.

I look forward to the day, Lord, when distraction is not even an option. Just Your love forever and ever. Amen. —Buck Storm

Digging Deeper: Matthew 18:1–14; 1 John 3:1

Sunday, January 21

Be careful not to practice your righteousness in front of others to be seen by them. —Matthew 6:1 (NIV)

As part of my church's hospitality team, I sometimes prepare and deliver comfort food meals to families experiencing medical convalescence or bereavement. Since I once cooked daily for my family of six, I easily plan and prepare entire dinners. Working around dietary restrictions or extra-large portions just adds to the creative challenge.

Perhaps the most satisfying part is chatting with the recipients, especially those who live alone: the new widow, the person in pain, the homebound. I like to think that my presence offers comfort along with the soup. And I confess I crave a little praise now and then. Or used to...

When I learned that a young father of six had died suddenly and the grieving family of seven included teen boys, I put on my apron and turned on the stove. Spaghetti and sauce, bread, salad, fruit, and pies. According to team protocol, I called the mother ahead of time. "I won't be home, but the boys will let you in."

But the boys didn't hear the doorbell. I left three totes of food on the porch. The next month, I prepared baked beans and ham, shredded coleslaw, extra rolls, and cake. I phoned Mom, who warned about icy steps. Again, no one received me. Again, I left food on the porch.

Praise? I've lost my taste for it. God knows I helped—and that's enough.

Lord, let me serve You without wondering who's watching. —Gail Thorell Schilling

---

Monday, January 22

**Don't speak evil against each other, dear brothers
and sisters. —James 4:11** (NLT)

Our family Bible study one evening focused on
the fourth chapter of James. My husband called
attention to the eleventh verse, then challenged us to
make more of an effort to build people up. "When
we find fault with someone," Dwight said, "how can
we instead say something positive?"

Our son, two daughters, and I sat silently, unable
to think of an answer. Finally, our son piped up. "I
guess when you want to say something like, 'He's
an idiot,' you could add, 'but that's what makes him
special in his own way!'" We all laughed, but it gave
me an idea.

"I'm going to try that this week," I announced.
"Whenever I catch myself saying something unkind,
I'm going to add that phrase to the end to call
attention to my negativity."

I had no idea what a humbling challenge I'd taken
on. I'd never before realized how casually critical I
could be.

While driving past our local college campus, I
commented, "These girls' shorts are way too short."
Then I added, "But that's what makes them special
in their own way." The kids were in the car with me,

and they laughed. Later on, we saw a personalized license plate. "What a dumb thing to put on your car," I said, quickly adding, "but that's what makes him special in his own way."

Before the week was out, my son's joke had become tiresome. "Mom," one of my daughters groaned, "it's not funny anymore."

How ashamed I felt that I'd made the words lose their punch through overuse.

I'm going to work on showing more grace—a truly wonderful and special way to be!

Lord, help me to be kind. —Ginger Rue

Digging Deeper: Matthew 5:22, 12:36

Tuesday, January 23

There is a time for everything, and a season for every activity under the heavens. —Ecclesiastes 3:1 (NIV)

I had waited twenty years to start pursuing publication. College, marriage, a career, and the birth of my daughters prevented me from taking the time. But I was finally staying home to raise my girls, so it seemed like the perfect opportunity to start writing again. I was several months into my first manuscript when I discovered we were pregnant with twins! My husband, daughters, and I were overjoyed to welcome two babies into our family.

But the day I heard the word "twins" was also the night I cried myself to sleep. Not because I was sad for this incredible blessing, but because I knew God was asking me to put my writing dreams on hold a little longer. How long? I didn't know. What I did know was that God had placed a calling on my life to worship Him through my words.

As I lay there in tears, I felt an overwhelming sense of peace. God whispered a promise to my heart that if I would honor Him in this season of life, He would honor my dream.

I never imagined that God would call me to pick up my pen again when my twin boys were not quite two years old. That was ten years ago, and in that time, I've had over twenty-five books published.

I learned an important lesson in that season of life. When we work on God's divine timetable and honor His plans, we step into the center of His perfect will.

Lord, when I get frustrated and impatient with delays, help me to remember that my times are in Your hands.
—Gabrielle Meyer

Digging Deeper: Psalm 31:14; James 4:13–15; 2 Peter 3:8

Wednesday, January 24

CELEBRATE!! Word of the Year
These things I have spoken to you, that my joy may be in you, and that your joy may be full.
—John 15:11 (RSV)

Many people mark the New Year, not with a resolution, but with a word intended to shape the days ahead. I'm doing that this year, and my word is *celebrate!!* with two exclamation points. *Celebrate!!* got woven into my spiritual life when I read Richard J. Foster's classic book, *Celebration of Discipline*. I was intrigued by the title that combined those two unlikely words.

According to Foster, discipline means doing what needs to be done when it needs to be done, and celebration is about recognizing God's goodness and pausing long enough to thank Him. The discipline turns the "thank You" into a habit that strengthens our faith.

As I stand on the edge of this New Year, looking at my new 2024 calendar, I'm reminded of blessing the blank pages of my new calendar years ago. I'd recently been diagnosed with cancer and faced a future of unknowns. My pastor stopped by to see how I was doing as I was adding the dates of my first rounds of chemotherapy. I confessed my fears about the outcomes of doctor appointments and treatments.

"You have to pray for the possibilities," he said, and then led me through a prayer, blessing those blank pages, trusting God's presence and protection, and ending by praying that I could focus on the possibilities.

I'm celebrating that memory today as I bless the blank pages of my 2024 calendar, especially praying for the possibilities.

Father, I am excited to discover the possibilities
You have for me in this New Year.
—Carol Kuykendall

Digging Deeper: 2 Samuel 6:14; Psalm 16:11

Thursday, January 25

Why, my soul, are you downcast? Why so disturbed
within me? Put your hope in God, for I will yet praise
him, my Savior and my God. —Psalm 42:11 (NIV)

It was dark and the road was blanketed with snow as
I walked home from visiting my mom next door. The
plow hadn't come through, and my path of footprints
from the way there were hardly visible. I shivered,
remembering another big storm was expected later in
the week. Winter, it seemed, had no end.

As the snow fell, I thought about dinner and
everything I had to do before the day's end. I was the
only one out on this frigid night, and the loneliness
of the season took hold in my heart.

I tugged my scarf up under my chin and noticed a
familiar scent that seemed so odd for a winter's night
that I almost didn't recognize it. The smell of hot
dogs and hamburgers wafted by me. I took a deep
breath, inhaling the scent of summer, most likely
from a neighbor's back porch barbecue.

I looked up at the beam of light from a streetlamp
in the distance. The falling snow made a hazy
rainbow around the lamp, and I found myself

walking lighter, excited to see the beauty of this night God had made, taking in every sense of the wintery moment.

Lord, thank You for unexpected gifts that lift my spirit away from cold thoughts to You, my Savior.
—Sabra Ciancanelli

Digging Deeper: Psalm 31:24; Romans 15:13

Friday, January 26

You shall have no other gods before me.
—Exodus 20:3 (NIV)

I woke up excited about getting a new car today—a rare event for our family. The whole car-buying process is fun for me. Our family enjoys spending time deciding the type of car, color, and options that best fit our needs. Once ordered, I look forward to the day the car arrives. Then we drive the car for a long time—usually ten years.

The excitement reminded me of an experience soon after getting our last new car. Pat and I drove the car to Texas to see our son. On the trip down, before even getting out of our home state of Ohio, a truck's wheel kicked up a rock, cracking the windshield. The evening we arrived, we went out to dinner. As Pat and Johnny walked toward the restaurant, I stopped to examine a noticeable dent in the driver-side door. Johnny came back to see why I had stopped. Totally frustrated, I fretted and fumed about both the windshield crack and dent so soon on a new car.

"Hey Dad, it's only a car! Are you really going to let a small crack and even smaller dent spoil our evening?" His point stung, but he was right; his comment helped get my priorities—and our evening—back on track.

I don't believe God has a problem with us having new things. But He certainly does care about our attitude toward anything, new or old, and their priority in our lives.

Dear Jesus, help keep my excitement about this new car in check, and when the first dent comes, help me not let it ruin my day with You or anyone else. After all, it is just a car! —John Dilworth

Digging Deeper: Deuteronomy 28:14; Jonah 2:8

Saturday, January 27

The LORD will guide you always.... You will be like a well-watered garden, like a spring whose waters never fail. —Isaiah 58:11 (NIV)

Writing has almost always been part of my life. My favorite school assignments were essays, sports reporting, and term papers. I wrote for Christian and farm magazines as a young mother, and I've been writing for *Daily Guideposts* (*Walking in Grace*) since 1979. But a couple of years ago, I wondered if it was time to quit. Did I still have anything relevant or encouraging to say? I prayed for guidance, but God seemed silent.

Then I got an email from my nephew Chris. He'd just finished reading my biographical sketch in the 2022 edition. The verse I'd quoted was Psalm 145:18, "The Lord is near to all who call upon him, to all who call upon him in truth." Then, when he opened his Bible, he was amazed to find the passage he'd bookmarked earlier was also Psalm 145:18! "Out of 1,189 chapters in the Bible and 730 days into my lumbering stroll from Genesis to Revelation," he wrote, "I arrived at Psalm 145 the exact same day I read your bio. I can only speculate about divine supervision or coincidence. But I am certain that God is working through your pen, experiences, and even the verse you chose."

Message received. The time will come when I put away my pen and computer. But for now, I'll keep on writing.

Thank You, Lord, for the amazing way you answered my prayer. Guide my thoughts and pen, that my words may bless others as their words have blessed me. —Penney Schwab

Digging Deeper: Psalm 25:4–5; Proverbs 16:1–3; 1 John 2:12–14

Sunday, January 28

...the Lord shall give thee rest from thy sorrow, and from thy fear.... —Isaiah 14:3 (KJV)

"Quarantined." A scary word, one you might imagine posted across a door in ancient times. Yet, here we were, quarantined, in the throes of a world pandemic. Our three younger children were home from school, and Harrison, our college student, had been assigned to remote learning.

Our investment office was now "work at home" status, and the stock market had crashed almost 35 percent in five weeks. It was a harrowing time. Stores were closed, meetings canceled, groceries were delivered to front doors.

Fear of the unknown was everywhere. We all suffered with those who were sick and mourned the dying. No one knew what was going to happen. Yet all around us, families began to settle in, reacquaint, and adapt to enforced isolation.

We were fortunate to have access to a rural farm, and Corinne and I decided to retreat to its safety. I had the equipment necessary to keep in touch with my clients' needs. Soon, we found ourselves taking long walks together, first because there was little else to do, and then because we had begun to love the beauty of God's creation, which we had so often failed to notice in the past.

It was on such an afternoon that my children Mary Katherine, Ella Grace, and David found a perfect spot for sitting on the trunk of a fallen tree. The sun fell across the woods behind them, making them beautiful.

"Daddy," Mary Katherine asked, "what's going to happen with the virus?"

I didn't have an answer to her question, so I responded with the only truth I knew: "I'm not sure, honey, but God is always with us."

Father, even in the midst of fear and uncertainty, You come. Stay close, Father, stay close. —Brock Kidd

Digging Deeper: Matthew 6:24; 2 Timothy 1:7

Monday, January 29

Devote yourselves to prayer, being watchful and thankful. —Colossians 4:2 (NIV)

Recently, I had an email from a former student. She'd sold her first short story to a children's magazine and wanted to thank me for the help I'd given her when she'd taken my writing course years ago. I was delighted for Gillian. More than that, I was touched that she'd reached out to say thank you. Very few students do.

I suppose it shouldn't surprise me. When Jesus healed ten lepers on his way to Jerusalem, only one of them returned to thank Him. One in ten. That's sad, isn't it? But thanklessness seems prevalent. Perhaps that's why magazines publish articles—usually in November—on the importance of having an attitude of gratitude. I've taken meals and disposable diapers to new mothers, delivered homemade cookies or flowers to shut-ins, and performed other acts of kindness without ever getting an email, text, or phone call to say thanks.

I didn't do these things to be thanked. I did them because the Lord would have me do so—to be salt and light in the world.

Why are we prone to take so much for granted? When my teenagers succumbed to grumbling or whining, I'd counter by asking them to share three things they were grateful for that day. Perhaps the attitude of gratitude is like a muscle that needs exercise to grow strong. I don't know. What I do know is that life is too short not to take time to thank the Lord for our blessings and to say thank you to those around us.

Dear Lord, I thank You for showering me with so many blessings that I can't count them all.
—Shirley Raye Redmond

Digging Deeper: 1 Chronicles 16:34; 1 Thessalonians 5:18

Tuesday, January 30

But he said to her, "Daughter, it is your faith that has healed you. Go home in peace, and be free from your trouble." —Mark 5:34 (PHILLIPS)

One day I visited a patient.

"Debra" soon confided, "My husband died a few months ago. I'm so lonely. I don't have anything to live for." As I listened, I prayed silently to receive the words the Lord would have me speak to this suffering woman.

Thankfully, the words came ever so gently. I told her, "I once had a brain tumor. I didn't think I could keep living feeling so bad. But then the Lord spoke to my heart."

"Yes?" she inquired.

"When you feel bad, you can't focus on anything else. So, when you pray, the first thing that often happens is you feel peace. Peace helps you to see life beyond the pain and helps you see that the Lord is always with you even in the worst of circumstances. That's what happened to me."

Debra touched my hand. "Tell me more."

I leaned in. "You took care of your husband in his last years as he lived with dementia. Even when he didn't recognize you anymore, you never left him alone. Your love for him was greater than his terrible illness."

She became teary. "How could I do anything else? Our vows . . . in sickness and in health. I loved him." She then looked out the window for a very long time. "Before you visited, I felt so alone, but now I feel hope. Thank you."

After I left Debra, I felt a renewed gratitude for how the Lord had carried me through my own illness. What I had once asked the Lord to spare me from experiencing was now my greatest blessing.

May Your understanding give us the peace
we all seek. Amen. —Adam Ruiz

Digging Deeper: John 14:27;
Romans 5:1–2, 10:14–15

God is love. Whoever lives in love lives in God, and God in them. —1 John 4:16 (NIV)

As a little girl, I enjoyed watching PBS shows when I returned home from school. I would burst through the door, throw my backpack down, grab a snack and some apple juice, and plant myself in front of "the tube."

One of my favorite shows was *Mister Rogers' Neighborhood.* I loved watching him return home, remove his suit jacket, and don a comfy cable-knit cardigan. I enjoyed his interviews with unique guests. Most of all, I loved his calm voice, a voice that exuded warmth and encouragement to children like me, seated in his virtual audience.

Recently, I attended a conference for people from various organizations serving vulnerable children. To my surprise and joy, a lady representing the Fred Rogers Center in Pennsylvania led a session that quickly became my favorite. The presenter spoke in the same calming tone of Mister Rogers, while sharing the ways his center continues his work in the world.

She closed with a clip of Fred Rogers, filmed decades ago, that transported me back to the little girl who found inspiration and joy in that kind face and gentle voice. The clip ended with this simple statement: "I like you just the way you are."

Those simple words—an embodiment of the truth of God's love that we don't hear often enough—filled my heart. Not only did I feel encouraged to live in authenticity and acceptance, but it also reminded me that every child in my life is yearning for this same affirmation. Every child needs to know that with all their struggles and imperfections, I like them just the way they are.

Dear Lord, help me to live in the truth that You love me just the way I am, and help me to gift others with kindness and acceptance. —Carla Hendricks

Digging Deeper: Psalm 17:7–8; 1 John 4:7–12

YOU WERE CALLED TO PEACE

1 _____

2 _____

3 _____

4 _____

5 _____

6 _____

7 _____

8 _____

9 _____

10 _____

11 _____

12 _____

13 _____

14 _____

15 _____

16 _____

17 _____

18 _____

19 _____

20 _____

21 _____

22 _____

23 _____

24 _____

25 _____

26 _____

27 _____

28 _____

29 _____

30 _____

31 _____

FEBRUARY

*For he himself is our peace, who has
made us both one and has broken down
in his flesh the dividing wall of hostility.*

—Ephesians 2:14 (ESV)

Open your mouth and taste, open your eyes and see—how good GOD is. —Psalm 34:8 (MSG)

I topped my bread with a basil leaf instead of butter. My Iranian-born neighbor, Shahin, was right. Delicious! During our lunch at her favorite Persian restaurant, Shahin not only showed me a new way to eat bread but also introduced me to *kefta* and taught me how to hold a sugar cube in my cheek while drinking strong tea. After we'd finished our Middle Eastern feast—with me oohing and aahing over every new dish—Shahin declared me a true *shekamu*.

Although *shekamu* is derived from the Farsi word for "stomach," it's sometimes translated into English as "fattie." Not quite the nickname I'd wanted to earn from my friend. But Shahin explained that being a *shekamu* wasn't synonymous with gluttony. Instead, it was someone who enjoyed a deep appreciation of food, almost like a gastronomical love affair. She had me pegged.

Although I didn't grow up in a family that said grace aloud before meals, I've always felt a deep, abiding gratitude for the gift of food—even long before I realized there was Someone to be grateful to. In the same way that seeing an awe-inspiring landscape, hearing the music of birdsong, smelling the scent of roses in a garden, or basking in the warmth of a friend's embrace all instinctively lead me to praise God, my sense of taste also leads me straight to God's throne. I'm grateful He created me a *shekamu*! It's just another way to "taste and see" that God is good.

Lord, thank You for my five senses and for how they reveal glimpses of Your creativity and provision, each and every day. —Vicki Kuyper

Digging Deeper: Psalm 107:9; Ecclesiastes 9:7; 1 Corinthians 10:31

Friday, February 2

Before a word is on my tongue you, LORD, know it completely. —Psalm 139:4 (NIV)

Alexa, what's the temperature?" I asked our Amazon speaker that chilly morning.

"Right now it's twenty degrees Fahrenheit. Today, expect a high of thirty-one degrees. Have a good day, Stephanie."

Stephanie? I felt surprised. My husband received the speaker as a gift years ago, but it has never called me by my name. *How in the world does that device know me?*

Touted as a virtual assistant, Alexa is capable of playing my favorite songs, streaming audiobooks, setting timers and alarms, giving sports scores, and turning on lights and our television. It can even play games and tell me jokes, although the jokes are seldom funny.

I'd recently heard that smart devices sometimes collected personal data, so I asked Alexa several questions like: *Who is Stephanie? What do you know about Stephanie? What does Stephanie like to order online?*

The first two questions yielded random answers that were read from Wikipedia, the online encyclopedia, and the last one elicited: "I'm not sure." Turns out, our brilliant smart speaker might know my name (since the account was set up with my first name), but it doesn't know me. In fact, it has no clue, at all, who I really am.

Thankfully, there's One who does. Not only does God know my name, but He also knows everything about me, even before I speak. And because of what's written in His Word, that's no surprise at all.

Dear Lord, You know all of my personal data, including my past, present, and future. I'm so grateful that I am fully known, and fully loved, by You.
—Stephanie Thompson

Digging Deeper: Psalm 139:1–16; Matthew 10:30; 1 Corinthians 8:3

Saturday, February 3

They approach and come forward; they help each other and say to their companions, "Be strong!"
—Isaiah 41:5–6 (NIV)

What on earth was I thinking? I'd invited two of my dearest friends, Lois and Tom, over for dinner when, during my kitchen renovation, I still did not have any countertops, no sink, no water, no garbage disposal, no stove, and no dishwasher. All I had at that point was new cabinets and a microwave. So I made the salad in the guest bathroom, where there's barely eight inches of countertop space. It wasn't easy considering the fact that you can't let anything, not even one tiny little piece of lettuce, slip down that drain.

Then I started thinking about whether the casserole that I had taken out of the freezer would stay hot enough heating it in the microwave. But the clincher was realizing I'd have to do dishes for three people in my bathroom sink with no place to set the clean ones. Sometimes I think in the dictionary under "nimrod" my picture is there. Thank goodness for friends you can call and say, "Can we just eat at your house and I'll bring the food?"

Lois and Tom greeted me with open arms, a set table, and a fabulous dessert she'd made in her, sigh, beautiful oven. We laughed over our flip-flop dinner plans, cleaned up the kitchen together, played cards, and enjoyed every minute of what a great friendship is all about.

The evening taught me to never be hesitant about asking friends, or anyone for that matter, for help.

Lord, sometimes I want people to think I've got it all together. Remind me that You are in the hearts of my friends and to never be afraid to walk into their arms.
—Patricia Lorenz

Digging Deeper: Psalm 118:13; Isaiah 41:6, 10

Iron sharpens iron, and one man sharpens another. —Proverbs 27:17 (ESV)

I gave my mom a jigsaw puzzle for Christmas that features very small vintage drawings of birds. The first day of February, she opened the box and began spreading out the pieces.

That night as we worked on the borders, Mom complained that the pieces didn't fit exactly right and she wasn't sure everything was where it should be. The next night was worse. Mom put her hands up over her face. "Four hours I spent on this puzzle, Sabra. Four hours and look, hardly any progress."

"Just put it away," I said. "I'm sorry it's so bad. It had top reviews, but if you hate it…"

"Nope," she said. "We're going to finish it."

About a week later, Mom had divided up what was remaining of the thousand pieces into small piles—one for each bird. "We have to do this first, but it's really hard. Sabra, I hate this puzzle."

Every night I worked on it with her. As we neared the end, Mom put a crystal bell on the table and when we placed a piece, we rang it and cheered. The worst puzzle in the world was turning out to be fun.

When it was finally done, I ran my hands over the puzzle and exclaimed, "We did it!"

Mom said, "Sabra, this was a terrible puzzle. One of the worst, if not the worst, I've ever done. Let's mail it to your sister up north to do with her family." And we laughed.

Heavenly Father, thank You for my mom, who still teaches me that finishing difficult things can be fun if you share the work with people you love.
—Sabra Ciancanelli

Digging Deeper: 1 Corinthians 3:9; Galatians 6:9

Monday, February 5

...In Your presence is fullness of joy....
—Psalm 16:11 (NASB)

My heart raced as I typed on the computer in my loft office. My job of brokering lumber in the wildly price-fluctuating market can be stressful. Suddenly, I heard a loud thud from my covered porch below—then more clattering. My German shepherd puppy was playing her favorite game, knock over the wood pile on the porch.

I leapt down the stairs, yanked the door open, and called out sharply, "Willow, you know better. Get in here now!" With her head drooping, she slunk in the door. I ushered her into her pen in the dining room that was piled high with her toys, then went into the kitchen to pour a cup of tea. When I walked out, I stopped. She was carefully piling up all her stuffed animals next to "Big Bear," her favorite three-foot-tall stuffie. She crawled on top of the pile, plopped down, and sighed. She'd created a place of comfort among her "friends."

I shook my head and thought, *That's what I need to do.* Instead of going back up to the office,

I disengaged from the stress by curling up in my favorite rocking chair with my Bible. After reading a bit and taking a couple of deep breaths, I felt led to call a friend. Her lighthearted chatter lifted my spirit. Before we hung up, we'd planned a late afternoon adventure of thrift-store shopping.

By the time I climbed the stairs to the office, I'd reset my emotions and was ready to go back to work.

Thank You, Lord, for being my Friend, as well as giving me friends, to be a place of comfort when the world around me is in turmoil. Amen.
—Rebecca Ondov

Digging Deeper: Psalm 138:1; 1 Peter 5:6–7; 1 John 3:19–24; Jude 24

Tuesday, February 6

And his name shall be called Wonderful, Counsellor, the mighty God, the everlasting Father, the Prince of Peace. —Isaiah 9:6 (KJV)

I've had a lifelong fascination with fashion, and I have collected vintage clothing labels for as long as I can remember. In high school, I aspired to become a fashion designer. But life—and illness—had other plans. My consolation prize was a glass-topped tray displaying labels I've snipped from Goodwill and estate sale garments. John Meyer of Norwich. Halston. Christian Dior...

When I was delivered from pain and prescription opioids, I wasn't expecting a new label to add to my collection. But one morning at the grocery store, I overheard a lady talking at the checkout lane. "Isn't she the one who took the pills?" she asked, pointing her head in my direction. It felt like the whole world was staring at me.

You've got yourself a new label, Roberta, I inwardly groaned. *And it sure ain't Ralph Lauren!*

I'd worn labels of one sort or another since childhood. Disfigured. Epileptic. Less Than. I hadn't counted on being the poster girl for opioid addiction. But labels are a funny thing. Just as a designer's signature on a pair of jeans turns heads, a label announcing God's redemption gets noticed. Gives a girl a chance to tell the story of second chances. Because sooner or later, we all need that second chance.

My glass-topped tray of vintage fashion labels is great for serving up coffee. But it can't hold a candle to my label with the Master Designer's signature. The One who changed my before into a forever after.

Your name is wonder-full, Lord, and I am Yours. That's the only label I need. —Roberta Messner

Digging Deeper: Isaiah 7:14; Acts 4:12; Philippians 2:9

Wednesday, February 7

Let anyone who desires drink freely from the water of life. —Revelation 22:17 (NLT)

"I can see the peace you have with your faith," Sue says, "but it's not for me."

"Why can't she see?" I fume at BlueDog in the passenger seat after I drive away. Sue's heart is hurting, and she is reaching out for help. With all my heart I want her to experience the light, love, and peace that is found in Christ. "How about we rope her and drag her to church?" I ask BlueDog.

But that's not how this works. God gave us all an enormous gift—the freedom of choice. This could be the most amazing feat He could have ever done. He made us and loved us beyond anything we could possibly imagine.

Then He left it up to us to love Him back.

My desire to force someone to align with my faith reminds me just how human I am. We cannot save anyone. We are called to disciple, to encourage, and to love without condition. God alone can save. I must leave this in His hands.

The old adage "you can lead a horse to water, but you can't make it drink" was never truer. "Here is a trough of sweet, pure, Living Water," I tell BlueDog. "Why won't more people drink from it?"

Lord, why did You give us freedom?

At that, it sinks in. That's how much God loves us. He loves us enough to offer us our complete freedom. Even though we make a mess of things. Even though we don't honor Him for it. That's a lot of love.

Trying to force someone to love isn't love. And God is love in its purest form.

Merciful Father, please help me to force less and love more. —Erika Bentsen

Thursday, February 8

We love because he first loved us. —1 John 4:19 (NIV)

When we learned that our son's family was going to
central Florida for winter break, we wanted to see
them. Normally, we only get to visit with them once
a year because they live several states away. However,
we are only eight hours from where they were going
in Florida.

Immediately, my husband, Chuck, said, "Let's
go!" He was ready to leave right away to see the
children and grandchildren.

But we hadn't planned the trip ahead of time. And we
already had commitments where we live. How were we
supposed to drop everything and go that quickly?

My first reaction was to say, *We can't*. You see,
I'm a planner. I plan my days, my weeks, and my
months, and I don't do well with impromptu events.
Much as I love my family and wanted to go see
them, the planner part of me argued that the timing
was wrong because I had too much stuff to do. I was
in the middle of planning a conference and meeting
writing deadlines, as well as leading a group at
church and hosting a book club.

But in my heart, I knew my priorities were
wrong, especially when I found this verse from
1 John on my mind. God's love is so strong it helps

us to reorder our own priorities. I set to rearranging our schedules. We booked a room, drove a day there and back, and had the most wonderful time. We played at the pool, on the beach, kayaked, fished, and played board games with the three grandsons.

Was the spur-of-the moment trip worthwhile? Absolutely! Everything else could wait. Spending time with loved ones was the most important use of my time.

Lord, thank You for love. Help me to always put the people I love first. —Marilyn Turk

Digging Deeper: Psalm 23:6; 1 Corinthians 13:1–5; 1 John 4:7–8

Friday, February 9

Your word is a lamp to my feet and a light to my path. —Psalm 119:105 (ESV)

I was getting ready for bed last night when my wife, Nancy, said someone was in our woods with a flashlight. I wasn't alarmed, but I did go out on the back deck to check. I've had to warn off more than a few trespassers or night hunters before.

The light seemed to be following some of the trails I've made through the woods. Since there was no sound of hunters or hunting dogs, I assumed it was one of my friends, so I went in and went to bed.

The next day, I saw my son-in-law Michael out on his morning walk. "Were you in the woods last night?" I asked. Indeed, he was. His later afternoon walk had gotten delayed, so he waited until dark to head out, guided by his flashlight.

On nights when the moon's full, there's plenty of light to traverse the trails. A full moon, especially in winter, even casts shadows of trees along the way. But this particular night, the moon was hidden by clouds and so a flashlight was needed—giving him just enough light for the few steps ahead.

Sometimes that's all I need in life too. I want the pillar of fire of God like the Israelites had on their exodus so they could travel through the darkness at night. That would really be helpful. But often I find God, in divine wisdom, gives me a spiritual flashlight. It provides just enough light to enable me to make my way.

That's all I need—if I trust my Guide, that is.

Guide me, O Thou Great Jehovah, as I pilgrimage in this sometimes dark land. Grant me, please, just the Light I need. Amen. —J. Brent Bill

Digging Deeper: Exodus 13:21–22; Nehemiah 9:19–20; Isaiah 42:16

Saturday, February 10

Here is a call for the endurance of the saints, those who keep the commandments of God and hold fast to the faith of Jesus. —Revelation 14:12 (NRSV)

My gig when I volunteer at our church's soup kitchen is to serve them coffee. Over time, I've gotten to know many of the guests, and if I'm lucky, I'll remember a name as I ask about a job search, a new apartment, kids and grandkids, workouts at the gym, and the prayers they want said.

I'm always struck by the different backgrounds people come from. I try to use any tidbits of foreign language I might have, but I struggled to communicate with one kindly guest, an older Chinese gentleman. One day, he dug into his pocket and took out an envelope.

"This is for you," he said, pausing, then gesturing to himself. "It's about...us."

I didn't have a chance to look it over till long after he left. Imagine my surprise to discover a brochure with a picture of a distinguished-looking cardinal, standing next to Pope John Paul II, blessing people. His name, "Ignatius Cardinal Kung, the Roman Catholic Bishop of Shanghai," ordained a priest in 1930, persecuted and imprisoned under the Chinese communist government, and allowed to immigrate to the United States in 1988, where he died in the year 2000.

I realized this was the man's way of sharing his faith journey with me. His English was limited, and he couldn't really explain it all to me, but he wanted me to know something about the God he served.

What a blessing. A reminder that every stranger has a story, ones you can never fully guess at.

What a rich world we live in, Lord. May my knowledge of it continue to grow. —Rick Hamlin

---

Sunday, February 11

**The purposes of a person's heart are deep waters,
but one who has insight draws them out.
—Proverbs 20:5 (NIV)**

"I try to put myself in the place of the person I'm
reading about in the Bible. Every one of them was a
real person."

Those words, spoken by the leader of a recent
Bible study I attended, caught my attention.

Of course, I know that everyone in the Bible was a
real person. Yet I generally skirt over that fact and just
note what they said or did. I don't always put myself in
their place or ask, "What were they feeling? Why did
they react that way? What were their thoughts, fears,
hopes, desires, dreams? How would I have felt? What
would I have said or done in the same situation?" In the
past, I've attempted to find the message but not tried to
more fully understand the people who conveyed it.

In my daily life, I'm much the same. Usually I just
react, rather than ask myself what a person is feeling
or what they might have experienced that prompted
their words or actions, especially when I am hurt or
angered by them. Too infrequently do I try to put
myself in someone else's place.

Author Stephen Covey said, "Seek first to
understand." Such good advice, but so poorly have

I followed it. Going forward, I'm going to try to place myself in the other person's shoes, both in my Bible reading and in my daily life. I feel certain that if I do, both my understanding and my compassion will increase.

Lord, help me remember there's a reason behind what people say and do. Help me look for and try to understand that reason, both in my study of Your Word and in my life. —Kim Taylor Henry

Digging Deeper: Proverbs 4:5, 20:27; Colossians 3:12

Monday, February 12

Be persistent in prayer, and keep alert as you pray, giving thanks to God. —Colossians 4:2 (GNT)

"Will you pray I find my pet snake?"

As a pastor's wife, I have been asked to pray for many things. For healing of broken bones and various ailments. For troubled marriages. For wayward children and grandchildren. But in all my years of praying, I had never been asked to pray for a reptile of any kind.

Not a harmless garter snake. Not a colorful rainbow boa. Not a camouflaged carpet python.

In fact, I was so surprised by the prayer request, I didn't find out details. Did the snake eat bugs, eggs, insects, or small mammals? Was it venomous? How long had she had the snake? Was it friendly or an isolated introvert? To be honest, I didn't ask because I didn't really care about her missing snake.

I tossed out a prayer, "Jesus, help my friend find her escaped snake," and then went about my day, unconcerned about the outcome.

But not so my friend. She kept me informed by ongoing text messages.

"She is a black, twenty-inch king snake, so she can hide anywhere."

I prayed again for the return of her pet.

"We have looked for four hours. No luck."

I prayed and checked my phone for updates.

"We are going to set a trap and see if that does the trick."

I prayed with fervor for a positive outcome.

The day ended with these simple words: "Snake found."

My heart rejoiced with my friend and at my newfound knowledge—persistence in prayer had changed my indifference to concern and caring, even for a lost pet snake.

Jesus, may Your gift of compassion wiggle its way into my heart. —Lynne Hartke

Digging Deeper: Luke 18:1–8; Romans 12:12

Tuesday, February 13

But I the LORD will speak what I will, and it shall be fulfilled without delay. —Ezekiel 12:25 (NIV)

The city was braced for a rare winter storm. Ordinarily, I would be satisfied to pull a chair near a window and wait like a second-grader for nature's dazzling show. But at this unlikeliest of times, a feeling of restlessness descended upon me.

Earlier, I had made a promise to my cousin—who'd been restricted by a stroke for years—that a portion of the next batch of seafood gumbo I made would be hers, and while there'd been no agreed-upon delivery date, I sensed today might be the day. What if my cousin, due to the imminent weather, was feeling alone? Maybe even a bit scared? For a Gulf Coast girl like her, gumbo would be just the thing.

I had previously prepared and frozen it. Suddenly, my perfectionist tendency kicked up its own storm. I'd forgotten the crabs! The logical thing would be simply to take my time, add the frozen crabs, and deliver the dish another day. But that strong, illogical prompt said no. I would go now, before the storm. I hurried across town only to find her in good spirits. What had the urgency been about?

Instead of perplexed, I felt euphoric. Turns out, *I* was the urgency. I needed my cousin's smile more than she needed the gumbo. The Spirit who anticipates my every mood had nudged me toward His will and my delight. What restlessness? I returned home feeling calm. Productive. Let it snow. Sleet. Whatever. I would have sweet rest.

Lord, help me to be discerning enough to move when Your Spirit does. —Jacqueline F. Wheelock

Digging Deeper: Psalm 119:60; Matthew 8:24; John 10:4

Ash Wednesday, February 14

For all who exalt themselves will be humbled, and those who humble themselves will be exalted.
—Luke 14:11 (NRSVUE)

I attend one of the churches where a smudge of ashes is placed on our foreheads every Ash Wednesday. I'm there each year, at noon, and the pews are full of my neighbors. I come forward and the ashes are marked on me in the rough form of a cross.

"Remember that you are dust, and to dust you shall return." Then I return to my pew. I can't help but look at those around me, all of us with smudges.

One of the Bible readings that day is from Matthew 6, in which Jesus instructs the disciples how to pray. He says go into your closet: "Go to your inner room, close the door, and pray to your Father in secret" (6:6, NABRE). This is because there were a lot of hypocrites praying in ways that would get them noticed by others. Jesus mentions these just one verse earlier, adding, "Do not be like [them]."

So, here I am with these ashes on my forehead. I've been told to keep them there; to walk back to my office, or to lunch, with my cruciform ashes on my forehead because it will be a witness to my faith in Christ. I'm not sure.

I've never felt this way before, but suddenly I can't reconcile those ashes with the humility that Jesus asks. So I wipe them off while walking down the street. And that night, and the next morning, I'm reminded to spend more time praying to my Father in secret.

Remind me, Lord, of the difference between showing off my faith and shoring up my faith.
—Jon M. Sweeney

Digging Deeper: Matthew 6:1–6, 16–18

Thursday, February 15

Bear with each other and forgive one another if any of you has a grievance against someone. Forgive as the Lord forgave you. —Colossians 3:13 (NIV)

Perhaps because it is Lent, I've been dwelling on forgiveness. What keeps coming up is one wound that has never healed. An injustice from years ago I don't have the space to share here and in fact is not all that terrible...except that I have never been able to forget it. It's like a thorn or a splinter: the more I dig at it, the deeper it goes.

All the touchpoints of my faith—the Scripture, the 12 Steps, meditation, and self-reflection—implore me to break free from the shackles of resentment if I am to attain true spiritual equilibrium. And I do. Except for this one ancient wound. Does clinging to it confer some sense of moral vindication? That I was done an irreparable wrong that merits me special victim status?

"I just can't forgive this one thing," I told a friend. "I don't think I ever will."

My friend, who knows me well, said with a smile, "Were you the one who hung on that cross?"

"I don't understand."

"Sometimes the best we can do is give our wounds to Christ, who died to forgive all our sins. What you let go of, He will take up. He can forgive what you cannot bring yourself to forgive. But you must let go."

I must let go. Not the first time I have been told that. But maybe the most important.

Let me always remember, merciful Lord, it is You who forgives even the unforgivable. It is You to whom I must turn when I cannot find the strength or desire myself to forgive. —Edward Grinnan

Digging Deeper: Genesis 50:16–17; Psalm 19:12–13; Micah 7:18–19; Matthew 18:21–22

Friday, February 16

Even to your old age and gray hairs I am he, I am he who will sustain you. I have made you and I will carry you; I will sustain you and I will rescue you. —Isaiah 46:4 (NIV)

I met with Anna, one of my students, to discuss her grad-school application. When the meeting was over, she said, "You've been so helpful. You remind me of my grandfather."

"Ah," I said. "I'll take that as a compliment."

Which, in fact, wasn't true. Oh, I'm sure her grandfather is a swell person, but apparently I'm much vainer than I thought because I don't want to be compared to *anyone's* grandfather, helpful or otherwise.

I shouldn't have been surprised by any of this. My hair has gone from mostly brown to mostly gray to mostly gone. My knees creak like an old Chevy with bad springs. In the words of Groucho Marx, I have the body of a twenty-year-old, but I should give it back because I'm getting it all wrinkled.

Yet somehow I still imagine myself to be young— OK, younger. Young enough to be Anna's dad but not her grandfather. (*Grandfather?* Seriously?)

This year, for Lent, I'm giving up pride. As I kneel to receive ashes on my forehead, I'll take to heart the admonition, *remember that you are dust, and to dust you shall return*. It's a reminder of what is important in our lives and what is fleeting, and a reminder to live accordingly.

Then again, when I stand up from the kneeler, my knees will creak. I'm getting all of the reminders that I need.

Lord, I want to stand among Your saints; give me the strength to stand, period. —Mark Collins

Digging Deeper: Job 12:12; Hebrews 12:9

Saturday, February 17

We know that all things work together for good for those who love God, who are called according to his purpose. For those whom he foreknew he also predestined to be conformed to the image of his Son.... —Romans 8:28–29 (NRSV)

We couldn't imagine a more beautiful day. My husband, Charlie, and I were in Key West, and while a blizzard raged at home in Connecticut, we strolled in bright sunshine, admiring the flowering plants that seemed to spring from the ground of their own accord.

A father and his daughter, who was probably ten years old, sat on a bench as we walked by. Seeing us, he jumped up, said, "Let's take a walk too," and pulled her to her feet. Surprised, and obviously not ready, she yelped, "Dad, what're you doing!" It was his turn to be surprised, and he backed away a little, waiting for her to collect herself, to see if she would follow.

I thought of how often God sits patiently with me, all-knowing, waiting for me to do something I probably know I should do but don't want to. There are times when He finally pulls me to my feet, and then I, like this child, often protest. Usually, He, like this father, draws back and waits, hoping I'll come to my senses, to His plan. Why do I hesitate? Fear? Uncertainty? Apathy? Weariness? All of the above?

Eventually, the girl rose, grumbling a little, and followed; as I watched, she eventually took her father's hand, and then they both walked more buoyantly, enjoying their time together. They reminded me of how much better I feel when I take my Father's hand and follow His lead.

Father, sit patiently with me when I need to rest, and then gently raise me to follow You.
—Marci Alborghetti

Digging Deeper: Luke 10:38–42; Acts 9:1–19

STAR WORDS: Star Singing

Now write down this song and teach it to the Israelites and have them sing it.
—Deuteronomy 31:19 (NIV)

Perhaps the most demoralizing restriction during the Covid-19 pandemic was not being able to sing together to avoid spreading the virus. Singing had been part of my life since childhood: musicals, choirs, chorales.

Now, nothing. Our imaginative church choir director launched "Quarantine Quire," which, at least, connected us online. She emailed music and audio clips for instruction, then she and her musician husband magically patched the separate parts into a "choir." Our harmonies sounded OK, but we had created them in isolation. We ached for spiritual closeness that only choral singing can provide. Several of us found our faith flagging.

To fill this gaping hole, I ordered a kalimba. Plunked it a few times and never played it again. I ordered a pennywhistle but didn't even open the box. Solitary music-making fell flat.

Then, during the first Lent of the pandemic, I blew dust off my guitar case and tuned the neglected instrument. I leafed through notebooks of yellowing music spanning fifty years, some in original handwriting. I'd played this music for folk masses from Boston to Wyoming. Back then, music connected me to my faith community and to God.

Credit God's mysterious—surprising—ways, but as I strummed an old favorite, it wasn't the song that spoke to me but the person who had taught it. Now the Swedish hymn evoked Ruthie; a reggae "Rock of Ages," Fr. Ho Lung; a "Magnificat," Nick…and dozens more. Alone in my room, this musical communion of saints surrounded me and lifted my weary spirit.

Lord, bless the music-makers who touch our souls.
—Gail Thorell Schilling

Digging Deeper: Psalms 63:7, 137:1–6; Isaiah 51:3; Colossians 3:16

Presidents' Day, Monday, February 19

I urge, then, first of all, that petitions, prayers, intercession and thanksgiving be made for all people. —1 Timothy 2:1 (NIV)

I was eleven years old when I first became aware of a US president. I didn't know the difference between a Republican and a Democrat; I just liked "Ike," as everyone called Dwight Eisenhower, our thirty-fourth president. He was mostly bald but with a boyish grin. His wife, Mamie, was well dressed and well liked.

During his term, Ike authorized the Interstate Highway Program. An engineer came to our school with a large wooden model of a cloverleaf interchange, and he showed us how it would work. Then, when Ike authorized the space program, I was very excited because my brother and I had been building model rockets. Now space travel would become a reality.

I once visited Ike's childhood home in Abilene, Kansas, and I was surprised at the humble white house he grew up in, much like my own house. It made me wonder if I could have been a president myself.

When I was in the seventh grade, Ike had a severe heart attack, and I was stunned. I didn't know presidents could get sick. Later, when I realized that Ike was not a perfect person, I was disappointed, but my mother said, "Pray for the president, Danny. He's just human, and he needs all the help we can give him."

That was when I learned that you don't have to be perfect to have a profound impact on the world.

I am thankful, Lord, that You can use imperfect people as our leaders. —Daniel Schantz

Tuesday, February 20

The workmen were honest and diligent.
—2 Chronicles 34:12 (MSG)

My True Temper SnoBoss twenty-six-inch shovel glided across the newly paved driveway. I scooped up heart-attack-grade, heavy-moisture snow with ease. Gratitude filled my spirit.

This was not always the case. For years, our driveway weathered in disrepair. I hesitated to call for estimates to resurface. Apprehension over extensive costs, discomfort about fitting the renovation work into schedules, or just plain pandemic-induced inertia held me back.

Then, while taking in recycling bins one morning, I detected a shallow, ten-foot-wide driveway depression, littered with broken blacktop. *Now* I had to call for a resurfacing job.

When a sporty E. Sprague Paving utility vehicle arrived for an estimate, my spirits rose. Spotting the "Paver Girl" New York state license plate, I had to smile. With good humor, this husband-and-wife team instilled confidence.

Their work crew polished off the hot-mix job with professional skill. Team members masterfully coordinated the five-ton truck asphalt unloading. Heavy-duty paver and road-roller compactor operators smoothly synchronized efforts. The resulting craftsmanship continues to gratify and inspire me— and to remind me that all parts of God's creation are worthy of our best efforts.

Now I'm energized by the even driveway surface. And, I'm inspired to pursue with excellence the work and tasks of the day ahead.

Creator God, we give thanks for work that is well done. May our efforts today be inspired by the beauty of Your handiwork and that of Your children. Amen.
—Ken Sampson

Digging Deeper: Psalm 90:17; 1 Corinthians 7:17; Revelation 14:13

Wednesday, February 21

CELEBRATE!! God's Personal Blessings
God is our refuge and strength, an ever-present help in trouble. —Psalm 46:1 (NIV)

Every part of our world endures its own damaging weather patterns. Tornadoes. Hurricanes. Floods.

For us in Colorado, it is loud high winds, which trigger my own version of PTSD. When I was a child, our neighbor's roof blew off on Christmas Eve. I vividly remember their broken Christmas tree and presents strewn amidst the debris. Years later, when we owned our own home, wind blew in a huge window at 2 a.m., filling our family room with shattered glass and debris. Worst of all, two years ago, Colorado's hundred-mile-per-hour winds triggered a record-breaking, horrifying wildfire in our drought-parched neighborhood that burned more than a thousand homes to ashes in about twelve hours. Our home survived, but we all still live with the physical and emotional scars.

No wonder that when the wind started blowing loudly yesterday, I pray-pleaded with God to stop it. By this morning, it had diminished to "breezy." As I sat at the kitchen counter, my early-morning-talk-to-God spot, I prayed for a day without the sound of relentless wind.

I sat quietly, just being with Jesus, until I heard a soft, slightly familiar sound, and soon realized it was the gentle sound of raindrops on the roof. Hallelujah! I raised my hands to receive the blessing, slowly inhaling and exhaling the sound of the soft rain that filled my wind-weary soul.

Lord Jesus, I will celebrate this memory of the way You calmed my fear of loud winds with the soft sound of gentle rain. I celebrate the personal blessing of Your answer to my prayer. —Carol Kuykendall

Digging Deeper: Isaiah 41:10;
Philippians 4:4–7

Thursday, February 22

...let us also lay aside every weight...looking to Jesus, the founder and perfecter of our faith...
—Hebrews 12:1–2 (ESV)

It's February. Here in northern Virginia, that means crocuses bloom and hope springs green. Not that that was evident this morning when a high-school neighbor girl phoned. "Miss Evelyn. It's snowing!" Yes, I said. "What if there's no cheerleading practice this afternoon?" The snow will soon turn to rain. There *will* be practice. "What if there's no school tomorrow?" It's going to stop raining and turn warmer. They will not cancel school. "What if there's no game"—it's the Big Game—"tomorrow night?" Before I answered, I heard a guttural, "Oy!" That telltale exhale communicated her distress. She hadn't heard anything I'd said—reasoned predictions of reasonable weather. Rather, her plans for two whole days were jeopardized by "what if?"

Those two words have rattled me far too often. Concerning day-to-day routines: What if my Internet crashes? What if my trusty old car dies? Occasional circumstances: What if I miss my plane connection? What if I get bad news from lab tests? Long-term prospects: What if my life lasts longer than my savings?

As an older man, Mark Twain admitted, "I have known a great many troubles, but most of them have never happened." His humorous quip eases my worried breath. It allows me to see "what if?" for what it often is, a weight that drags down my reasonable reaction and redemptive hope.

Lord, when "what if?" threatens to ruin an hour or a day, help me to lay aside the worry and put my trust in You, the foundation of my hope, the founder of my faith. —Evelyn Bence

Digging Deeper: Matthew 25:25–34

Friday, February 23

For You formed my inward parts; You covered me in my mother's womb. —Psalm 139:13 (NKJV)

Although my mother has been gone nearly twenty years, one of the things I miss about her most is the fun times we had shopping together. Mom was tiny. At 4 feet 11 inches, she carefully maintained her weight at 108 pounds for most of her life. On one occasion, Mom and I were at a well-known department store, and she tried on a lovely outfit. Coming out of the dressing room, she looked at herself in the mirror, sighed, and said, "I am so fat." I couldn't help it; I burst out laughing at how ridiculous that was.

I learned a valuable lesson that day. No one is happy with how they look. We're never satisfied by our appearance. Like my mother, I am judgmental and critical of myself too. I want the perfect body. Oh, how I wish God had made me taller. I'd love to have a cover model's beauty. My reflection is a painful reminder of how far I fall short. Is it any wonder that in the world of nonfiction books, the two top-selling categories are cookbooks and diet books?

And yet when I read Scripture, I am reminded that God created me in His image. The wise, loving, creative genius that is our God carefully knit me together in my mother's womb exactly the way He wished. Now when I look in the mirror, I smile and tell myself I am the daughter of the King, and He loves me exactly the way I am.

Dear Heavenly Father, please help us to see our worth and our beauty in Your eyes, not in our own or the world's. —Debbie Macomber

Digging Deeper: Romans 12:2; Colossians 3:12

Saturday, February 24

Write it down before their eyes, that they may faithfully follow...all its laws. —Ezekiel 43:11 (JPS)

One of the high points of Shabbat morning services for me is to touch the Torah as it is carried through the congregation. For the months of lockdown in Washington State, the synagogue was closed to in-person services, so I only saw the Torah on a computer, a tablet, or a phone. I missed it a lot. It's not just the words—I have seven or eight different translations of the Hebrew on my bookshelves, and I could read them and compare them any time I wanted. I missed the physical presence of the beautifully dressed scroll itself, the only ritual object of ours that has to be perfect in order to be used for prayer.

I thought that touching the Torah and kissing whatever we used to make the contact—a prayer shawl, a book, even our fingers—was the way of honoring it, and I couldn't do that virtually. For several months, I complained to myself about that, and then it occurred to me that maybe—just maybe—God was telling me, "Thanks, but no thanks. You need to start doing more with the words than just getting more versions of them."

I realized that honoring the physical Torah, while beautiful and appealing, was not a substitute for honoring what it meant and what it was saying. What mattered, really, was engaging with the text, not just touching it and then going on with my day.

Lord of all that is hidden in the words and in the world, I meet You in my heart. Thank You for showing me that meeting You in the Torah is really important as well. —Rhoda Blecker

Digging Deeper: Deuteronomy 1:5; 2 Kings 22:8

Sunday, February 25

Take the helmet of salvation and the sword of the Spirit, which is the word of God. —Ephesians 6:17 (NIV)

When I was growing up, our preacher, Brother Jerry, would often make a request of the congregation before he began his lesson. "Hold up your Bibles," he'd say. "Hold them up high and let's see them!" It troubled him that so many people would show up for worship without having brought their Bibles, and I suppose he thought this would help us get into better habits.

I can remember thinking, *What's the big deal?* It wasn't like Brother Jerry wouldn't be reading the scriptures to us anyway. Why did we need to read along?

Over time, I began not only reading along but also keeping a pen in hand to take notes. I love that

I can now look back through my old Bibles and see passages I marked and my comments beside them. Some of those notes come straight from Brother Jerry's lessons. I now have the Bible app on my phone and can read Scripture anywhere, but I'm most engaged when I can mark the text myself.

Recently, our Sunday school teacher told us how his mother would ask the same question every time they were about to leave for worship service: "Do you have your sword?" As he explained, the Word is the only offensive weapon listed in the Scriptures about the full armor of God; everything else is for defense, protection. I'd never thought about that before.

I now see what Brother Jerry understood: a soldier should never be without his or her weapon. Especially in a battle where the stakes are so high, affecting eternity.

Father, thank You for Your Word. Let me never take it for granted. —Ginger Rue

Digging Deeper: John 17:17; 2 Timothy 3:16–17

Monday, February 26

...he be not far from every one of us...
—Acts 17:27 (KJV)

Deep in sleep, I woke up with a start. Something was terribly wrong. An urgent need to pray enveloped me.

"Father, someone needs You. Send Your angels to surround them," I prayed into the dark, quiet night.

After a while the sirens came, and I knew something bad had happened on the highway at the foot of our hill. My prayers were more intense now because I realized God had involved me in something beyond my imagining.

Finally, everything grew quiet, and I drifted back to sleep.

A few days later, I saw a makeshift memorial had risen up by the road. Someone had died there. Had God used my prayers to summon angels to comfort them?

Still, there was more. I was haunted by the memorial, and though I resisted at first, I finally made my way down to the place where flowers, notes, and sentimental objects had been placed. Searching the poignant leavings, I pieced together the story of a teenage girl's short life.

Now came the angel whispers. "Call her mother. Write her a note."

No, I responded. *Her mother must be in shock. She might think I'm crazy. I don't want to add to her pain.*

I would have left it there, but the angel whispers (yes, some interpret them as the Holy Spirit) wouldn't leave me alone. So finally, I wrote the letter. I described the sudden awakening and all that followed. I held my breath and mailed the letter.

The call came several days later. "Thank you, thank you, thank you," a mother sobbed. "I haven't stopped praying for a sign that my daughter wasn't alone when she died. You have answered my prayer."

Father, Your goodness follows me. Thank You.
—Pam Kidd

Digging Deeper: Proverbs 15:3; Jeremiah 23:24

Tuesday, February 27

Because your love is better than life, my lips will glorify you. I will praise you as long as I live, and in your name I will lift up my hands. —Psalm 63:3–4 (NIV)

My wife's family and I gathered around my mother-in-law, Nereida, before she was taken off the ventilator and medicines keeping her alive. Life wasn't easy for Nereida. She buried four children, her husband, and a grandson, and overcame breast cancer. Her faith and prayer life sustained her in good and bad times.

As she lay on the bed with machines monitoring her breathing and heart, I decided to play her favorite Christian song on my phone, "Levanto Mis Manos" (I Lift Up My Hands) by the Christian artist Samuel Hernández. The song is about how when we lift up our hands, our burdens are gone, and God gives us new strength.

As the song played, my wife, Elba, lifted Nereida's left hand and her granddaughter, Jasmine, raised her right hand. Slowly Nereida gained strength and began to move her head left and right. Her lips moved without sound as she sought to sing along. Tears streamed down her cheeks. She was praising the Lord and singing her song one last time with all the strength she could muster up.

Several hours later, Elba and I watched her take her last breath. Even at the end, she was teaching us the same lesson she had taught us throughout her life—that she belonged to the Lord, in life or death.

Lord, let us praise You till the day You call us home.
—Pablo Diaz

Digging Deeper: Psalm 66:17; Habakkuk 3:17–18

Wednesday, February 28

The LORD is my shepherd; I shall not want.... He restoreth my soul: he leadeth me in the paths of righteousness for his name's sake.
—Psalm 23:1, 3 (KJV)

The year after my husband Don's death, my house fell apart. The furnace quit, followed by the hot-water heater and oven. The breakdowns weren't unexpected; those appliances were nearly forty years old. But the oven had to be ordered and didn't arrive for four months. Then a freak windstorm slammed a storm door open forcefully enough to rip off part of the door frame. A few nails and lots of duct tape held the doors together during the two-month wait for replacements. My dog, Pepper, tore up three sections of molding. The roof developed a leak, the ceiling fan quit, and the built-in vacuum cleaner died. To top it off, the cellar flooded and partially collapsed, shorting out the water-well pump and wiring.

The roof and ceiling fan aren't yet repaired, but there have been many bright spots. Welding and an inexpensive part fixed the furnace. An efficient hot-water heater was quickly installed. Nephew Jeff and wife, Yuki, gave me a toaster oven complete with an air fryer. Grandson David replaced the molding. The new doors fit better than the old ones. And the well repairmen worked after-hours to repair and relocate the pump and restore running water.

As I adjust to life without Don, there are times when I feel like I'm falling apart just like my house. But visits, messages, and practical help arrive when I most need them. And always, our loving Lord and Shepherd restores my soul.

Thank You, Lord, for those who fixed my house and those who are healing my heart. —Penney Schwab

Digging Deeper: Psalm 23; 1 Thessalonians 5:12–13

Thursday, February 29

Beloved, let us love one another, for love is from God, and whoever loves has been born of God and knows God. —1 John 4:7 (ESV)

My grandpa held up a worn photograph. He pointed to people preserved in black and white.

"Our family immigrated to the United States in the early 1900s," he said. "This picture was taken shortly after."

My grandpa and I had spent the evening sifting through old photographs at my request. My heritage is important to me. I wanted to better understand where I came from. I reached into the photo box and pulled out a picture of two boys. One boy held a simple runner sled. The other stood nearby, boots planted in snow.

"Who are they?" I asked.

My grandpa inspected the picture. "The boy with the sled is my uncle Arthur," he said. "The other boy is my father."

My chest tightened. My grandpa rarely talked about his father. I knew that the two had been close. I also knew that, when my grandpa was a young man, his father had passed unexpectedly. I waited for words. Maybe a story about my great-grandfather. But there was only silence.

My grandpa tilted his head, viewing the boys through bifocals. Then he smiled softly. That smile spoke what words never had. My grandpa lost his father a lifetime ago. But he still loved his father deeply. Age. Time. Death. None of these could change my grandpa's love.

I had desired to know where I came from. Now I did—a family who loved relentlessly. My grandpa carefully set down the picture of his father. And I prayed that I would learn to love as deeply as my grandpa did.

Lord, let my love for others be timeless, boundless, and endless. —Logan Eliasen

Digging Deeper: Proverbs 3:3–4;
Ephesians 3:16–19

YOU WERE CALLED TO PEACE

1 _____

2 _____

3 _____

4 _____

5 _____

6 _____

7 _____

8 _____

9 _____

10 _____

11 _____

12 _____

13 _____

14 _____

15 _____

16 _____

17 _____

18 _____

19 _____

20 _____

21 _____

22 _____

23 _____

24 _____

25 _____

26 _____

27 _____

28 _____

29 _____

MARCH

*How beautiful on the mountains are the feet
of those who bring good news, who proclaim
peace, who bring good tidings, who
proclaim salvation, who say to Zion,
"Your God reigns!"*

—Isaiah 52:7 (NIV)

Friday, March 1

They will still bear fruit in old age, they will stay fresh and green. —Psalm 92:14 (NIV)

Surrounded by a host of family and friends, my Aunt Dorothy danced in the center of the circle as we sang Stevie Wonder's "Happy Birthday." We danced while we sang, but no one could outdance the eighty-year-old birthday girl.

I smiled as I witnessed the joy my aunt exuded, her arms raised, hips swaying, fingers snapping. Her contagious joy gave no evidence of the rough road she had walked over the past decades. She had battled and overcome breast cancer. She lost her husband during her middle-aged years. A few years later, she lost her forty-four-year-old son suddenly, due to his struggles with seizures. And the year before her eightieth birthday, she lost another son, age fifty-five, to cancer.

My aunt has walked through heartbreaking years. And still, her remarkable spirit clings to God's promises and manifests joy and contentment. Sure, she lives with the same aches and pains that the average octogenarian suffers, but she continues to laugh—and dance—through it all.

As I watched Aunt Dorothy sashay across the dance floor, stopping only to greet her guests and enjoy her birthday meal, I made a promise to myself. No matter the hardships I face in life, no matter the trials I endure, I made a commitment to just keep trusting in God...and to keep dancing. And, since my aunt's party, on the days I feel my spirits dropping, I tell Alexa to play some good R&B and practice my favorite kind of therapy. I dance until I feel the joy bursting through like a ray of sunshine.

Father, may I find joy through all the days ahead, whether they bring sunshine or rain. And give me strength to dance through them all.
—Carla Hendricks

Digging Deeper: Psalm 1:1–3; 2 Corinthians 2:16; Philippians 4:4

Saturday, March 2

…for while bodily training is of some value, godliness is of value in every way, as it holds promise for the present life and also for the life to come. —1 Timothy 4:8 (ESV)

I sucked in a breath as sharp pain zinged through my lower back. I paused midway up the basement stairs and gripped the railing, waiting for the pain to subside. I knew what this particular pain meant—weeks, possibly months, of nursing my angry muscles until I'd be able to function normally without severe discomfort.

"What do you think caused it?" my mom asked when I told her I'd reinjured my back.

I tried to remember if I'd done something unusual that day, like heavy lifting or twisting the wrong way. "I didn't do anything that could explain this much pain."

"Didn't you say you haven't had time for massage lately? If you ignore those things for too long, they'll get out of control."

And grow so bad that I couldn't ignore them anymore. My heart finished the thought as her statement struck a deeper chord than she'd intended.

Back pain wasn't the only thing that had flared up lately. An old fear had returned, interfering with my sleep and daily life. Had I neglected my spiritual health too? I hadn't spent as much time in the Word and prayer recently as life's demands increased. But, like the back pain that seized my attention because of neglect, that sinful fear was a signal I'd failed to care for my soul.

I thanked my mom with the promise to take time for better health. First up, an appointment with my Bible and the Lord.

Father, help me to stay disciplined in cultivating godliness through time spent with You. —Jerusha Agen

Digging Deeper: 1 Timothy 6:11–12;
2 Timothy 3:16

Sunday, March 3

Truly my soul finds rest in God; my salvation comes from him. —Psalm 62:1 (NIV)

I was invited to speak at a church up in Iowa, but it was a six-hour round trip, with rain in the forecast. Reluctantly, I agreed to go.

Rainy days depress me, and I felt as though I bungled my talk on "God's Grace." Chagrined, I was weaving my way through the crowd to escape, when an old farmer in bib overalls came up to me and hugged me. "Thank you for explaining grace," he said, and then he told me about his family: three boys and one girl. When he got to the girl, his voice tightened, and he said, "She died…when she was only thirty-three…she was the best of the lot…everybody loved her…I blame myself…I wasn't a good father…I was harsh…I didn't know the Lord back then…will God ever forgive me?" Tears slid down his sunburned face.

I hugged him and assured him that God would indeed forgive him. He wiped his eyes with a red bandana, and then his tense face softened into a portrait of peace. His old eyes seemed calm and rested.

On the way home, I was thinking, "God, you didn't send me up there to speak, did you? You sent me there to listen, to one man whose heart was crushed."

Then I thought of all the people I pass by every day who may also be struggling with regret. The gentle *swish, swish, swish* of the windshield wipers reminded me that I need to slow my pace and be ready to listen to people in need.

For the peace that comes only from forgiveness, Lord, I give thanks. —Daniel Schantz

Digging Deeper: Romans 5:1; Jude 1:2

Monday, March 4

CELEBRATE!! A Meaningful Milestone

So do not fear, for I am with you. —Isaiah 41:10 (NIV)

When our son Derek was nine years old, he was diagnosed with type 1 diabetes. At that time, in the 1980s, this diagnosis was especially difficult for a child to accept and manage. Lots of finger pricks to test blood sugar and insulin shots two or three times daily, with careful attention to choosing the right amount of insulin. These responsibilities sometimes overwhelmed us, but the challenge felt especially hard when diabetes began chipping away at Derek's self-image.

We could help with the physical responsibilities, but these new realities also threatened him emotionally. Before diabetes, he had seen himself as an athlete who could win races and score baskets. Now he felt less confident. He didn't want to go to a friend's birthday party because he couldn't eat cake and he didn't want to be "different." I began fervently praying, "Lord, please don't allow diabetes to change Derek's choices or self-confidence. May this challenge strengthen, not diminish, him."

He faced some difficulties in his growing-up years but chose a college far from home where he learned to handle his challenges and lean on his friends and faith. On the twentieth anniversary of his diagnosis, he planned a celebration in Colorado to thank God and his friends and family for their support. His hardy group of friends climbed one of Colorado's "fourteeners" (mountains that reach higher than

14,000 feet) and offered prayers of gratitude at the top of that snow-covered mountain.

That night, we hosted a dinner for the group. I looked around the room and silently thanked God for His answer to a mother's prayer, demonstrated by Derek's choice to mark this milestone with a truly joyous celebration.

> **Jesus, this memory always strengthens my faith. Thank You for Your faithfulness.**
> —Carol Kuykendall

Digging Deeper: Romans 8:24–25; 1 Peter 5:10–11

Tuesday, March 5

Do not neglect to do good and to share what you have, for such sacrifices are pleasing to God.
—Hebrews 13:16 (ESV)

One thing I love about our neighborhood is Bible Club. For years, parents have hosted grade-based, gender-divided Bible Clubs before or after school each week. That means that every Tuesday morning, my backyard fills with two dozen third-grade girls. They gather before school for forty minutes to hear a Bible story, pray together, and then walk into school as a group. Two other parents and I serve breakfasts that range from smoothie bowls to store-bought muffins, while we fill their spiritual cups with Old Testament stories and reminders of God's love.

Because we meet outside, we have a rule that we cancel if it's below forty degrees; that would just be too cold for these Alabama girls to sit and focus!

For several weeks in a row, I would check the weather and see it was hovering right at forty-one. *Are we crazy to press on, Lord? Should we just pause until spring?*

The next day, at our grocery store, the bulk containers of hot chocolate were on sale. *I see what you're thinking, Lord!* I grabbed a canister and headed home, ready to face the next morning.

The girls showed up, ready to learn, and I made twenty-four servings of hot chocolate, exactly the number of mugs in my cabinet.

Sometimes it's hard to know if you're making the right decision; you just have to move forward in faith. On that morning, I felt God give me a high five as I whisked that cocoa, blessing our efforts to pour into these sweet girls.

Lord, blessed am I when I have the chance to share Your Word and love with others. Thank You for affirming me when I'm indecisive. —Ashley Kappel

Digging Deeper: Matthew 25:23; Galatians 5:13

Wednesday, March 6

Do not be anxious about anything....
—Philippians 4:6 (NASB)

I recently decided to have LASIK surgery. In most circles, this is considered a well-tested and safe procedure, but I wasn't altogether comfortable with someone whaling away on my eyeballs with a light saber. Still, the initial consultation went well, and the doctor assured me everything looked like clear sailing. She also said I would have to come home following the procedure and keep my eyes shut for a minimum of five straight hours, no exceptions.

I suppose a person could put a positive spin here. An opportunity to listen to an audiobook or maybe take a long nap. For me, forced blindness only added to the unease.

My family, on the other hand, bless their evil hearts, immediately began discussing what kind of practical jokes could be accomplished in my closed-eyed state. I had to admire their creativity. The conversation started with cold water, then Sharpies, and went as far as an Internet search for live snakes.

In the end, it didn't matter. I don't get along with snakes but, as it turns out, I don't get along with Vicodin either. I stumbled into my bedroom feeling like a half-dead sponge.

Let the pranks begin.

My wife helped me to the bed. My daughter started an audiobook for me.

I love those guys.

Isn't it funny, even little things in life can take us out of our depth. But guess what? I woke up after five hours and saw trees and clouds clearer than I have in years. Sometimes being out of our depth is how God brings us blessings.

And not a Sharpie or snake anywhere.

Lord, thank You for even the small trials. And how much clearer we can see afterward to reflect on Your faithfulness on the journey. —Buck Storm

Digging Deeper: Proverbs 3:24; John 14:27

Thursday, March 7

I said, LORD, be merciful unto me: heal my soul.... —Psalm 41:4 (KJV)

The killing of George Floyd was a day of reckoning for many Americans. I count myself in that number. It was tough to realize that I was living in a privileged world only because of the color of my skin. I felt ashamed.

Over a business lunch, I found an unexpected community with two friends who expressed similar feelings. "My parents always stressed that social justice was a responsibility of our faith," I explained, "and here we are, the three of us recognizing injustice." It was then and there that we pledged to do something to make our world at least a little bit better. Between us, we contacted other like-minded business friends and invited them to join us in forming a group.

Every person who we invited showed up. We shared feelings of our inadequacy and brainstormed ways that we might work as individuals to bring change. We invited speakers from depressed communities to educate us. Even the great civil rights icon Bernard Lafayette agreed to speak to our group, explaining that his resolve came when as a child he saw his grandmother mistreated because of her color.

We found that each of us had power to influence the future in some way. Scholarships for minority students were underwritten, steps were taken to address diversity in our businesses, and mentorships with children of color were formed.

In all this, we discovered that the dream for equality reaches far beyond what money can buy. For don't we all have the power to look into the eyes of each child of our God and see His hope for humankind there?

Father, I saw a clip of George Floyd's daughter saying, "My daddy changed the world." I thank You, Father, that he changed mine. —Brock Kidd

Digging Deeper: Proverbs 23:7; Matthew 6:22

Friday, March 8

People do not light a lamp and put it under the bushel basket; rather, they put it on the lampstand, and it gives light to all in the house. In the same way, let your light shine.... —Matthew 5:15–16 (NRSVUE)

There I stood on the subway platform, waiting for a train. Like the other people standing there, I kept checking my phone, then peering down the tracks to the long, dark tunnel where the uptown train should appear. Any moment now. The first sign would be a faint glow in the distance, then the headlights coming our way with a fierce rumble.

Light, I thought. *That's what we're all looking for.* How well Jesus understood this, saying, "I am the light of the world. Whoever follows me will never walk in darkness but will have the light of life" (John 8:12, NRSVUE). He showed us how in faith we, too, could be a source of divine illumination, as he says in the book of Matthew: "You are the light of the world" (5:14, NRSVUE).

I looked around me at the other passengers and thought, *Yes, us. All of us.* We all have that potential, to be a source, to be something that could signal a new journey, a light-filled one, taking us to destinations that we might never imagine. Not without that light.

Finally, it came. The light at the end of the tunnel. The train came to a halt, the doors opened, we stepped inside, and the doors closed, the train heading on its way. Here we were, all together, shepherded by a driver and the electric power that came beneath the tracks. Bonded for a moment in waiting for a light.

Help me, Lord, to cultivate all the gifts and talents You have given me to let my light shine.
—Rick Hamlin

Digging Deeper: Psalm 119:105; Isaiah 60:1; John 1:5

But the greatest of these is love.
—1 Corinthians 13:13 (NIV)

The news that one of my books was a finalist for an award was an unexpected honor, so I made arrangements to attend the conference where the winners would be announced. But I assured myself that even if I didn't win, I would be thankful for the recognition.

Arriving at the conference with a happy heart, I soon encountered one disappointment after another. From registration to miscommunication, things went downhill. Still, I hoped the book would do well. However, the night of the awards, not only did I not win, but also my finalist certificate was misplaced.

Needless to say, I returned home discouraged, feeling like the biggest loser ever.

The next day, my adult son Bret, whose hobby is writing music, singing, and playing his guitar, invited my husband and me to watch him perform at a local restaurant. Naturally, I wanted to go and support him.

We arrived at the outdoor venue, giving Bret and his wife, Sara, a hug before taking a seat near the stage. Then Bret surprised me by dedicating the next song to us for our anniversary. When he sang "Stand by Me," I couldn't help crying, knowing he was telling me he appreciated the years I had done just that. Words can't express how full my heart was from the way he recognized my importance in his life.

As I compared the lows of the previous week to the mountaintop experience of my son's tribute, I realized there was no greater award that I could have received.

Lord, help me appreciate the things in life that really matter, especially the love of my family.
—Marilyn Turk

Digging Deeper: Psalm 127:3; 1 Corinthians 13:1–13

Sunday, March 10

…Jesus said, "…you will know the truth, and the truth will set you free." —John 8:31–32 (NIV)

Last week, I visited my mother in her nursing home. She is one hundred years old and still sharp and witty. It was a lovely day, and she asked if I would push her in her wheelchair through the beautiful garden outside of her window. As we gazed at the spring flowers, I groused about growing older. Mother suddenly turned, looked me in the eye, and in a regal voice exclaimed, "Scott, age is only your perspective on things. You can be as young as you want to be—and I'm living proof of it!" She spoke with the authority of experience. And, for once, I surprised us both and really listened!

The balanced truth is that my father died at forty-six from a sudden heart attack, leaving my mother a forty-three-year-old widow with two young children. For years, I had secretly harbored the fear that I might die young too. This anxiety often made me an intense and driven young man. Finally, after jogging hundreds of miles, gobbling bottles of vitamins, and consulting multiple cardiologists during my thirties, I slowly realized that I was not destined to die young. More than that, I'd spent so much of my young life consumed with worries about death that I'd forgotten to focus on *living*.

My mother's wise perspective contains the powerful truth: whether we are young or old, we must live each day with the full expectation that life is good and promising. Death will come when it comes. But we can live every day to the fullest, confident that the Spirit of all life walks with us, even into eternity.

Father, may I make the choice this day not to fear death but to embrace life. Amen. —Scott Walker

Digging Deeper: John 6:35; Romans 12:2; Galatians 2:20

Monday, March 11

The LORD would speak to Moses face to face, as one speaks to a friend. —Exodus 33:11 (NIV)

When I studied for the ministry, we were required to have a spiritual director.

In one direction session, I asked Fr. Fernando to explain prayer. He replied, "Above all, prayer is good friends spending time together, getting to know one another."

Not convinced, I asked, "Why do we have to tell God about ourselves if God knows all things?"

He smiled. "True friendship isn't about having *to do* something. Rather, it's a willingness to let the other person into our hearts; letting them see us as we are. Perhaps you are friendly with God but not yet friends?"

Taking a walk that evening, I noticed two students, Tony and Keith, sitting on a bench talking. Their voices were carried by a gentle breeze toward me. I couldn't make out a word they were saying, yet I was transfixed by how animated they were, obviously enjoying each other's company. I could even hear joy in their laughter.

And then a thought formed in my mind: this is what Fr. Fernando was referring to when he spoke about friendship with God. Always present, just beneath the surface, was my constant fear that God would ask something of me that I could not do. But when I saw Keith and Tony together that evening, I knew what I now wanted: I wanted to be friends with God.

Starting that night and continuing to the present day, one of my daily prayers is for God and me to become good friends. I'm happy to report: so far, so good!

Lord, teach me how to be a good friend to You and to others. Amen. —Adam Ruiz

Digging Deeper: Proverbs 17:17; Luke 5:20; John 15:13

And let us run with perseverance the race marked out for us. —Hebrews 12:1 (NIV)

My nerves were getting the best of me, even from the metal bleachers at my son's high school stadium. It had been over thirty years since I'd set foot on a track, but seeing him lined up among a cluster of mid-distance runners brought back memories.

Although my son was a sophomore, he hadn't participated in an organized sport in several years, favoring band as his extracurricular activity. Others on his team and the opposing teams probably had more running experience. They may have trained in other sports that would give them an athletic advantage.

Yet my instructions to him were simple: Run your race. Focus on doing your best. Cross the finish line.

When the starting pistol was shot, the runners moved together in a tight pack. By the time they rounded the first curve, some of the runners had begun to pull away. I watched as my son fell behind. I cheered him on from the stands—probably embarrassingly loud—but my pride swelled as I watched him not only do something he'd never done before but also persevere.

We all have a race to run, knowing that God is cheering us on. He doesn't compare us to other people but expects us to run the race He set before our individual lives. And to do it well. And though by the sports-world standards my son came in last, from a mother's eyes, he was victorious simply because he didn't give up.

Lord, help me stay focused on the race You've given me to run. I pray that I run it well and that my faith and love for You carry me to the finish.
—Tia McCollors

Digging Deeper: Psalm 119:32; Isaiah 40:3; 2 Timothy 4:7; James 1:12

Wednesday, March 13

"My grace is sufficient for you, for my power is made perfect in weakness." —2 Corinthians 12:9 (NIV)

All my life I've struggled with ADD, now known as ADHD or attention deficit hyperactivity disorder. I've always been what I call spontaneous, but you might term impulsive. A mind that's curious, wandering, dreaming, and scheming. Pain caused by tumors on the nerves of my face and mouth kept facial expressions and talking to a minimum. But that didn't keep me from thinking about what I'd say if I could.

When I was delivered from tumor pain, thoughts tumbled out of my mouth so fast and frequently, I didn't know who I was anymore. A word-nerd with thoughts squirreled away has a lot to say.

At a wedding reception, I was seated beside a wonderfully engaging lady. For two solid hours, she talked and talked and talked, never asking a thing about me. She was interesting, but she wasn't interested. That evening, I prayed: "I want to give others a chance to speak, Lord, to be more thoughtful. To channel this sudden urge to babble into something that matters."

My answer to that prayer was so stunning, it stilled me. I began to pay close attention, to really notice others. When I observe something I know will shape me forever, I find a way to quietly tell the folks involved. Ask them to hold it in their hearts, as will I.

Now nudges, I call them. Can you believe it? God is using my ADHD impulsivity to slow me down, to focus. To better love the people in my path.

Who but You, Lord, would have a strength in mind for my every weakness? —Roberta Messner

Digging Deeper: Psalm 73:26; Isaiah 40:29; Romans 8:26; 2 Corinthians 12:10

Thursday, March 14

God is our refuge and strength, a very present help in trouble. —Psalm 46:1 (KJV)

I'd had a rough day at work and was unwinding by the fire, with my nose in a book, trying to get lost in the story.

"Mom! The front door is open!" my son Henry yelled. "The cats are outside!" He opened the door and quickly corralled one in. Although we live on a rural road, the highway is nearby and we keep our cats indoors all the time just to keep them safe.

I ran outside to see Gillie, our big, fluffy orange tabby, standing in the icy snow, fur puffed up, eyes wide. I approached him slowly, hoping he wouldn't run as Henry went after Kirby, Frank, Woopy, and Sherry. It only took a few minutes, but by the time we got them inside, I was freezing and my nerves were spent.

We counted all five cats three times to make sure we had everyone inside and then sat on the couch by the fire.

"Look at Gillie," Henry said. "His eyes are still huge." They were. Since we had adopted Gillie two years ago, this was the first time he had ever ventured out. Who knows what he thought?

Henry picked Gillie up and gave him a hug. He wrapped Gillie in a soft blanket and sat on the couch, softly petting the fur between his ears. "He just needs to know he's safe where he belongs," Henry said. "He's home."

Gillie closed his eyes and fell asleep—and taking his cue, I let go of my bad day, closed my eyes, and prayed.

Lord, when I am feeling lost and upset, confused about the world and my place in it, remind me I am safe in Your arms. —Sabra Ciancanelli

Digging Deeper: Psalms 16:8, 28:7

Friday, March 15

David said to Saul, "Let no one lose heart on account of this Philistine; your servant will go and fight him." —1 Samuel 17:32 (NIV)

A couple years ago, a team from little Saint Peter's University in Jersey City, New Jersey, nearly made it to the finals of the NCAA men's basketball tournament. Even casual fans like me pulled for them.

What makes us root for the underdog? I mean, who rooted for Goliath except his fellow Philistines—and I bet even a few of them were secretly pulling for David. I think what we see in the underdog is ourselves, up against forces that often feel overpowering.

Wasn't Jesus himself an underdog? He wasn't the progeny of a revered rabbi. He wasn't born to royalty. He was the son of a humble Hebrew carpenter, brought into this world by a Jewish woman of even more modest origins. He led a ragtag squad of unemployed laborers in a small corner of the Middle East spreading a simple gospel of love and justice that would change the course of history.

If ever there was an underdog religion, it was early Christianity, whose adherents were persecuted and martyred, whose faith was outlawed by the Roman Empire. And yet Christianity prevailed, built upon a rock I can't help pointing out was named Saint Peter.

Christianity is still an underdog religion. Practiced as Jesus commanded, we champion the poor. We defend the defenseless, feed the hungry, clothe the naked, house the homeless, love the unloved.

Many of us feel like underdogs faced with the problems of the world. And yet every time we do the things our Christianity asks of us, we triumph. We overcome. We are David against Goliath.

Lord, our faith is our power. Your strength is ours when we follow Your teachings. —Edward Grinnan

Digging Deeper: 1 Samuel 17; Matthew 16:18–19

Saturday, March 16

If I go up to the heavens, you are there; if I make my bed in the depths, you are there. —Psalm 139:8 (NIV)

My bicycle sliced through the March air. As I approached an intersection, I called back to my friend Oscar.

"Which direction?" I asked. I hadn't been in Perry, Iowa, before, but this was Oscar's hometown. Oscar coasted parallel to me.

"Hang a left," he said. "I want to show you something."

I let Oscar take point. We turned left, then rode straight for several blocks. Oscar slowed as we approached a small church. A marquee sign displayed a sermon title in English and Spanish. I wondered why Oscar had stopped here. The church was ordinary. It didn't have stained glass windows or a bell tower. The building wasn't old enough to be historic or new enough to be impressive.

Oscar smiled. "This is where I met Jesus," he said.

I recalled Oscar's testimony. As a boy, he had emigrated from El Salvador—leaving his friends and much of his family. His first few years in the United States had been difficult. He struggled to adapt to a new life and to learn English through immersion. Then, one Sunday, Oscar wandered into a church. There, he heard the gospel for the first time. And once again Oscar's life was changed.

To most, this church was an ordinary building. But for Oscar, it was holy ground. It was where Oscar learned of the Savior who left his home in heaven to save the world. The Savior who understood Oscar completely and loved him unconditionally.

I stood before the humble church where a young boy had met the Lord.

"It's truly beautiful," I said.

Jesus, thank You for reaching hearts in chapels and cathedrals and anywhere else Your people are.
—Logan Eliasen

Digging Deeper: Exodus 3:1–5; Ezekiel 1:1

St. Patrick's Day, Sunday, March 17

The words you say will either acquit you or condemn you. —Matthew 12:37 (NLT)

This spring, I taught a creative nonfiction workshop, in which students learn to delight and instruct us with stories from their lives. As always, their peers praised whatever they wrote—So relatable! What a good metaphor!—while I tore it apart. My complaints are pretty much the same every year: they want to explain lessons they've learned from whatever happened, but I want them to tell the story itself and let us get there on our own.

As it happened, I was concurrently reading St. Patrick's fifth-century account of his life and ministry. Though it's only eleven pages long and says more about God than himself, it's surprisingly engaging. My students would call it "relatable," though they've had nothing like Patrick's experience: enslaved, carried off to a foreign country, somehow managing to escape and cross the ocean back home to Britain, then returning to minister to those who enslaved him.

Historical articles focus in on these exciting events, but Patrick barely touches on them. Instead, he goes on about being an unlearned bumpkin who, but for God's calling, wouldn't be the converter of souls he became.

If Patrick were in my workshop, I'd tear up his writing. "Where's the dialogue?" I'd ask. "I want to *see* those slave traders."

Even so, I found myself copying passages—like him calling himself a stone mired "deep in the mud" whom God prized out and set atop a wall—and pasting them into a document for future mulling. Other writers, even my own students, have so much to teach me!

Thank You, Lord, for the voices of those who've loved You from the beginning of time until today. Help me hear them, value them, learn from them. —Patty Kirk

Digging Deeper: Luke 1:1–4;
2 Timothy 3:14–17

The good man does not escape all troubles—he has them too. But the Lord helps him in each and every one. —Psalm 34:19 (TLB)

It was almost lunchtime—time for my big excursion to the mailbox. I love unlocking that tiny little door. It's like receiving a surprise package six days a week. Tucked inside, there could be a note from a friend, a catalog filled with lovely things I'll never purchase, or maybe a coupon for a new restaurant I've wanted to try. I never know what's going to be hiding inside. At least, I didn't until a few months ago, before I turned sixty-five.

I opened the door and peered inside. My joyful anticipation morphed right into an eye roll. I didn't even need to open the envelopes. I could tell what they held: more advertisements for insurance. There were offers to supplement my Medicare; insure my life, home, car, and appliances; help cover long-term hospital or cancer care; provide extended warranties; protect my credit card; and prepay future funeral expenses. It felt as though turning sixty-five meant I was suddenly on the brink of tragedy and disaster. Apparently, with enough insurance coverage, I could allay any fears I might have about the future.

But insurance isn't assurance. God assures me that whatever lies ahead, He'll be with me and guide me. Yes, I'll strive to be financially responsible as I age. But I don't need to fear getting older. I'd rather focus on celebrating God's gift of each day, regardless of what it brings.

Lord, You're my only true source of security. I willingly put all of my tomorrows into Your capable hands.
—Vicki Kuyper

Digging Deeper: Deuteronomy 31:8; Isaiah 46:4; John 14:27; 2 Corinthians 4:16

Tuesday, March 19

Confess your sins to each other and pray for each other so that you may be healed. —James 5:16 (NLT)

Beloved missionary Amy Carmichael once wrote, "Let nothing be said about anyone unless it passes through the three sieves: Is it true? Is it kind? Is it necessary?"

Reading those words on my devotional calendar gave me a pang of guilt. I'd spoken harsh words about another woman to my friend Pam over coffee and croissants just the day before. Those words had not been kind and were certainly not necessary, as I let my frustration flow unchecked. There's a verse in James warning us that, "no human being can tame the tongue. It is a restless evil, full of deadly poison." I'd certainly spewed poisonous words into my friend's ear yesterday, and now I felt convicted by the Holy Spirit.

I asked God for His forgiveness. With a contrite heart, I called Pam, asking for her forgiveness, too, for speaking as I'd done. It had been gossip—perhaps even malicious gossip—and I was ashamed of myself. I'd let my exasperation with another person's behavior get the better of me. Pam quickly reassured me of her forgiveness and understanding, even admitting that she, too, had been guilty of similar behavior in the past. Pam promised to keep me in her prayers. I promised to do the same for her. Confessing brought healing to my heart as well as a closer relationship with Pam—my sweet, understanding Christian friend.

Dear Heavenly Father, thank You for being slow to anger and, most of all, for Your gracious mercy to me when I come broken in spirit with a contrite heart.
—Shirley Raye Redmond

Digging Deeper: Psalms 32:1–5, 51:10

Wednesday, March 20

All Scripture is God-breathed and is useful for teaching, rebuking, correcting and training in righteousness.... —2 Timothy 3:16 (NIV)

Here's a confession: I am a news junkie. I listen to radio news most of the day, read several online newspapers daily, and never miss my evening local news report. As a trained journalist, it's important for me to know what's happening in the world.

When the news is pleasant, it's fine to submerge myself in the goings-on of the day. But when the reports detail upsetting or unnerving stories, I can become stressed and start to have a negative outlook. But when you have a desire to be well informed, what's the middle ground?

A recent devotional study offered an alternate plan: learn to put the Word before the world! So instead of waking up to the local news, scanning headlines, and *then* reading my Bible, I flipped my priorities.

Simply switching my Bible study to start my day, rather than beginning with the news, gave me a sense of peace and grounding. It even helped me to become more consistent about reading the Word, as putting this first has made studying the Bible more of a habit than an obligation.

Sure, there are some days when I succumb to my news addiction and turn on the radio to find out the results of an election or to find out some other outcome. But never do I feel as good about that as I do when I face the news and the day with the protection of God's Word around me.

Dear Lord, thank You for Your Word; it covers me with spiritual armor to face whatever comes my way each day. —Gayle T. Williams

Digging Deeper: 1 Thessalonians 2:13; 2 Timothy 3:16–17

Thursday, March 21

If I must boast, I will boast of the things that show my weakness. —2 Corinthians 11:30 (NIV)

My daughter is learning to play the recorder. Sometimes, during practice, she'll make a few mistakes and absolutely melt down. I've always tried to teach her mistakes are a valuable part of learning. So why this extreme distress?

As if in answer, my own relationship with mistakes decided to show up.

A friend and I had made plans to play our trumpets together in public. "It'll be fun!" he insisted, but on the morning of, I was terrified. I just knew I was going to mess everything up. My friend would regret asking me to play. The people listening would wish I'd be quiet.

"How do I make this awful fear go away?" I asked my brother.

"You have to stop caring about the mistakes," he said. "It's inevitable. You're going to make them. So what?"

Literally impossible, I thought in reply. There's almost nothing that scares me more than asking others to accept my weaknesses. Because...what if they don't?

But then, I remembered the first time I'd heard the Fairbanks Community Band play. I'd been in their audience, wondering if maybe, just maybe, after twenty years, I'd finally found a place to play my instrument again. I still remember a few of that performance's lovely "mistakes" because what they said to me was: "There can be a place for you here."

I'm sure the musicians who made those "errors" wished they hadn't. Little did they know, they'd played exactly what I'd needed to hear. I'm so grateful they did.

Thank You, God, for this powerful reminder that my idea of what constitutes a mistake and Yours are not always the same thing. —Erin Janoso

Digging Deeper: Isaiah 53:1–5; 2 Corinthians 12:9–10

Friday, March 22

My times are in your hand.... Make your face shine on your servant; save me in your steadfast love! —Psalm 31:15–16 (ESV)

Being present and on time was important to my pastor dad. This sensitivity fueled his hobby of making grandmother clocks for us kids. My clock, crafted from walnut he'd salvaged, was my first piece of furniture. The planed boards framed a golden clock face above the enabling pendulum and weights. Though recently silent, needing repairs, my clock has kept watch over my dining room for decades.

There's a family understanding that the clocks will be passed down to the next generation. It took months to get used to the idea, but—considering that my trusty repairman was up north, near my family—the timing seemed right. When a sister visited from "back home," we packed up the treasure for transport to an awaiting niece. "It's a kindly presence," I explained, thinking of our family ties and spiritual heritage.

When I let the heirloom go, my older sister surprised me with the gift of a wall-hung "school clock." She'd bought it in the 1960s from our natal church when someone complained of its loud ticktock. "I haven't wound it in decades," she said. "But let's try."

As we leveled the timepiece, I mused, "Think of it—this clock would have cued Dad to end his sermons—on time." We smiled when the pendulum kicked in. I miss the handmade clock but not as much as I had expected. I hear a reassuring note in the loud and slightly offbeat ticktock that someone once deemed distracting. It's as if a peaceful presence is saying, "I'm *here*. I'm *here*." I'm sure of it.

Lord, thank You for tangible reminders that we are loved and not alone. —Evelyn Bence

Digging Deeper: Psalm 31:14–24

Saturday, March 23

But when you give alms, do not let your left hand know what your right hand is doing, so that your alms may be done in secret, and your Father who sees in secret will reward you. —Matthew 6:3–4 (NRSVUE)

Years ago, my wife and two daughters and I were out to breakfast with friends in a town an hour from home. Our friends lived in another direction, and we'd chosen a diner located roughly midway between us. None of us had ever been there before.

The food was good. I like breakfast out. We were there for ninety minutes, talking, drinking multiple cups of coffee, when I saw a sign behind the counter: "Cash only. No exceptions."

I leaned over to my wife and pointed to it, and said, "Oh no. I don't have cash, do you?" She looked, and she didn't.

I mentioned the sign to our friends. Did they have any cash, and could they perhaps loan us some? They didn't, either. So, we made a plan: the men would get in the car and go find an ATM, then return to pay the bill.

Just then, our server came over. "I'm sorry," I began saying, assuming she wanted us to pay the bill and go, "we will pay the check really soon. We need to go and get some money."

She said, "No, you don't. That's why I stopped by— to tell you that the people sitting behind you, who left a few minutes ago, paid your bill."

After that, I began to reconsider my own ways of giving. Now I give more freely, and often, and sometimes anonymously. And often without worrying about tax-deductibility.

God, make me a more kindhearted, g enerous person. —Jon M. Sweeney

Digging Deeper: Proverbs 11:25

SEEKING JOY IN A TIME OF GRIEF:
Holding On to Hope

"Out of the mouths of infants and nursing babies, you have prepared praise for yourself."
—Matthew 21:16 (NRSV)

Eyes bright, Mom gestured at the green sprouts in the bulb garden basket we'd sent to arrive before Easter. Recognizing the look on her face, I held my breath joyfully, hoping she would describe how it would look when fully bloomed. She knew so much about flowers, gardens, everything. But then her eyes glazed, fingers fluttering down.

Approaching year seven with dementia, she would be giving no more flower lessons. No more buying extra eggs tomorrow with the Paas Easter Egg dye kit. No more clandestine searches for those hidden eggs that she, I, and my sister, Lori, much preferred: the chocolate ones.

That stab of joy mocked me, an improbable hope that everything would be OK, that God was answering our prayers, that our family would be restored, saved. But, oh, how I yearned to live in that joy! I wanted the Palm Sundays of my childhood, when we heard at church about the wild rejoicing as Jesus entered the temple's east gate, and held our palms up to be blessed, and brought them home to tuck among dried flowers or forsythia. I wanted Mom to prepare us for the solemn week ahead and offer hints about hidden chocolates and dyed eggs and joy to come.

Like the Jews on that original Palm Sabbath, I wondered how joy would come as I quietly drew Mom's attention back to the bulb garden, asking about the different stalks. Gently, she smiled.

Loving Father, thank You for gently bringing me joy when I least expect it. —Marci Alborghetti

Digging Deeper: Nehemiah 1:9–10; Psalm 119:143–147

Monday, March 25

The steadfast love of the LORD never ceases; his mercies never come to an end; they are new every morning; great is your faithfulness.
—Lamentations 3:22–23 (ESV)

Olivia, eight years old, loves her birthday. When she was younger, she would ask, "When is it going to be my birthday?" I'd reply, "When the flowers bloom."

Each year, she looks to our yard as a countdown. March brings green tips; April brings tall tulips. "They're blooming!" she would announce the morning they finally showed their colors.

So you can imagine my heartbreak when, in January, I remembered I had never planted the tulips. I know that tulips are perennials, but our yard is basically a buffet for squirrels and chipmunks, so we typically plant at least sixty bulbs each fall in hopes of sprouting a dozen come spring.

I frantically searched for bulbs. *What do I do?* I prayed. *I know this is a small thing, but it is huge to Olivia.*

In March, I gave it one last shot. *Should I just transplant blooming tulips?* I pondered, desperately browsing our local garden store. When I pulled in the driveway that day, I paused to look at our yard. Where once I had noticed weeds and dry patches, something else now caught my eye: green shoots.

I hopped out of the car and walked up to the beds. There, just in front of the bushes, where I always plant our bulbs, were green shoots. When Olivia got home that day, she squealed with delight. "The countdown is on!" she hollered, as she ran inside.

I feel like God blessed our tiny yard and its dry beds to show me that you can continue to reap from years of sowing, even if you fall short one year. Grace grew in my garden that year, and I'm forever grateful.

Lord, Your mercies are new every morning and in every season. Thank You for blessing me so.
—Ashley Kappel

Digging Deeper: Matthew 6:26, 10:29–31

Tuesday, March 26

Every good gift and every perfect gift is from above. —James 1:17 (ESV)

My dad has always had it on his bucket list to see the northern lights.

And so, when we went to Finland in 2019, we hired an aurora hunter (yes, that's a thing) and paid him $500 (yes, a whole lot of money) to take us out. Together, we drove around lakes, up hills, down dirt roads, and trekked across snow-covered lakes and through icy ravines. The weather seemed perfect, and it was the right time of year but no luck.

We were so disappointed. I was sad for myself, of course, but even more so for my dad, who felt as if he was leaving a bucket-list item unchecked.

Fast-forward three years. I was scrolling around online and I saw an ad for flights to Finland. They were cheap. I called my dad. Should we try again?

We decided to go for it. Three weeks later, we were back at the arctic circle. Only this time, the weather forecast called for clouds and "minimal chances of aurora sightings." We braced ourselves to be disappointed yet again.

We were eating dinner when the waiter said to us that there was a break in the clouds and an aurora outside. We ran out to find the entire sky lit with dancing light. It continued for hours. The people at our hotel said it was the best northern lights they had seen in decades.

God unexpectedly lit up the sky for us—right when we thought it was something we would never see.

God, thank You for beautiful, surprising gifts that come at the perfect time. —Erin MacPherson

Wednesday, March 27

For everything there is a season, and a time for every matter under heaven. —Ecclesiastes 3:1 (ESV)

"Look, it's back." My husband was calling attention to the once-dead fern near our front door.

This foxtail fern rooted in our yard was cherished, so I was gutted when winter led me to believe it died by turning it brown and brittle. I was having a short period of ennui, and I think my husband was sweetly trying to help me focus on hope. Laying eyes on those baby shoots peeking from the dead stalks, I immediately felt a spark of hope and joy.

I cherished the foxtail fern because it was a gift from my mom. Knowing I admired the fern and wanted one of my own, Mom lovingly dug it up from her own yard, placed it in a planting pot, and loaded the large fern unexpectedly in our trunk as we packed up to leave on a visit home. So, the baby sprouts coming up really stirred hope within my soul. The new fern shoots were hope for what was thought lost, hope not just for a cherished plant's life but also for the other places in my life where I need to hope in God's enduring and life-changing love.

Now that I better understand the natural seasons of the fern's life, I know the desolation of winter will lift and tiny green sprouts will peek out in the spring. Like the fern, my spiritual life will experience transitions. Periods of stagnant faith can be followed by periods of spiritual growth. God binds our lives, our faith, and foxtail ferns in hope.

Loving Father, may I always hope in Your love and grow through the seasons of my faith.
—Jolynda Strandberg

Digging Deeper: 1 Samuel 1:26–28; Proverbs 31:26–27; Isaiah 66:13

Maundy Thursday, March 28

SEEKING JOY IN A TIME OF GRIEF: Learning How to Serve

Peter said to him, "You will never wash my feet." Jesus answered, "Unless I wash you, you have no share with me." —John 13:8 (NRSVUE)

During the years of Mom's dementia, my sister was my parents' primary caretaker. Dad wanted Mom home without outside care, and he and Lori worked hard. One thing I did, until Covid-19 made it dangerous to visit regularly, was care for her feet.

I'd sit, working from the same floor where I'd played decades before; she'd sit in her chair facing the large window. Eventually, her toes overlapped, toenails thickening. No ointment could soften them. Toe separators became useless. Sometimes she'd become restless or want her socks back on. When she dozed, she could abruptly shift position, so I stopped using clippers and resorted to just filing everything, including calluses. Our favorite part was rubbing cream all over her feet and ankles afterward.

Years before, when the custom of foot washing first came to church in imitation of Jesus at the Last Supper, Mom adamantly refused to participate. Although I sometimes went through the motions at Maundy Thursday services, I was Mom's daughter and always felt uncomfortable.

Years later, I think she was still uneasy with me sitting at her feet. But it felt right to me. I finally understood the kind of sacrificial love it takes to tend to someone's feet and how necessary it is for the one being washed to feel vulnerable before such humbling and powerful love. I understood why Jesus asked us to do it, literally and figuratively, for each other.

Jesus, help me to be vulnerable, serving You by serving others, and to be served by You through others.
—Marci Alborghetti

Digging Deeper: John 12:3, 7–8; 13:2–20

Good Friday, March 29

SEEKING JOY IN A TIME OF GRIEF: The Comfort of Christ

Jesus cried out with a loud voice, "Eloi, Eloi, lema sabachthani?" which means, "My God, my God, why have you forsaken me?" —Mark 15:34 (NRSVUE)

Just when Mom started to precipitously decline, the floor collapsed in my own life. Long months of feeling vaguely ill culminated in emergency surgery, infection, months of complications, headaches, medication reactions, and more infections. Mom, of course, had no idea of my situation, and I shared few details with Lori and Dad, knowing their plates were full. We were living, individually and together, through a long, agonizing Good Friday.

Where was hope?

We couldn't know Mom's mind; she seemed barely aware of us, much less our problems. Then one Friday afternoon, just before she died, I went to visit her. I was thin, pale, and felt wretched physically, emotionally, and spiritually. But I smiled, spoke heartily, and read to her. She was agitated, sitting up, lying down, gesturing, silent. Suddenly, she leaned forward and reached out her arms. I thought she was silently pleading for me to take her home, but when I moved close to try to comfort her, she clasped my body and gently pulled me to her. Stunned, I realized that somewhere in the depths of what was left, she knew how sick I'd been and was; she was mothering me, loving me.

I hope I comforted her that day. I know she comforted me.

Jesus, even on the Cross, helped me through Mom. As He does for all of us, even when we don't realize it.

Loving Lord, help us remember, during all of our Good Fridays, that You are present, helping, comforting, loving us. —Marci Alborghetti

---

Holy Saturday, March 30

SEEKING JOY IN A TIME OF GRIEF:
Quiet, Expectant Faith

**For all who exalt themselves will be humbled,
and those who humble themselves will be exalted.
—Luke 14:11** (NRSV)

Dad wants you to write Mom's obituary."

My sister sounded weary on the phone. Having done the lion's share of work in Mom's last years, Lori was capably handling the death arrangements in the age of Covid-19. Because there could be no service, we wanted the obituary to convey not only that she was gone but also who she'd been. Grieving during my own health and spiritual crisis was difficult; condensing Mom's story in too few words seemed impossible.

I couldn't sit at the computer. Spotting a lone chickadee on the porch, looking for seeds we'd put out last winter, I remembered Mom protecting the littlest birds from starlings that would drive them from the bird feeder. A few scraggly daffodils reminded me of her filling the house with forsythia and daffodils because they were Dad's favorites, though she disliked the color yellow. A mail appeal from Appalachian Christians made me think of how she'd let us "help" write checks to that very same nonprofit, cautioning us to "never let the right hand know what the left is doing." Warming leftovers, I could hear her admonishing us to clean our plates because children were starving all over the world.

Mom wasn't a "showy" Christian; her Holy Saturdays were calmly patient, perhaps spent planting bulbs or ironing Easter clothes. I can't remember one lecture on Jesus. But in all those quiet Holy Saturdays, those myriad "normal" moments, she was teaching us how to wait for Him.

I was ready to write.

Jesus, thank You for great teachers, especially the quiet ones. —Marci Alborghetti

Digging Deeper: Matthew 6:1–4; Luke 8:1–3

Easter Sunday, March 31

SEEKING JOY IN A TIME OF GRIEF: Victory in Christ

Supposing him to be the gardener, she said to him, "Sir, if you have carried him away, tell me where you have laid him, and I will take him away." —John 20:15 (NRSVUE)

Dad was gazing at the floor. Finally looking up, he asked, "Will I recognize Mom in heaven? Will she recognize me?"

When we lose someone we love—in Dad's case for sixty-nine years, just a few years longer than Lori and I had loved Mom—we must proceed by faith.

Oh, we have theologians and preachers who describe what it will be like to be Risen in and with Christ, even offering ideas about our "new" bodies.

But because we do not witness our loved ones' new life, we cannot yet be like Mary Magdalene, whose weeping became worship upon recognizing her Gardener; or Peter, still ashamed when Jesus taught him what forgiveness really meant at breakfast by the sea; or the devastated, beloved John, almost afraid to enter the tomb and exult; or even Thomas, doubting and then overcome by joy.

When we grieve in the light of Christ's rising, we remember that for that glorious event, we have disciples who provided us written witness. Wonderful, joyous, breathtaking witness! With such evidence, it is easy—necessary—to cry, *alleluia*.

And we can imagine what these blessed witnesses felt facing these moments, days, years, before we meet Jesus and our beloveds: Mary's despairing, dogged sense of duty, Peter's guilt at denying Jesus, John's sorrowful loneliness, Thomas's gnawing doubt.

Today, on Easter, Lori, Dad, and I can witness the witnesses, joyfully anticipating the day when the One Who overwhelmed them with sudden joy brings us all together again.

Risen Lord, today we feel the joy and victory we have in You! —Marci Alborghetti

Digging Deeper: Luke 24:13–35; John 21:1–8

YOU WERE CALLED TO PEACE

1 _____

2 _____

3 _____

4 _____

5 _____

6 _____

7 _____

8 _____

9 _____

10 _____

11 _____

12 _____

13 _____

14 _____

15 _____

16 _____

17 _____

18 _____

19 _____

20 _____

21 _____

22 _____

23 _____

24 _____

25 _____

26 _____

27 _____

28 _____

29 _____

30 _____

31 _____

APRIL

*Now may the God of hope fill you with all joy
and peace in believing, that you may abound
in hope by the power of the Holy Spirit.*

—Romans 15:13 (NKJV)

SEEKING JOY IN A TIME OF GRIEF:
Following Jesus Every Day

Lift up your heads, O gates! and be lifted up,
O ancient doors, that the King of glory may come
in! —Psalm 24:7 (NRSVUE)

"You spent all that time trying to help, and she
hasn't even answered your messages!" I groused to
my husband about an acquaintance who'd called
weeks ago seeking assistance. After Charlie had done
research, arranged a meeting, and then tried to reach
her, there'd been no response.

I forgot about it until we saw her in our doctor's
waiting room later that spring. Looking tired and
pale, she immediately apologized for not following
up. She'd been ill, her son was having trouble, and
she was putting her mother, who had dementia, in
hospice. As she described her mother's situation, I
grew increasingly uncomfortable. Though it was
hard to relive seeing Mom in hospice, there was
more to it.

I felt guilty. While I'd been busily aggravated
at her not getting back to Charlie, she'd been
experiencing the kind of personal and family crises
that I was living through. How many people in
my life were puzzled or annoyed at *my* inability to
respond or even be present?

Here I was, not even a week into the Easter season, fearfully fleeing the foot of the Cross, denying those dark nights of waiting, only to smile vaguely at the open tomb. Grieving takes a long time; so does learning—and living—the message of the Cross and Resurrection. No matter what, Jesus is always present to us. He always responds.

The next day, I prayed for her and her family. A small start.

Risen Lord, gently help me follow You through the pain and joy of the life to come.
—Marci Alborghetti

Digging Deeper: Ecclesiastes 1:22–24; John 20:24–31

Tuesday, April 2

...they will call him Immanuel (which means "God with us"). —Matthew 1:23 (NIV)

Succumbing to peer pressure, I began watching a new television series. "It's an excellent series," one friend said. "It's not a horror. More of a thriller," another added. So every evening, I tuned in to the series that had me immediately hooked.

Somewhere around episode four, however, the story took a turn, living up to the network's description of "dark and ominous." My pulse quickened and eyes bulged. I fought the inner voice advising me to stop watching. I just had to see how the story would end.

That night, a creepy feeling overtook me. I began peeking around dark corners. My only consolation was my large family of six. Seldom am I alone.

Then the day came. I had finished the series, which ended horrifically, and this particular day, I was alone. It also happened to be a Saturday, so I didn't have work to distract my racing thoughts. I prayed, asking God to calm my spirit, to remind me that I had witnessed a fictional story and that He is in control, in spite of evil in the world.

After praying, I looked outside my kitchen window while washing dishes. On my fence sat a beautiful, majestic bird with a breast full of furlike feathers. I watched with awe and amazement. After an online search, I discovered my bird-friend was a Cooper's hawk, and further research revealed that the presence of a hawk can be interpreted as a sign of protection.

Suddenly, I felt as though God had sent a messenger my way when I most needed one. My feathery friend reminded me that God is always with me, protecting me from evil. There's no need to be afraid. He is God with us.

Thank You, Lord, for being ever present in my life.
—Carla Hendricks

Digging Deeper: Isaiah 8:8–10; Romans 8:31

Wednesday, April 3

Guide me in your truth and teach me, for you are God my Savior, and my hope is in you all day long.
—Psalm 25:5 (NIV)

Today I am TK years sober. TK is journalistic shorthand for information to come.

I write these devotions two years in advance of publication, and therein lies the paradox. Sobriety as I practice it is a day at a time. Even though the members of my twelve-step fellowship celebrate our yearly anniversaries, we do so only after we attain them, always remembering that we are sober through the grace of God, a day at a time.

I would certainly be dead by now if I hadn't gotten sober. I was living on and off the streets, unemployed and unemployable, hustling change and cigarettes on lower Broadway. I was suffering both the extreme physical and psychiatric effects of alcoholism, in and out of hospitals, rehabs, and detoxes. Worse, I was alone. Drink and drugs were supposed to swallow up all that loneliness.

Then I found Guideposts, which I had never heard of and assumed was a travel magazine. Substitute *journey* for *travel* would be more like it. Somehow Guideposts gave me a job. I wouldn't have hired me.

By the grace and love of my Higher Power and by miracles I can't count, I had my last drink, God willing, on April 3, 1996. It has been a day at a time. It always will be so. Which is why it will always be TK.

Dear Lord, I am led on this journey by You: a power greater than myself, greater than my addiction, the only power that could save me, a day at a time, by the miracle of sobriety. —Edward Grinnan

Thursday, April 4

He will yet fill your mouth with laughing. . . .
—Job 8:21 (NKJV)

It was still dark out when I stepped out back to throw a bag of trash into our overloaded dumpster. I braced my flashlight hand on the edge of the trash bin, and with my right hand I heaved my sack of trash up on top, but in the process I dropped my brand-new, expensive flashlight, which tumbled down into the bottom of the dumpster.

"Oh, great, just great!" I unloaded the entire dumpster, but when I got to the bottom, my flashlight was not there. Mystified, I began refilling the dumpster, watching for my flashlight as I went along. When I threw the last bag up on top, my flashlight fell out of it, and dropped, once again, down into the bottom of the bin.

"Oh, no, not again!" Once more, I unloaded the dumpster, climbed inside, and retrieved my light, then refilled the dumpster. I was almost done when an overstuffed bag of trash burst open and showered me with wet garbage.

I was sweaty, exhausted, and sore all over. I reeked of broccoli and coffee grounds. I plopped down on the curb to rest, and my eyes filled with tears, but after some rest, I began to see how entertaining all of this actually was, and I began to laugh out loud.

Since then, I have been trying to look for that entertaining spot in every hard day, that fleck of funny that God sends to help us rewrite a tragedy into a comedy.

And that flashlight I dove through garbage to save? It no longer works. Turns out that's not a tragedy.

Thank You, Father, for our ability to reframe our woes with humor. —Daniel Schantz

Digging Deeper: Genesis 2:6; Proverbs 15:15

Friday, April 5

…woe to one who is alone and falls and does not have another to help. —Ecclesiastes 4:10 (NRSVUE)

Here in Wisconsin, near the lake cabin we use, is a small Amish community. I like to support their industries, so I visit to buy things. Canned pickles and jams mostly but also a sauerkraut my wife says is good. When I first stopped, I saw on the table at the farm a sign next to mason jars filled with "dandelion jelly."

I wanted to be friendly, not just lay down cash and go. So I asked the woman at the farm stand a foolish question, unsure how to relate to people living so differently from me. "Dandelion jelly, how do you use it?"

She paused, then said, "Well, I take a piece of bread, and I put it in the toaster. When it comes out, I put butter on it," using hand motions to show me the spreading of butter with a knife. "Then I put on the dandelion jelly." I smiled, said thanks, and paid her. Since then, I try not to ask dumb questions, and we've come to know each other better. I sometimes stop, now, just to talk.

One afternoon, her husband was digging a hole to "plant" an enormous birdhouse in the front yard as I pulled up. He knew my name by then, and as I emerged from the car, his birdhouse began to falter. "Jon!" he yelled, and I ran over to help him catch it from hitting the ground.

I'm grateful for the ways God gives me to help, and be helped, and to be a friend.

Lord, may my path be filled with simple ways of being a friend today. —Jon M. Sweeney

Digging Deeper: Hebrews 12:14

Saturday, April 6

For wherever I am, though far away at the ends of the earth, I will cry to you for help. When my heart is faint and overwhelmed, lead me to the mighty, towering Rock of safety. —Psalm 61:2 (TLB)

As a volunteer at the Tampa International Airport, I answer questions for the thousands of passengers arriving in baggage claim on Sunday mornings. I call airport police when someone loses or finds a purse, bag, cell phone, stuffed animal, or computer. I hand out coloring books, crayons, pens, sunscreen samples, and Tampa Bay vacation literature. I answer questions about how to get to the car rental center or "Where can I tell Uber to pick me up?" Or, "What's the easiest way to get to Clearwater Beach?"

But mostly I watch excited families arriving for their first vacation to sunny Florida. Business travelers. Groups of ladies heading to the beach for their first-ever all-girls trip. Young people anxious to explore the nightlife in Tampa Bay. People in a hurry, all going somewhere to meet someone, start their vacation, or just happy to be back home at last.

Sometimes I see people struggling with wheelchairs, or trying to corral three or four small children, or maneuvering way too much luggage. That's when my airport job reminds me to be thankful of my own blessings, like the opportunity to travel to visit my children, grandchildren, other family members, and friends scattered around the country. I am blessed to travel as much as I do and also blessed that home is the best place of all and that there are always kind people everywhere to answer questions and relieve fears.

Father, whether I'm traveling or working at the airport, help me to be kind, calm, and willing to help anyone during times of stress. —Patricia Lorenz

Digging Deeper: Luke 5:7;
Acts 20:35

STAR WORDS: Surprise—Leo

…for I have learned, in whatsoever state I am, therewith to be content. —Philippians 4:11 (KJV)

When my son and his wife invited me to Baltimore to care for my grandson, age four, I started packing. My presence would allow them to travel to Europe for job interviews at a prestigious university. Best of all, spring flowers already bloomed in the Chesapeake area, while winter dragged on in New Hampshire.

My arrival on March 15, 2020, coincided with the closure of Leo's preschool for a few days due to a new flu bug going around. Little did any of us anticipate that the coronavirus would upend our lives. Not only were the interviews switched to online, but also my son and his wife began to teach remotely and the preschool shut down permanently. In short, the Covid-19 lockdown changed my two-week stay into two months.

Surprise!

God had positioned me exactly. Even as I read about grandparents sheltering in place, bereft of grandkids, I reveled in bonding with the grandson I'd enjoyed for only a few hours at a time. While his parents taught, Leo and I explored the pretty park outside his door and learned about spring flowers. We planted seeds, drew with chalk, played make-believe. Indoors, we made cookies, artwork, and jokes. We read and laughed. Gosh, we laughed.

Once the semester ended for Leo's parents, I returned home. The photo book I created of our time together seems especially precious now that the family has moved to Singapore for a few years. I bless the surprise of our time together when so many families were thrust apart.

**O God, You order all things in their time.
May I trust Your wisdom. Amen.**
—Gail Thorell Schilling

Digging Deeper: Proverbs 3:5–6, 17:6;
Ecclesiastes 3:1

Monday, April 8

...do good....—Psalm 37:27 (KJV)

"Be good," always followed my mother's goodbyes. I was seven, hopping out of the car for school. "Be good," she'd say. On my way to a friend's, or later, starting a new job, marrying David, or holding our first child, always the same at parting, "Be good." During my mother's last earth days, in ICU, while she could still speak, each visit ended the same: "I love you, Pamela...be good."

Whether all mothers say this to their children or if it's simply a Southern thing, I'm not sure. But over time, these two words have become much more than a "goodbye" for me. They are my inspiration, not just for trying to fulfill my mother's vision for me but for pleasing God.

So, what exactly is "good"? The dictionary offers everything from "dandy," "decent," and "peachy" to "morally admirable." But if we really want to get specific, we need a guide. Could that be the Bible?

Consider the Ten Commandants. Or delve into Matthew 25 or the Beatitudes. All about good. Don't kill people, or steal, or tell untruths, or covet our neighbor's stuff. Show honor to others and make God number one in our lives. Caring for others is really important, like welcoming strangers, feeding the hungry, and generally watching out for the "least of these."

There are more directives. Things that take us to what, in a sacred sense, we might call our "happy place." Straight from Jesus's mouth, true happiness comes from feeling compassion, for extending forgiveness, grace, love, and humbleness to others. And that's just His short list.

Realizing that I "get it," my mother surely smiles down from heaven. So, I echo her words to you: "Be good."

Father God, help us to remember Your way— help us "be good." —Pam Kidd

Digging Deeper: Isaiah 1:17; Luke 6:45

Tuesday, April 9

Hope deferred makes the heart sick, but a longing fulfilled is a tree of life. —Proverbs 13:12 (NIV)

I had been planning my fortieth birthday for several months and had made plans to celebrate away from home. In our family, birthdays are some of the most important days of the year. But my fortieth was in April 2020. About six weeks before my big day, we went into lockdown. For weeks, I prayed the pandemic would pass us by. I was missing my friends and family, but I especially wanted to mark my birthday with something memorable.

As the date grew closer and closer, I had to accept the fact that I wouldn't get the celebration I had wanted. I tried to make the most of it and planned a good meal to enjoy with my husband and children at home.

The morning of my fortieth, I woke up feeling melancholy and hopeless. I thought it was going to be a day like all the others we'd been having.

But I was in for a few surprises. In the middle of the night, my dad had put a huge sign in our yard to tell the neighborhood it was my special day. My sister had brought gifts and dropped off a cake at the end of the driveway. It was later that day, when my husband called me outside, that I got the biggest surprise of all. He had organized a drive-by parade, and dozens of friends and family dropped off gifts and wished me a happy birthday.

What started as the saddest birthday turned into the sweetest as I was showered with God's love and the love of family and friends, and I learned our life doesn't have to be extravagant to be meaningful.

Lord, when I'm disappointed and my expectations aren't being met, remind me that Your plans are always better than my own. —Gabrielle Meyer

---

Wednesday, April 10

I will sing of your steadfast love, O LORD, forever; with my mouth I will proclaim your faithfulness to all generations. —Psalm 89:1 (NRSV)

I'd gone to a voice therapist because my larynx needed help. I figured whatever exercises she'd give me would be quiet because making a loud noise would tire my voice.

How wrong I was. There in her office, she asked me to go "ahhhhh" as long as I could and as *loud* as I could a few dozen times. After repeating some stentorian sentences, I had to proclaim a passage at top volume. "Why so loud?" I asked.

"That way you build up the muscle," she said. Sort of like lifting weights with my vocal cords. The kicker: I was supposed to practice these exercises at home, including reading—loudly—a passage of my own choosing.

We live in an apartment, and as dutifully as I did the exercises, I hated making so much noise. "I'm so sorry," I said to our downstairs neighbor. "I don't hear a thing," she said. I was sure she was just being polite. *Why not go outside?* I thought.

I did just that, crying out in the open air. When it came to picking a passage, I clicked on my favorite Bible app, turning to the Psalms. I read verse after verse, *loudly*, smiling to myself. "For who in the skies can be compared to the Lᴏʀᴅ? Who among the heavenly beings is like the Lᴏʀᴅ?" (Psalm 89:6, NRSVUE). No scaring the birds or squirrels or even disturbing a branch or a leaf. We were all one here, on the Lord's terrain. The perfect place for making a joyful, LOUD noise.

> **May I never be shy about making a joyful noise to and for You, O Lord, singing Your praise.**
> —Rick Hamlin

> **Digging Deeper:** Psalm 110:1;
> Hebrews 2:12; James 5:13

Thursday, April 11

"For I know the plans I have for you," declares the Lᴏʀᴅ, "plans to prosper you and not to harm you, plans to give you hope and a future."
—Jeremiah 29:11 (NIV)

Being a high-school senior in the midst of a pandemic was anticlimactic. What should have been a fun year for my daughter, Micah, was burdened by safety regulations and event cancellation. I was thankful that school administrators took precautions, but I hated that Micah's last year of high school didn't go as planned.

I remembered back to her second semester at her small Christian school, when the staff had a mother/daughter tea and blessing—an opportunity for moms to share a prayer with their daughters. I'd read blessings in the Bible, and I crafted one for this occasion. On the appointed day, I met Micah at the church that adjoined the school.

After the tea, we entered the vacant sanctuary. Micah sat in a chair near a giant wooden cross as I read her blessing: "My precious daughter, your dad and I chose your name, Micah, because of the meaning, 'one who is like the Lord,' and because of the verse Micah 6:8. After you were born, the Lord gave me a prophecy that you would do great acts to glorify Him and to further the Kingdom of God. This is your destiny. Nothing can thwart the will of God."

I put my hand on her shoulder and prayed that she would always love the Lord and walk with Him. I kissed her cheek, and we hugged.

Micah's senior year didn't go the way she, or I, planned, but no matter what happens, I have faith in the promise of her name. God still has a very special plan for her.

Father God, please bless Micah and hold her close. Help her, and me, to always trust Your plan for her life. —Stephanie Thompson

Digging Deeper: Psalm 33:11; Jeremiah 1:5; Micah 6:8

Friday, April 12

As each has received a gift, use it to serve one another, as good stewards of God's varied grace.... —1 Peter 4:10 (ESV)

Olivia, my eight-year-old daughter, has always been a gatherer. Given the chance, she would spend every moment of her life surrounded by friends and family doing, well, anything.

As you might imagine, her birthday party is a challenge each year. For years, we held it at the park so she could invite anyone she wanted. Then her friends outgrew bounce houses and playgrounds, and friends started to shift toward smaller parties, gathering groups of friends for the skating rink or a trampoline park.

Not Olivia. She wants everyone.

For too long, I fought it, trying to sway her toward fun, smaller options, before realizing that this is Olivia's gift. She is a gatherer of all people, so of course her birthday party should be a celebration of that.

We're trying to plan her upcoming birthday now, and I've tried to convince her to maybe invite just the girls in her classroom. "No, Mom. Charlie told me he hasn't been invited to a birthday party since first grade. That's two years! He has to be invited," she insisted.

Well of course he had to come to our party. We still haven't found the perfect spot yet, but we will. It will be open and easy and likely have only a huge sheet cake and ice cream because pizza for thirty is going to get out of hand quickly.

Olivia has taught me many things, but my most precious lesson so far has been to look for God's gifts within my children. To see them, to honor them, to celebrate them.

Lord, open my eyes to the gifts You provide to those around me. —Ashley Kappel

Digging Deeper: Romans 12:4–8; 1 Corinthians 12:4

Saturday, April 13

I was filled with delight day after day....
—Proverbs 8:30 (NIV)

My young granddaughters squealed and laughed as their dad waved a bubble wand and transparent globes flew into the air. Big bubbles, little bubbles, single bubbles, double bubbles, each iridescent in the sunshine. The bubbles were short-lived, but each brought a sparkle of joy before vanishing.

Seeing the girls chase the bubbles, then watch as each popped, then disappeared, I thought of the joy bubbles God puts into my life. The bubbles he sends me are fleeting moments of delight, bursts of blessing that take many forms. My bubbles have included sitting in front of a blazing fireplace reading and eating dark-chocolate chips, receiving a hug from a loved one, catching a glimpse of a butterfly lighting on a flower, feeling sun warmth seep into my skin, and seeing an ice cream–smeared grin from my two-year-old granddaughter.

The other day, while shopping, I saw four small, unique flowerpots, just right for my décor. I bought two of them and put them on my windowsill. I then got an idea. I could fit four on the sill and make a small herb garden! Since I'd purchased them at a store where when something's gone, it's gone, I jumped in the car and drove back to see if the other two were still there. They were! Smiling, I snatched them up. "Thank you for the bubbles, Lord," I said.

> **Lord, now that I'm looking, I see so many bubbles You send floating into my life, flashes of pleasure that brighten my day. Thank You, Lord, for the bubbles!** —Kim Taylor Henry

Digging Deeper: Psalm 4:7; Isaiah 55:2

Sunday, April 14

For where your treasure is, there your heart will be also. —Matthew 6:21 (NIV)

Rain poured down outside, and I was feeling a little down with the house empty, the kids off and about, as I straightened up. Putting away clothes, I rummaged through my top dresser drawer—a catchall for important mementos. I spotted my oldest son's baby pacifier. Almost two decades old, the rubber plastic nub had grown brittle and dark amber with age. Holding it in my hand, memories flooded back of the days when we couldn't leave the house without a pacifier.

Solomon was extremely particular about binkies. Even as a newborn, he had a favorite type and rejected anything that wasn't right by pouting his delicate lips and pushing it out with his tongue. It was one of his first likes and dislikes. I was captivated by this quirk and fascinated that the right pacifier held the power to peaceful sleep.

Beside Solomon's binkie is my sister's last grocery list, written on the back of an envelope the night before she passed in her sleep. Lettuce, asparagus, milk, honey, seltzer. Back when I was trying to figure out what happened or why, I read the list over and over, looking for a sign or a message, some way to rearrange the letters into a goodbye.

Next to that was a ceramic heart-shaped paperweight I made for my dad on Father's Day in elementary school. As I closed the drawer containing my treasures, the house no longer felt empty but filled by beautiful experiences, relationships, and, most of all, God's love.

Lord, thank You for the magnificent gift of memories that flood my heart with love and treasured keepsakes that remind me of my many blessings!
—Sabra Ciancanelli

Digging Deeper: Psalms 9:1, 143:5–16

Monday, April 15

Eli would bless Elkanah. —1 Samuel 2:20 (JPS)

Spring announces itself in several unmistakable ways at my house: the daffodils start blooming; the frogs down at the creek begin singing; and I start facing every morning with an increasing number of sneezes—all of them my own.

When my husband, Keith, was alive, he started holding off saying "God bless you" to me until I had sneezed at least twice. A little later, he upped the count to three sneezes, then to five. "I don't want to be saying it every ten seconds," he told me. I didn't blame him, but I had no control whatsoever over the sneezing. It was just a spring thing.

All by myself during the quarantine, I dreaded the inevitable nose-related part of the season, which not only meant keeping a box of tissues in every room for handy access but also not having anyone to say "God bless you" to me. It made me sad—all those lost opportunities to be blessed gone because neither the dog nor the cat is verbal.

For weeks on end, I muttered resentfully after every spate of sneezing, wishing spring was over already. Then one morning, I awoke to the fact that there was someone verbal in the house: me. And I finally changed my morning routine so that every sneeze ended with me saying, "God bless me!" It's not as satisfying as when Keith used to say it to me, but it's comforting to have so many occasions for prayers.

Did You create pollen as a roundabout way of encouraging us to pray, God? Subtle! (And maybe sneaky, as well.) —Rhoda Blecker

Digging Deeper: Psalm 67:2;
Malachi 3:10

Tuesday, April 16

**Blessed are the pure in heart, for they shall see God.
—Matthew 5:8 (ESV)**

Planting will begin soon. The field next door will either be seeded with corn or soybeans. At the same time, all the trees are blooming and leafing out. The prairie grasses are reaching toward the sky. By midsummer, the wide-open vistas I've enjoyed will have disappeared behind the growing vegetation.

No longer will I be able to look out the window from my living room and see the creek winding through the woods. I'll have to trek through the woods to see it. The western woods will be hidden by tall cornstalks that also block my line of sight down the road as I try to pull out of our farm lane to head to town. And the six-foot-tall prairie grasses will hide the fox and rabbit burrows—giving those critters protection from the prying eyes of prey.

I could mourn the loss of the big landscape...or let it be an invitation to see new things. New wildflowers springing up in the prairie—with their attendant butterflies, bees, and red-wing blackbirds. The delicate seedlings in the fields sprouting, growing, and beginning to produce grain or beans to feed a hungry world.

It is an opportunity to remember that the wonder of God is not present just in the big things but also in the tiniest milkweed sprout or a small West Virginia White butterfly. The wonder of God surrounds us constantly, whether it be in country vistas or cityscapes.

Praise be to God for His presence everywhere. Let he who has eyes see.

All-Seeing God, my eyes are open all the time, but I so rarely really see. Help me learn how to behold You all around me. Amen. —J. Brent Bill

Digging Deeper: Psalm 63; Jeremiah 29:13

Wednesday, April 17

So do not fear, for I am with you; do not be dismayed, for I am your God. I will strengthen you and help you; I will uphold you with my righteous right hand. —Isaiah 41:10 (NIV)

"Papi, are you cold?" I asked my father on the airplane. I was already pulling a hat over his ears before he said yes.

I sat back in my seat, feeling the hum of the aircraft transporting me to a place in my life I thought would never come. When my father was first diagnosed with dementia, my family discussed what would happen when my mother could no longer care for him.

"He'll live with me," I said, annoyed with the subject. I didn't want to think about my father getting worse or even hear the words *nursing home*.

For years, I was able to feed my delusion that he would live out the rest of his years healthy and self-sufficient, yet on that flight from Florida to NYC, I prayed for the strength to face his illness, his mortality, and my promise to care for him.

As I care for my father now, I believe God has heard my prayer. I accept my father's illness as part of his incredible life story. My fear of his mortality has made way for gratitude in each moment spent together, and tasks I thought would be uncomfortable are simply an expression of love—the same love and care he's given to me my whole life.

Lord, thank You for the precious gift of human life. Prepare our hearts for everything that comes with this mortal gift, including its end, and the promise of eternal life with You. —Karen Valentin

Digging Deeper: Isaiah 46:4; 1 Corinthians 15:55

Thursday, April 18

Heal the sick...freely ye have received, freely give. —Matthew 10:8 (KJV)

I, um, *liberated* a pair of aluminum crutches from my neighbor's trash this week. I have no current use for crutches, nor (God willing) future plans. I imagined the crutches for a new purpose: as legs to support an aluminum clock that I bought at a garage sale.

This crutch-clock design worked on paper— but only on paper. After some spectacularly messy results, I figured out that the crutches worked best upside down, bolted onto a metal tray. I'm happy with the results—an oddly shaped postmodern grandfather's clock, if your grandfather happened to be either oddly shaped or postmodern.

I don't know how the crutches landed in the neighbor's trash. I hope that whoever used them is now walking this earth unaided and pain-free—but the truth is I don't know what necessitated the need for crutches. Maybe I should be more attuned to my neighbors' lives.

I wonder how many lives are turned upside down by the sudden need for crutches, for canes, for walkers. I was able to reuse them for another purpose; I hope my neighbor's family was able to find purpose in their new, unasked-for phase of life, where the once steady suddenly become unsteady.

I, too, have experienced that phase. One hard lesson is giving up your pride and learning how to lean on more than just crutches. You learn how to lean on Someone who can help you find your footing so you can walk by yourself again...but never, ever walk alone.

Lord, our flesh is sometimes weak; give us the strength to walk in Your ways. —Mark Collins

Digging Deeper: Isaiah 40:30–31; Luke 14:13–14

Friday, April 19

He has made everything beautiful in its time. —Ecclesiastes 3:11 (NIV)

We set out bright and early for our family trip with high hopes. For my fortieth birthday, I felt I deserved a reward, after struggling through several years of deep pain and grief.

Ten hours into the road trip to my dream cabin in the Tennessee mountains, I was met with dark, rainy skies, arguments with my husband, and steep, winding cliffside roads. Frustrated, I took the next curve much too close to the edge. I was losing control of my emotions and of the car. I wanted so badly to have the view at the top, without any hurdles on the way up.

I sat with the car parked on the roadside, with a decision to make. I could hold onto the bitterness I felt about the road being hard and long. Or, I could face it with courage and keep going. In that moment, it meant I had to let my husband help me figure out how to maneuver the car out of the tight spot. I couldn't be the bossy one in charge of it all. I had to let my kids see that even their strong mom sometimes sheds tears and needs encouragement and guidance.

By the grace of God, we arrived at the cabin shortly after. I have often wished the roads of my life were shorter or easier to navigate. I know I need more time to process through past hurts. I am grateful that God allowed me to achieve getting to this beautiful mountaintop amidst my challenges. It encouraged me to keep going and to reach for more.

Father, thank You that Your love breaks through both metaphorical and literal mountains in my life and rescues me. —Nicole Garcia

Saturday, April 20

...man looks on the outward appearance, but the
LORD looks on the heart. —1 Samuel 16:7 (ESV)

Four years ago, my new neighbor—we share a
stoop—told me in broken English he'd planted two
watermelon seeds in my flower patch. Not pleased, but
not eager to complain about borders and boundaries,
I tilled over his interlopers and broadcast zinnia seeds
across the five square feet of God's good earth that I
tend. The flowers flourished.

This year, my seed-spreading efforts weren't as
successful. Nothing sprouted quickly. I intended to try
again after a rain. In the meantime, I kept checking,
hopefully. Then on two mornings, I noticed a patch of
damp dirt. *Is somebody watering one spot? Is an animal
stopping by?* Then a leafy plant appeared. *What? A
melon?* I wasn't amused and assumed the sometimes
bold and brash neighbor was up to his old tricks. I
reacted slowly, prayerfully contemplating my next
move. When I saw him on the sidewalk, we chatted
amicably enough that I felt comfortable pointing.
"Did you plant something over here? A melon?"

"Where? No," he answered, then ventured, "it's a
zucchini. Maybe my mom..."

Hmm. His mom. She speaks no English. She's
given me a bright turquoise shift from her country.

She hands me dinner plates of lamb and couscous. Or sometimes a selection of homemade sweets with dates. If I add her smiles and hello waves and kind gestures into our relational equation, it's suddenly easy for me to set aside my pique. Beyond a trespass, I can see and appreciate a thoughtful, fruitful gift.

God, open my eyes and heart to see a neighbor's best intentions. —Evelyn Bence

Digging Deeper: James 1:16–21

Sunday, April 21

When I consider Your heavens...What is man that You are mindful of him? —Psalm 8:3–4 (NKJV)

The night sky fascinates me. I grew up in the tropical Philippine Islands, and my missionary father, a seminary professor, often took me on evening walks high in the Sierra Madre Mountains on the island of Luzon. As we gazed at the luminous stars in the dark Pacific sky, he frequently quoted Psalm 8: "When I consider Your heavens, the work of Your fingers, the moon and the stars, which You have ordained, what is man that You are mindful of him, and the son of man that You visit him?" (Psalm 8:3–4, NKJV). These words still permeate my thoughts sixty years later, and the mystery of God grows deeper and more beautiful.

I am particularly captivated by the sight of a full moon. Only recently did I learn that the dominant opinion held by current scientists and astronomers is that our moon was once part of planet Earth millions of years ago. The earthen substance that now forms our moon was violently severed from Earth when a "Mars-sized" object violently collided with Earth, throwing vaporized chunks of matter into space. Gravity slowly caused these ejected bits of matter to coalesce over millions of years and form a moon that orbits around Earth. In fact, the composition of the earth and the moon are almost identical.

Last night, my grandson and I went for a stroll by the ocean, and as we gazed at a full moon, I introduced him to Psalm 8. Our awareness of Almighty God must always be tinged by the awesome mystery and amazement that we are in a personal relationship with the Creator of the Universe.

Father, You are holy. You are mystery. You are personal. You are Almighty God! Amen. —Scott Walker

Digging Deeper: Psalm 19:1, 136:6–9, 147:1–4; Isaiah 40:26–29

Monday, April 22

The earth is the LORD's, and everything in it....
—Psalm 24:1 (NIV)

As a collector of vintage artifacts, I'd amassed my share of stuff. When Covid-19 hit, clutter closed in on me. I revisited my stash of discards I'd picked up curbside or at yard sales, relegating items to one of four categories: Keep. Toss. Donate. Sell. The objects I determined no one would want ended up in thick Hefty bags destined for trash day.

Then my neighbor lined up an array of castoffs at the edge of her lawn. She taped a "Free to a Good Home" sign on each one. They weren't anything *I* wanted. Nothing like a good cleaning frenzy to curtail your acquisition inclinations. Besides, that divided thing on rollers would confound the wise. Was it a file cabinet or a laundry sorter?

I didn't need to wonder long. A woman in a shiny red SUV slammed on her brakes and jumped out. Like a horse at the starting gate at the Kentucky Derby, she flew toward the object that had my head shaking. Next thing I knew, she'd called someone on her cell, shrieking, "You won't believe it! The organizer on wheels we saw at HomeGoods is on Aracoma Road. There's a Free sign on it." She snapped photos of everything, then made fast work of loading it all into her vehicle.

I got to work as well, pulling junk beyond redemption out of those Hefty bags. One person's trash really is another's treasure. Made Mother Earth smile too.

Teach us to care for Your creation, Lord.
—Roberta Messner

Digging Deeper: Genesis 1:1;
Psalm 89:11

Tuesday, April 23

CELEBRATE!! Kindness
Do for others what you want them to do for you.
—Matthew 7:12 (TLB)

"Lord, help me find a parking place!"

I felt guilty saying those words. I have friends who think people who pray for parking spaces are wasting God's time. But I was desperate. My husband, Lynn, had an appointment at this hospital and we knew the importance of being on time.

After circling around two filled parking lots, I finally left Lynn at the door of the hospital with his new walker and told him I'd meet him in the doctor's office. But when I had no luck circling the fourth and final lot, I wasn't sure what to do next. As I rounded the final corner of that lot, I saw a man wearing a bright orange vest getting out of his pickup. He looked official, so I rolled down my window and asked if he could suggest where I might find a parking space.

"I've been through all four lots," I said.

"Probably on the streets," he said, gesturing in the opposite direction of the hospital.

"Thanks," I sighed.

"Wait," he said. "You take my spot and I'll go find one." I started to object, but he was already in his truck, backing out and waving.

"Thank you!" I called.

Who does that? I asked myself, pulling into his spot and jumping out of my car as I answered my question. *Jesus dressed as a kind hospital workman who answers prayers.*

Lord, I want to celebrate this act of kindness by passing on the gesture. Please give me the opportunities. —Carol Kuykendall

Digging Deeper: Matthew 7:7–11; 2 Peter 1:5–9

Wednesday, April 24

But watch thou in all things, endure afflictions, do the work of an evangelist, make full proof of thy ministry. —2 Timothy 4:5 (KJV)

It had happened for years. My blood pressure was perfect at home, but when I got to the doctor's office, it shot a hole in the roof, resulting in a feeling of defeat and embarrassment. How could I call myself a witness for the Lord if I didn't have enough faith to "believe" my way out of what is commonly called "white coat syndrome" (when a person's blood pressure is only high in the doctor's office)?

Finally, one day the Lord whispered to my heart: *Pride. What you're trying to do is not to prove your ministry but to salvage your pride.* Unwittingly, I was misappropriating what Paul meant when he wrote to Timothy that he should "make full proof of [his] ministry."

Pride opposes godly ministry, but it is sometimes cunning in its manifestation. It is not always the image of a strutting rooster. Who would have thought that my attempt to witness to the healing power of God would somehow become tainted with a self-driven effort to show my Christian beliefs? Paul says we should not "frustrate the grace" that God provided for us through His Son. I began humbling myself each time I had an appointment, finally seeing that, for me, this was not about my blood pressure. It was about humbling myself under the mighty hand of God.

Though my pressure is still a challenge, I have learned that proving my ministry is not about showing spiritual muscle. It's about showing a willingness to trust God.

Jesus, help me to see my next step, not through prideful vision but through the eyes of the Spirit.
—Jacqueline F. Wheelock

Digging Deeper: Proverbs 11:2; 1 Peter 5:6

Thursday, April 25

Then Jesus suggested, "Let's get away from the crowds for a while and rest." —Mark 6:31 (TLB)

My home used to feel like a retreat, a place of peace and rest. Then I started watching my three granddaughters. Now, my closet door's been slammed off its hinges, there's macaroni and cheese ground into my dining room carpet, and the neck of No Drama Llama (a stuffed animal who resides in my bedroom) has been almost twisted completely off, thanks to the "love" of Lula, Shea, and Taylor.

Sometimes, making memories is synonymous with creating chaos.

I adore my granddaughters, but my heart and soul also long for a place of peace. But where in my small townhome could I find an oasis? I thought of the tiny balcony right off my bedroom. Sure, it overlooks six lanes of traffic and is covered in snow for a portion of the year—but, so far, it's remained untouched by tiny fingers.

I purchased a brightly patterned outdoor rug and a lounge chair the color of a tropical sea. My oasis was open for business. Now, while Taylor's napping and the older girls are in school, I plug in the baby monitor, sit in the sunshine, and read a book or pray. When it's chilly, I wrap myself up in a blanket like a proverbial burrito. After a few minutes, I no longer hear the buzz of the traffic below. All I notice is the sun and the azure sky. As my heart and mind grow quiet, I can hear God's voice above the din of life once more.

Jesus, remind me to take time out when I need it, seeking little respites of peace to help quiet my heart and soul. —Vicki Kuyper

Digging Deeper: Psalm 29:11; Matthew 11:28–30; 2 Thessalonians 3:16

Friday, April 26

Sympathize with each other. —1 Peter 3:8 (NLT)

With a heavy heart, I pushed my grocery cart into the express lane line and glanced at the mob of people in the store. Ever since the TV show *Yellowstone* had been (and was being) filmed in my town, hordes of out-of-state folks were moving in. The small-town kindness was being displaced by icy-faced folks who honked horns and who wouldn't even nod hello.

After placing my items on the belt, I watched the first man in line shrug his shoulders. The machine wouldn't read his card for payment. Immediately, the woman in front of me said, "Sir, that's OK. I'll pay for your groceries." The clerk's jaw dropped, and the customer's head whipped around in unbelief. Quickly, he reinserted his card. Again it failed. The woman insisted, "That has happened to me before. Sir, just take your groceries and go, I'll pay." Wide-eyed, the man shoved the card into the reader, that time with success.

Once the man gathered his groceries and left, I thanked the woman. She'd warmed my heart and showed me what I needed to do. Even though the small-town kindness seemed to be disappearing, it didn't have to disappear from within me. There were opportunities all around me to melt those icy gazes with simple gestures that say, "I care."

I may have gone into the store for groceries, but I came out with a deeper understanding of the impact of sharing God's love in a practical way to those around me.

Thank You, Lord, for placing people of good example in front of me. Amen. —Rebecca Ondov

Digging Deeper: Ephesians 4:32, 5:2

For where your treasure is, there your heart will be also. —Matthew 6:21 (NIV)

"What has a head and a tail but no body?" my grandson, Micah, asked me when I answered my phone. He jumped in with the answer—"a penny"—as we both laughed.

"I got your package," he continued, referring to a box I had sent to break the tedium of lockdown due to the pandemic. I had made simple finger puppets out of felt for his siblings, ages seven and five, but knew puppets were too juvenile for a nine-year-old boy. Unsure, I had settled on a penny collection, including the folders for one-cent coins from 1909 to the present day and a baggie of loose change from a jar in our bedroom. Could a penny collection interest a boy in this fast-paced, digital world?

Apparently, it could. Micah's mom, Rachel, called to report, "The penny collection has *saved our lives* during lockdown, as Micah has meticulously cleaned each penny—all three hundred of them—with a small pink eraser."

Several months later, when restrictions had lifted, Micah sat with my husband, Kevin, at our kitchen table. Kevin's boyhood penny collection—retrieved from a battered box stored in the back room—lay next to Micah's as they opened several rolls of 1950s coins.

"Here's one from 1954," Micah said, as he put it in his penny folder. "And from 1952." Two heads, one dark-haired, the other salt-and-peppered, conferred over Lincoln one-cent pieces for hours, lost in the world of old coins as they unpacked much more than pennies. What a blessing to see my husband connect with our grandson in the common currency of time spent together.

Jesus, only You can take a pile of pennies and turn it into a treasure. I like how You do math.
—Lynne Hartke

Digging Deeper: Luke 6:38; 2 Corinthians 4:18

Sunday, April 28

...you were sealed and marked [branded as God's own]....—Ephesians 4:30 (AMP)

Branding calves is a chore performed in the spring on most ranches in the West. Nobody brands cattle for the fun of it; it is done to provide a lifelong proof of ownership that helps deter theft. If nobody rustled cattle, then nobody would have to brand their livestock.

At the same time as branding, calves are vaccinated against illness and bull calves often become steers according to their intended use in the future. Studies have been done that indicate the temporary separation from their mothers is more stressful than any of the procedures performed. This has always motivated me to work as quickly as possible to return the "worked" calf to its mother.

When I read Ephesians 4:30 during branding season, it resonated as never before. God not only calls us by name, not only writes our names in the Book of Life, but He also seals us with the Holy Spirit. In essence, He brands us, permanently, with a mark that no one can steal away. I reread that part with joy. I belong to Him.

In the book of Revelation, it is prophesied that the devil will demand everyone on earth to take his mark. But unlike cattle, and even before the last days, it is entirely up to us to choose our Owner. If we belong to God and accept Jesus as our Savior, nobody can separate us from life with Him.

I release the freshly branded calf and watch him reunite with his mother. She tucks him close to her side.

Precious Father, life is simply being separated from You long enough to decide which brand we will wear for eternity. Here I am. Make Your mark.
—Erika Bentsen

Digging Deeper: Romans 8:39;
Ephesians 1:13; 1 John 4:6

Monday, April 29

Take the helmet of salvation and the sword of the Spirit, which is the word of God. And pray in the Spirit on all occasions with all kinds of prayers and requests. —Ephesians 6:17–18 (NIV)

Before I was recently diagnosed with cancer, my friend John's wife was having delicate neurosurgery. Weeks before the surgery, he asked me to pray for her. Early the morning of the surgery, I received his text, "Surgery will begin soon." I texted back, "Are you there by yourself?" He replied, "Just me and my Bible."

Due to the pandemic protocols, John was waiting through a stressful time without the company of his family or friends. Throughout the day, as I prayed for his wife, I also prayed for John, thinking how hard it must be waiting alone through a long surgery. Hours later, John texted that the surgery was over. All had gone well, but the recovery and healing would take time. "Keep praying," he requested. After months of ups and downs and uncountable prayers, her healing came.

As the uncertainties of my own surgery to remove cancer approached, I thought of how John and his wife dealt with a very difficult situation for an extended time: armed with the Word of God and relying on prayer. And the words from John's text, *Just me and my Bible*, became a centering phrase and reminder when I felt anxious or alone that God, prayer, and His Word—"the sword of the Spirit"— would see me through. And I found His peace!

Thank You, Lord, that whenever we draw close to You, You draw ever closer to us, and when we're by ourselves, You are there watching over and providing our care! —John Dilworth

Digging Deeper: 2 Samuel 22:31; Isaiah 40:8; Ephesians 6:14–15

Therefore, as God's chosen people, holy and
dearly loved, clothe yourselves with compassion,
kindness, humility, gentleness and patience.
—Colossians 3:12 (NIV)

A recent Facebook post caught my attention: "In
a world where you can be anything, be kind." After a
bit of research, I found that the source of the quote
was likely the Ven Peter Leonard, former Archdeacon
of the Isle of Wight. He wrote it following the
suicide of a public figure who had been besieged by
negative comments and threats.

Would kind words have prevented that tragic death?
I don't know; thankfully, I haven't been the target of
verbal abuse. So my thoughts turned to the kind words
and actions that have had a positive effect on my life
since the death of my husband, Don. Family and
close friends provide practical help and comfort. But
I've also received blessings from unexpected sources.
Martha, a talented pianist and *Walking in Grace* reader,
sent a disc of favorite hymns she'd recorded; it included
my favorite, "Amazing Grace." The night before
Mother's Day, a neighbor and her married daughters
brought me a lovely rose corsage. "Our husbands each
bought three corsages," she said, "so we're sharing the
extras." Another neighbor plowed my drive after a
heavy snow. A busy young mother texted a Christmas
invitation; she wanted to be sure I wasn't alone.

Kindness, I realized, isn't complicated. It's simply
being aware of those who need a prayer, a word of

encouragement, an unexpected visit, or a small gift. But what a difference one small thing might make in someone's life!

Jesus Savior, etch the words on my heart:
"In a world where I can be anything, be kind."
—Penney Schwab

Digging Deeper: Galatians 5:22–23; Ephesians 4:22; Titus 3:4–8

YOU WERE CALLED TO PEACE

1 _____

2 _____

3 _____

4 _____

5 _____

6 _____

7 _____

8 _____

9 _____

10 _____

11 _____

12 _____

13 _____

14 _____

15 _____

16 _____

17 _____

18 _____

19 _____

20 _____

21 _____

22 _____

23 _____

24 _____

25 _____

26 _____

27 _____

28 _____

29 _____

30 _____

May

Finally, brothers, rejoice. Aim for restoration, comfort one another, agree with one another, live in peace; and the God of love and peace will be with you.

—2 Corinthians 13:11 (ESV)

For by grace you have been saved through faith. And this is not your own doing; it is the gift of God. —Ephesians 2:8 (ESV)

It's perfect weed-growing weather, and I should be out battling weeds in the prairie. But I went golfing instead. While I was walking up one of the fairways, the thought occurred to me that I may care more about weeds than God does.

My feelings come from remembering a joke about a man who bought a farm overgrown with bushes and weeds. With a lot of work, the man turned the farm into a showplace—weed-free and verdant. One day, his minister came to visit and observed, "Well, friend, you and God have done a marvelous job on this garden."

The farmer replied, "You should have seen it when God had it by himself."

If I stop my weed wars, then in a few years, my farm would be bushy and weedy again. And God would not seem to care. Birds would still nest, coyotes would make their dens, deer would tramp down the tall grass for their beds, bees would zoom around the pokeberry, and life would go on. It would still be good.

And I wonder—do I worry too much about weeding in my life? Weeding the teeny-tiny sins out? The fact is, sometimes weed seeds blow in. And God does not seem to be overly upset with it. From my reading of Scripture, that's what grace is all about.

It's not by our works (weeding) but by His work that we are saved. And by saved, I mean become a beautiful garden for God.

> O Lord, sometimes there are weeds in my soul.
> Work with me to clean them out and help me not
> to obsess about them. Instead, lead me to deeper
> trust in You. Amen. —J. Brent Bill

Digging Deeper: Titus 2:11–14

Thursday, May 2

My command is this: Love each other as I have loved you. —John 15:12 (NIV)

When Gary, a senior citizen friend who lived alone, stopped responding to phone calls from myself and others from our church, we all became very concerned. Several members of his church family stepped in: We searched the Internet to try to locate his daughter, who lived in another state. We called all the neighbors we knew. Finally, we were able to get local officials to go in and check on Gary.

Whispered prayers remained on our lips as we made calls, scoured sites, and tracked down neighbors. And most of all, we were resourceful! Our pure love for our church brother helped us uncover a variety of methods to help deal with this challenge. Without knowing what the outcome would be, we knew we had to try every available way to get someone into Gary's apartment to help him.

Within hours, authorities entered Gary's apartment. He had fallen, and unable to get up, he had spent four days on the floor. Praise God, he was alert, awake, and alive. It is only by God's grace that Gary was found in time. Our "rescue team" did a little praise dance upon receiving word that Gary was found safe.

Certainly, life will throw us trials and hardships to overcome. But using our God-given resourcefulness—and banding together with our brothers and sisters in Christ—will always help us to push through.

Father, I thank You for our church family and for their dedication to our brothers and sisters at all times. —Gayle T. Williams

Digging Deeper: Galatians 6:2; Ephesians 2:10

Friday, May 3

I am the true vine, and my Father is the gardener. He cuts off every branch in me that bears no fruit.... —John 15:1–2 (NIV)

It's a lovely day to be outside in my garden. I delight in the springtime sunshine on my face and shoulders and in the scent of warm, damp earth rising up to greet me.

Crouching next to one of the beds, I prepare a spot for a tomato plant that needs to be transplanted. It's gotten leggy and overgrown in its now-too-small pot, so I dig its hole extra deep.

Next, I pick the plant up, and—after giving it an appraising look—I use my fingernails to pinch off its middle and bottom branches. Now I'll be able to nestle most of the plant's height into the hole I've prepared. Roots will grow along the length of the buried stem, stabilizing it and helping the plant take up more of the water and nutrients it needs.

Pausing, I suddenly register the weeping wounds left by the missing branches. It occurs to me that, while what I've done is positive and helpful, the plant's experience at the moment is one only of injury.

So often, periods of transformative growth seem to begin with wounding. It's only later that it becomes possible to look back and understand why the cuts were necessary.

I look again at the small plant in front of me, freshly situated for its next stage of life, and I know the plans I have for it are good. As God's are for my life too. Even when His pruning hurts.

I'd avoid pruning it if I had a choice, God. But You are a wise gardener. Thank You for making the cuts You must, so I can continue to grow. —Erin Janoso

Digging Deeper: Jeremiah 29:11;
Romans 8:28

Saturday, May 4

Produce fruit in keeping with repentance. —Matthew 3:8 (NIV)

As a tenth-generation Southerner, I thought myself an expert on down-home sayings. But recently an elder at our church taught me a new one.

Growing up, when Rick and his siblings got caught doing wrong and would apologize, their mother would often reply, "Sorry don't feed the bulldog." She wanted her kids to understand that, while it's right to admit mistakes, the apology doesn't magically wash away whatever damage the transgression has done.

As I turned the words over in my mind, I wondered why this saying linked repentance to the satiety of a bulldog. And why a bulldog and not another breed?

I thought back to Fudge, the bulldog my uncle had when I was a child. Fudge, a watchdog, was fantastic at his job. I was terrified of his bark and his snarl—at times I wondered whether I might be his next meal! Thinking on Rick's mother's words, I imagined that Fudge with an empty stomach would've probably been even fiercer than Fudge with a full belly. The aftermath of foolish decisions can be fierce too—I've been bitten enough to know. The consequences of our sin don't suddenly disappear in this life; we still have to face the often formidable messes we've made.

Sorry may not feed the bulldog, but how incredibly blessed we are that "godly sorrow brings repentance that leads to salvation and leaves no regret" (2 Corinthians 7:10, NIV). God is quick to forgive. Like the father in the parable of the prodigal son, He is always rushing to welcome us home no matter what we've done wrong.

**Lord, thank You for Your amazing grace.
Help me to live wisely.** —Ginger Rue

Digging Deeper: 2 Chronicles 7:14; Proverbs 12:21

Sunday, May 5

**Be kind and compassionate to one another....
—Ephesians 4:32 (NIV)**

"Don't hit your brother with that branch!" I yelled as we arrived in Central Park.

"We're fencing," my oldest said, assuring me it was just a tap. I sat on the grass with my book and my sons climbed a nearby hill clustered with trees.

Balancing my role as the cautious mother and fearless father figure wasn't a job I'd asked for. Divorce and a mostly absent father left me to weigh my need to protect while also allowing my sons to learn through adventure and risk.

As I turned the page of my book, my oldest yelled for me to come. I ran toward the hill, imagining the worst, feeling guilty for letting them fence with branches.

"We found a dead baby squirrel," Brandon said when I arrived out of breath, "and we buried him right here."

"Don't worry," Tyler reassured. "We didn't touch him with our bare hands. We used leaves to move him."

The boys had sprinkled yellow flower petals over the mound and made a wooden cross of twigs. As they stood over the grave in silent reverence, the only thing I questioned now was how much I continually underestimate my children and the work I do as their parent. God has given me more strength and love to face those challenges than I ever realized.

Lord, help me remember You will give me all the tools I need. —Karen Valentin

Digging Deeper: Deuteronomy 11:18–19; 2 Corinthians 12:9

Monday, May 6

This is the day the LORD has made. We will rejoice and be glad in it. —Psalm 118:24 (NLT)

My recipe box is one of my prized possessions. When Bill and I evacuated our home due to a raging forest fire, that little box was one of the first things I seized from the kitchen shelf to take with me. My husband laughed and said, "You're taking that old thing?" I nodded emphatically. Nearly fifty years old, the box contains treasures: recipes for Mom's macaroni pie, Sharon's cheesy sausage balls, Nita's chocolate brownies, Irene's peanut butter pie. Most of these recipes were written by the giver, making them even more precious as many of these beloved ones have passed away.

The recipes are more than instructions for various culinary delights. Each brings back fond memories of time spent together at Terri's picnic table, on Aunt Blanche's kitchen stools, or shelling pecans on Theresa's porch. We shared jokes and Bible verses and advice on everything from cooking to parenting and stain removal. These women willingly shared a part of themselves with me. I treasure that.

I also treasure a life lesson I learned from these special encounters: that our time here on earth is all too brief. It's important to enjoy the present, the *right now*. Pay attention to those around you. Listen to them—really listen. That's what Jesus did. Whether speaking with Nicodemus in the middle of the night or enjoying a noontime conversation with the woman at the well, Jesus fully experienced the here and the now of any given moment. We should too.

Dear Lord, help me to keep worries about the future and disappointments of the past from distracting me in the present. —Shirley Raye Redmond

Digging Deeper: Matthew 6:34; James 4:13–14

Tuesday, May 7

You are my refuge and my shield; I have put my hope in your word. —Psalm 119:114 (NIV)

"What happened to your umbrella?" I asked my daughter as she slid into the back seat of the car. Her sweatshirt hood was drenched and rain puddled around her.

"I left it at home," she confessed. Her eyes avoided mine. That morning I'd warned my children of imminent heavy storms that were forecast for the afternoon.

Such is life. We all experience seasons of joy and sunshine; none are shielded from the storms of life. But those who are aware of the goodness of God can find peace and lasting refuge in times of trouble.

Recently, when I learned that the cancer my mother fought five years earlier had returned, I sought shelter in God's arms. I needed His security, compassion, peace, and lasting refuge. "God is my refuge and strength, a very present help in trouble" (Psalm 46:1, KJV). Had I learned that verse during weekly Bible study, during summer vacation Bible school, or had I picked it up listening to my mom? All I know is that I'd been prepared for the storms, even when I didn't realize it.

Whether it was sitting in a doctor's waiting room, keeping my mother company by her bedside while she slept, or crying silent tears at night, the negative thoughts and fears would be pushed out by the scriptures I'd read, jotted down on note cards, or memorized. Unlike my daughter being without her umbrella during the torrential downpour, I didn't have to worry about leaving home without the Word of God. It's hidden in my heart.

God, thank You for giving me Your Word to hide in my heart and for being a shelter in the time of storm.
—Tia McCollors

Wednesday, May 8

...but set the believers an example in speech,
in conduct, in love, in faith, in purity.
—1 Timothy 4:12 (ESV)

"My mother is so demanding." My fellow shopper in
the Mother's Day section of the store leaned closer.
"She has to get exactly the right thing, or she won't
be happy."

I reached for another card as I conveyed my
sympathies. I'd just met the woman, but I already
had a clear picture of her eighty-two-year-old
mother, who was so dissatisfied and exacting that her
sixty-something daughter approached shopping for a
Mother's Day card with fear and trembling.

I stared at the card in my hand, but the words
blurred. I couldn't stop thinking about the woman
whose experience as a daughter was so different from
mine. Her words struck me—with gratitude for my
wonderful mother and with personal conviction.

Although I'm not a mother, I am a teacher of
children and teens, a mentor and instructor to budding
writers, a counselor to friends and family. What kind
of impact am I having on others? Am I leaving a legacy
of love and faith or one of bitterness and unkindness?

I wonder how those who know me think of me
and how they'll remember me when I'm gone. Most

importantly, will others be spurred on to serve and glorify Christ because of the example they saw in me?

Thanks to the Mother's Day shopper, whenever I interact with those I'm in a position to influence—which, in truth, is everyone I encounter in life—I try to remember I'm leaving a legacy. Will it be a positive one?

Father, help me to leave a legacy of love, faith, and purity that will point others to You.
—Jerusha Agen

Digging Deeper: John 13:14–15; 1 Corinthians 10:1–11; Philippians 3:17

Thursday, May 9

And thine ears shall hear a word behind thee, saying, This is the way, walk ye in it, when ye turn to the right hand, and when ye turn to the left.
—Isaiah 30:21 (KJV)

Laughter always erupted among my family as we rehearsed an old joke about a preacher who was pulled over and chastised by a policeman for driving in the wrong direction on a one-way street. "But officer," the reverend argued, "that's what I was doing: driving *one* way!"

Life imposes its own one-way direction, and no matter the ups and downs, there are no exceptions to eternity as our destination. Often, though, in our observance of more popular Christians, we can confuse *where* we are headed with how many miles we've racked up along the way. It's tempting to rubberneck, watching others' accomplishments and convincing ourselves we should at least be as far along as they. Dreaming of an impressive foreign mission added to our ministry, we sometimes forget to check on our neighbors.

In my quest to do good, I have sometimes found myself flying headlong toward the future—thinking so much about meeting tomorrow's self-imposed quota that I forget a standard simple assignment for today, like "Rejoice forevermore" (Isaiah 65:18, NET). We may be at different places in our walk with God, but we are all headed toward a prepared place of infinite joy. Just as we reach adulthood at different heights, weights, and accomplishments, so will we reach eternity. That's where God's grace comes in, making us all glorious in that day. Meanwhile, we could just be grateful for—and diligent about—our assignment right where we are.

Father, God, help me to do with joy what You have assigned me to do this day.
—Jacqueline F. Wheelock

Digging Deeper: John 14:6; 2 Corinthians 10:13

Friday, May 10

Encourage...older women as mothers, younger women as sisters. —1 Timothy 5:1–2 (ESV)

A neighbor with developmental delays and immigrant roots calls me her "extra grandma." She looks to me for social cues. She's blossomed from a girl unable to articulate a full paragraph to a teen who chats with track-team friends. Last week, she mentioned an upcoming Monday outing, from noon till three, with six of those mainstreamed girls— meeting at a grocery store to buy ice cream and bananas, then eating in a nearby park.

Not until Monday morning did she mention that *she* had initiated the gathering. *Oh dear, she's in over her head.* But hadn't she helped me host coffee hours? I let hope slip in alongside worry. To facilitate success, I asked questions and gave suggestions. "Who will bring bowls? Spoons?"

"We'll buy them," she responded. Hmm. Costs and calculations—not her strength.

From my picnic basket, I handed her some plastic supplies and a sturdy tablespoon. "Take along your UNO game." I prepared her for disappointment: "If they go home early, just thank them for coming." And even disaster: "If no one comes, you'll feel sad; try not to be angry." With a silent prayer for God's best, I wished her well. And anxiously awaited a call.

"It was a blast!" she reported, at 1:30. It was less time than she'd planned for the outing to take, but she was satisfied with it.

"How many came?" She named four. That, too, was "enough." Her positive take—itself an evidence of new maturity—turned my apprehension to applause. "Did you do anything more than eat?"

I asked. When she answered, I smiled and thanked God for UNO.

Lord, as I encourage others, may some encouragement slip back to me. —Evelyn Bence

Digging Deeper: Ruth 2:8–13

Saturday, May 11

If you come with us, we will share with you whatever good things the LORD gives us. —Numbers 10:32 (NIV)

When my family moved from New York to Indiana, it was painful to say goodbye to friends we'd known our entire lives.

I asked God to bless my friends and to help us stay connected.

As I packed all those boxes, I looked out at the perennials I'd lovingly planted and tended. I mourned leaving them too. What if I left a part of myself, some of those flowers, with my friends? They gladly accepted my flower gifts; I imagined them thinking of me every summer.

Some summers I visited my New York friends or they visited me. Sue brought me perennials from her garden, and Linda let me dig up perennials from hers. When I planted them in Indiana, I called it my Friendship Garden. I see Sue's face in her coreopsis, Linda's in her lily of the valley, Carol's face in her periwinkle, and Pat's in her columbine.

I began to share my Friendship Garden with my Indiana friends and neighbors. In return, some shared their perennials. Now I smile when Joyce's morning glories bloom next to Maureen's delphinium, Sydney's old-fashioned daffodils, and Martha's iris.

I rang the doorbell at Cheryl's house, my new friend from the Y. I held up a bag. "Would you like some lily of the valley?" Cheryl broke into a delighted grin and gave me a hug. "I know just where to plant them! We had some out back years ago, and I miss them!"

My Friendship Garden keeps growing, just like my friendships!

Dear Lord, thank You for friends and flowers, both new and old. They are all beautiful.
—Leanne Jackson

Digging Deeper: Song of Songs 2:12; Matthew 7:12

Mother's Day, Sunday, May 12

From the lips of children and infants you, Lord, have called forth your praise. —Matthew 21:16 (NIV)

How'd it go?" my husband asked as I climbed into the waiting car.

I sighed. I'd been in a school board committee meeting and—as always, it seemed—much of what had been discussed had been hard. There were so many important perspectives to consider. Sometimes it felt impossible to take it all in at once. I often ended up feeling as though I didn't contribute as much as I should or wanted to.

"It was OK, I guess," I answered. "I wish I could find it within myself to speak up more."

My nine-year-old daughter piped up then from the back seat: "It's alright, Mom. You don't talk much there. But you are watching and listening so you can think about it all later."

I froze, stunned, as the truth of her words resonated and sank into my mind. I'd never thought about it quite like that before.

"H–How do you know that, Aurora?" I asked, unable to keep astonishment from my voice.

"Becauuussse Mom-Silly," she answered, "you've taken me to bazillions of your meetings!"

"Someday," an older friend had said to me recently, "when the others have gone, it'll be your daughter who knows your story best."

Looking in the rearview mirror, I marveled at the wisdom of the child sitting in the back seat, who tonight had shared with me a part of myself and my story I hadn't yet even realized was there.

On this Mother's Day—and every day, God—I am grateful beyond measure for the treasure that is my daughter. For all that she is, all that she sees, and all that she teaches me about myself, about the world, and about You. Thank You. —Erin Janoso

Digging Deeper: Psalm 8:2; Matthew 18:1–3; Mark 10:14

The Lord is close to the brokenhearted and saves those who are crushed in spirit. —Psalm 34:18 (NIV)

Our black Labrador, Darby, was twelve. We'd been treating her diabetes with insulin for over a year, but she had gone blind and become arthritic. We made the decision to say goodbye at the end of June, and though it was the hardest decision we've ever made, we also knew it was the kindest thing to do. Darby was the sweetest companion we had ever known, and she loved us fiercely. We didn't want her to suffer anymore.

When we arrived at the country vet, he let us say goodbye to Darby outside, in the grass, under the bright blue sky. After he administered the anesthetic, we had ten minutes before she fell asleep. The six of us circled around Darby and loved on her like never before. She was so happy as we told her what a good girl she was and how much she'd meant to each of us.

After Darby was gone, my oldest daughter went to the car to be alone, my second daughter wanted to talk through her tears, and one of my boys clung to me and wept. It didn't take my other son long to wipe his tears and become my husband's helper. I wondered at his lack of tears. *Wouldn't he miss her? Wasn't he sad? Why wasn't he showing it?* I soon realized that he was dealing with his grief by being useful. He taught me that God has made each of us unique and there is no wrong way to say goodbye.

Lord, when our hearts are breaking, help us remember that it's OK to grieve the loss of a loved one in our own way. —Gabrielle Meyer

Digging Deeper: John 16:22; Philippians 4:13; Revelations 21:4

Tuesday, May 14

For he satisfies the thirsty and fills the hungry with good things. —Psalm 107:9 (NIV)

Can I have your chicken and rice recipe?" Kelley, a former student, called from her college dorm room while I sat staring at my Bible, uninspired to begin my morning devotions.

I knew exactly which recipe Kelley wanted. When my husband was a youth pastor, we often took students to the Havasupai Canyon during spring break, a beautiful location in Arizona known for its turquoise water and spectacular waterfalls, an area only accessible by helicopter, mule, or a long hike down a canyon. On our limited budgets, it was always on foot for us, with everyone carrying all they needed for four days in a backpack.

Packaged ramen, oatmeal, dried fruit, and beef jerky filled out most people's menus as every ounce was weighed and considered. On the last evening, we planned a potluck so people could share remaining food. Nobody wanted to carry the additional weight to the van at the trailhead—ten miles uphill.

Knowing most hikers would offer reconstituted dry food, I served chicken and rice, a one-pot dish that consisted of minute rice, almonds, and the unheard-of luxury of canned chicken and canned pineapple. The teens had dug into it as if they had never seen food before, scraping the pan until not one grain of rice remained. At the enthusiastic, five-star reviews, I could easily have believed I needed to quit my day job and become a chef if I had not known the simple ingredients.

"Food tastes better when you are hungry," Kelley said as we laughed about my recipe.

I contemplated her words as I hung up the phone and opened my Bible with a renewed conviction to feed on the words on the pages.

May I long for You, Jesus. —Lynne Hartke

Digging Deeper: Psalm 17:15; Matthew 5:6

Wednesday, May 15

I lie down and sleep; I wake again, because the LORD sustains me. —Psalm 3:5 (NIV)

Every so often, I get up in the wee hours to use the bathroom. When I return, the warm spot I left behind in the bed is occupied by Gracie.

Moving a seventy-five-pound golden retriever back to her own bed is no small task. I knock over something, making a racket, which startles me.

Meanwhile, Gracie is sleeping limply in my buckling arms. I lay her in her own bed only to have her leap up and beat me back to my spot. I'm fully awake now.

"You win," I whisper.

I hear a satisfied sigh as I wander off in search of a place to rest and read a book and maybe nod off, except I left my book on the nightstand. I make myself a cup of coffee instead and stand at the window, staring into the dark and thinking of nothing until quietly, almost magically, night yields to a breath of light in the east.

All at once, I am mesmerized by the miracle of the obvious. Night becomes day as day will become night, the earth turns and turns, and God is in His heaven.

And in our lives. All around me I can see His hand, in the rising of the sun and the turning of the earth, in the song of the bird, and in the patter of paws behind me, a hungry and well-rested golden retriever sitting demurely asking for breakfast.

Maybe this is the way God reminds me of His glory, to wake me up to witness the miracle of another day.

You win, Lord. I will gladly surrender a little bit of sleep for more time with You. —Edward Grinnan

Digging Deeper: Isaiah 50:3–5; Revelation 3:2–4

Thursday, May 16

Then he said, "I tell you the truth, unless you turn from your sins and become like little children, you will never get into the Kingdom of Heaven." —Matthew 18:3 (NLT)

This morning, I jumped on my bike and peddled down the road. It's a route I've traveled hundreds of times since I was young. As I coasted down Jenny's Hill, named after the woman who lived there forty-some years ago, I took my feet off the pedals and straightened my legs, balancing and swerving, whooshing down the bumpy hill as I'd done as a child.

I felt ineffable joy.

Perhaps it was being on the same road that I grew up on and coasting down the same hill that gave me that feeling of being a kid again, that wonderful, wordless excitement of being both connected and carefree, young and old, all at the same time.

I pondered the word *ineffable*: unable to describe, beyond expression. Growing up, that vocabulary word challenged me. I was convinced everything could be described. There was nothing that couldn't be unraveled and harnessed with words. Every experience could be expressed through language, and saying you couldn't find the right words was just plain lazy.

I pedaled up the next hill faster and faster and tried to put the ineffable feeling of coasting down the hill and reexperiencing my childhood joy into words. Like God Himself, like faith, there are some things I still can't find the words for. I laughed at myself for being decades older and still trying to attempt the impossible.

I let go of trying to capture the magic and let joy flow through me, coasting in the breeze.

God of Wonder, maker of the ineffable, thank You for innocent childlike joy and a million other experiences that are too beautiful, too wonderful, too amazing to put into words. —Sabra Ciancanelli

Digging Deeper: Psalm 118:24; Philippians 4:4

Friday, May 17

Offer hospitality to one another without grumbling. —1 Peter 4:9 (NIV)

I struggle with inviting people into our home. With three kids, both adults working, and a pup, the clean laundry piles up, waiting to be folded, and the house looks, well, lived in. *I want to be the person who flings open my doors to Your people, Lord. How do I do that when it looks like this?*

I tried cleaning more, enlisting the help of the kids, and setting up routines, but nothing really made a dent.

As I lamented my lack of hosting to my girlfriends, one of them said, "You know, the gospel comes with a housekey," reminding us of the name of a book she'd recently read. "To love people, you need to invite them in—into your heart and into your house, even if it's not perfect."

Those words etched on my heart. How true they were! God never calls us to be perfect before coming to his altar; why would my house need to be perfect before sharing it with others?

The next week, I hosted my coworkers on my back deck for a going-away party. Did I work several hours to clean up the deck? Sure. Did I also cheat by not having them in my house? Maybe, but this felt like a step forward.

I know my house is not magically going to be clean when I need it to be, but I've learned I'd rather have gatherings that make others feel loved than prove that we live in a frozen state of no-dust-bunny perfection. These days, the words "the gospel is a housekey" rings in my ears whenever I hesitate to invite others in.

Lord, thank You for softening my heart and removing the desire to be perfect. Help me to always welcome others. —Ashley Kappel

Digging Deeper: 1 Timothy 5:10; Hebrews 13:2

Saturday, May 18

So those who went off with heavy hearts will come home laughing, with armloads of blessing. —Psalm 126:6 (MSG)

Ah…what delight I felt opening the recently purchased twenty-five-quart Miracle-Grow more-blooms-for-more-color potting mix. I was preparing our window boxes for spring. I pictured healthy vines and exuberant morning glory blossoms thriving in the rich soil.

After filling the boxes with the nitrogen-infused compost, I delicately sowed seeds left over from last year's planting. With my wife Kate's steadying hand on our stepladder, I positioned the planters under our sun-bathed front windows.

Oh, the profusion of sprouts that burst forth. Vines reached the rooftop. Abundant heart-shaped leaves, lush and full, overflowed the compact boxes. But no blossoms.

Figuring my miserly ways—using old seeds—were the difficulty, in late spring I picked up a fresh packet of "Heavenly Blue," intense-blossom morning glory seeds. Only after I inspected the packet's "gardener's notes" did I realize the source of my no-flower problem.

"Soil should not be too fertile or moist. High fertility causes excessive vegetation, but few flowers."

Morning glories require hardscrabble dirt to flourish. Blossoms appear only after vines are tempered by roots made strong in difficult soil.

This spring, I'm filling the planters with loose, unfertilized dirt. And I'm welcoming disruptions that break into my routines. After all, if morning glory flowers flourish in coarse ground, maybe I, too, can see difficulties as opportunities for blessing and growth.

Abundant God, we thank You for difficulties that steel and fortify us. Enable us to blossom forth with your renewing and glorious power. Amen.
—Ken Sampson

Digging Deeper: 2 Corinthians 4:17; Philippians 3:12–16

I was glad when they said to me, "Let us go to the house of the LORD!" —Psalm 122:1 (NRSV)

We were always taught in Sunday school to think of the church not as a building but as the people in it. We'd sing the little ditty "We Are the Church" by Richard Kinsey Avery, and know that when we gathered together, we become the church.

And yet, when I'm in the church where we've worshipped for almost forty years, I feel my heart warmed by all the visual clues. Angels shimmering through stained glass, the image of Jesus on the cross in the back, that window of Martha and Mary, the words "I am the bread of life and all who come to me will not hunger" over the altar, the Bible on the lectern.

If it weren't for all those souls and the trust they gave and the sacrifices they made, the old building wouldn't be here. We give to our church, not just to keep the lights on and cover some modest salaries but also to keep the building standing. To make it a welcoming place for all who enter. Those beloved neighbors who get a great meal at the soup kitchen, the kids who show up on Monday nights for homework help, the musicians who come to sing, the Sunday schoolers who get the rudiments of faith—as I did many years ago.

In fact, those stained-glass windows say a lot. For it's not light bouncing off them that helps us see the images, it's light that shines *through* them. Like the light that shines through all of us worshipping in faith.

How glad I am to have this place where I've seen that Light shine.

Let me continue to help make this place Yours.
—Rick Hamlin

Digging Deeper: Matthew 18:20;
Romans 12:5; Ephesians 2:20

Monday, May 20

Mightier than the thunder of the great waters, mightier than the breakers of the sea—the LORD on high is mighty. —Psalm 93:4 (NIV)

My husband, Lonny, had been working across the pond in Belgium all summer. My biggest worry while he was away was the safety of our sons, some of whom were young drivers. They spent more than a few hours a week on the road. I prayed without ceasing, but anxiety crept close. Lonny and I have always worked through things together. I didn't want to have to handle something difficult alone.

My fear came to fruition one early morning when fifteen-year-old Gabriel called after he'd left for school. "Mom, I'm alright," he said. His voice wavered. "But someone hit me. The car is totaled. I'm on River Road."

I arrived just as the ambulance did.

"He'll need to go to the hospital," the paramedic said after checking Gabe. "But if you'd rather drive him, it will be OK."

And it was OK. There was grace after grace. The policeman was kind and reassuring. The paramedic held the clipboard when I shook so hard I couldn't sign. A tow truck driver just happened to drive past, and he was compassionate. Before I'd arrived, passers-by had stopped to comfort Gabriel and the young man who'd hit him too. Gabriel would need surgery on his hand, and cars had been crumpled, but both boys walked away.

When Lonny and I talked on the phone that afternoon, he said, "I'm proud of you for handling this alone."

Only I hadn't.

The mighty Lord, mightier than the breakers of the sea, had met our every need. Mighty mercy in gentle, compassionate waves.

Lord, You are mighty when I'm afraid, and I praise You. Amen. —Shawnelle Eliasen

Digging Deeper: Psalm 33:6–8; Ephesians 1:19

Tuesday, May 21

...that you may become...children of God without fault in the midst of a crooked and perverse generation, among whom you shine as lights in the world.... —Philippians 2:15 (NKJV)

In the early morning darkness, I was riding my bicycle downtown, when I passed an old church with a lighted bulletin board out front and a beautiful scripture displayed on it. Later that day, I saw a young woman changing the scripture, so I stopped and introduced myself. "I want to thank you for these scriptures," I said. "They are truly helpful to me."

The lady blushed. "Well, I sometimes wonder if anyone ever reads them, so thank you for that feedback."

I, too, often wonder if anyone notices my feeble acts of kindness.

One evening, I came across some poetry by British author Francis Bourdillon, whose most famous poem begins with, "The night has a thousand eyes…"

As I thought about that, I could see that the darker the world around us, the more our Christian witness stands out.

Like the other day, when I was having lunch at a little downtown restaurant, and some middle-aged ladies were seated nearby. When their order arrived, they joined hands, and one of them began saying grace. Suddenly, inexplicably, the noisy restaurant grew perfectly still, just long enough that everyone could hear every word she prayed.

The night does, indeed, have a thousand eyes…and a thousand ears.

After witnessing this prayer, I no longer wonder if what I do affects others. I know the best thing for me to do is to concentrate on doing good and to trust God for its effects.

Lord, help me to remember that my work shines brightly in this dark world. —Daniel Schantz

Digging Deeper: 2 Chronicles 16:9; Proverbs 15:3

Wednesday, May 22

Commit your work to the Lord, then it will succeed. —Proverbs 16:3 (TLB)

After my husband, Jack, died in 2019, I'd floundered like a fish flopping on a sidewalk, out of place and with no purpose. So I decided to visit my son Michael and his fiancée, Monica, in Ohio. Monica had taken up beekeeping as a hobby, and I couldn't wait to see the 30,000 bees she'd purchased.

Monica suited us up in head-to-toe Star Wars–like white beekeeper suits with elastic at the wrists and ankles. Then she pulled a number of frames covered in bees out of the bee boxes until she found the one with the queen. "See? She's bigger than the others with longer legs."

Monica explained the different roles each bee has. "The nurse bee feeds the young. The architects build the comb. Cleaners, organizers, and honey makers do exactly what their name says. The foragers are the most important because they are the pollinators in a three-mile radius. Guard bees with mature stingers keep intruders out of the hive. The queen bee's only job is to lay 2,000 eggs a day. The drone bees mate with neighboring queens to spread healthy genes.

The undertakers clean out the dead bees and debris from the hive."

Just then, one of the guard bees stung me on my ankle through my sock. I got the message. I also got God's message—we all have a role and a purpose in life. Back home, I got back to my purposeful life: writing, giving speeches, painting, driving people to the airport, socializing more, sending handwritten notes to all those I love, volunteering…things I'd let slide for a few years.

Father, You created me with a purpose in mind. Help me stay on track. —Patricia Lorenz

Digging Deeper: Psalm 103:14–15, 22; Isaiah 40:6–8

Thursday, May 23

CELEBRATE!! Ring the Bell!
Come, everyone, and clap for joy! Shout triumphant praises to the Lord! —Psalm 47:1 (TLB)

My friend Heidi rang the bell a few weeks ago, surrounded by people clapping and cheering. She had just finished twelve rounds of chemotherapy treatments and celebrated in the way that has become a tradition in cancer treatment centers around the world. Patients loudly ring a bell to mark the end of their treatments, a sound that becomes a symbol of hope for everybody in the treatment center who hears it.

According to Heidi, the time spent getting infusions can feel lonely and long. "For me, it was one of the hardest realities of having cancer," she told me. "But it was also a spiritual experience. I knew I was never alone. God was clearly with me and helped me get through it. I thanked Him for His goodness when I rang that bell."

Heidi claims that the bell ringing has become even more meaningful as she keeps remembering it. "I'm now a survivor, and we are important reminders for all those coming along behind us. When we ring the bell, we are telling them there is an end to their treatments. And they, too, will ring the bell someday soon. They are walking on hope as they continue their treatments."

I especially like Heidi's story because I, too, am a cancer survivor. I finished my twelve chemotherapy treatments before the bell-ringing tradition was established. I know there are no guarantees that cancer won't ever come back, but I join Heidi in celebrating God's goodness.

Lord, I celebrate Your blessing upon every cancer patient who rings that bell at the end of their treatments. May they know Your presence in celebrating with them. —Carol Kuykendall

Digging Deeper: Psalm 126; Ephesians 20–21

Friday, May 24

For your heart will always pursue what you esteem as your treasure. —Matthew 6:21 (TPT)

"Happy birthday, eight months early!" my ever-generous sister said, handing me a small box.

As our tour bus pulled away from the souvenir shop, and we continued our journey to Masada, Israel's ancient hilltop fortress, I excitedly opened my unexpected gift. Inside was a bronze coin, set in silver. My sister explained it was found in Masada and minted almost 2,000 years ago. Less than five years after the Jewish coin was made, the Romans conquered Jerusalem, and Jewish rebels fled to the safety of Masada. After a months-long siege, when the Roman army finally breached the city's walls, they found only two women and five children alive, hiding in a cistern. Rather than be captured by the Romans, 960 Jews had taken their own lives.

My sister knew me well. Long before I'd wanted to be a writer, I wanted to be an archaeologist. Instead of writing stories, I'd longed to uncover other people's stories by studying what they'd left behind. This little piece of history I held in my hands set my mind racing. *Who had held this in their hands? What were their last days in Masada like?*

Then my mind made a U-turn. I began wondering what the relics of my own life had to tell future generations about me. Would my "treasures" hold clues as to my faith, generosity, courage . . . or materialism? That one tiny coin, a "rebel's mite," became a touchstone for me, a reminder to be ever mindful of where my true treasure lies.

Lord, teach me how to hold loosely onto my possessions and tightly onto what matters most to You. —Vicki Kuyper

---

Saturday, May 25

And in the early morning, while it was still dark, Jesus…went away to a secluded place, and prayed.…—Mark 1:35 (NASB)

There's an old saying I often hear tossed around Christian enclaves regarding our petitions to God: "Don't worry, the answer isn't *no*, it's just *not yet.*"

This was actually my own response years ago when my kids started asking me to help them build a treehouse. "It's not no, guys, just not yet." After all, I was busy. On staff at a church, often on the road with my music. Hey, I had to make a living, right?

But the asking didn't stop. Looking back, I'm ashamed how long it went on.

God has a gentle and wonderful way of speaking to us in a way we can't help but hear. For me, it came the day I was asking Him for some important thing (so important I can't remember what it was now) and "just happened" to glance up at that very treehouse-less tree outside the window.

"Seriously? You think that's the priority?" I asked Him.

We built a treehouse.

Of course, you already know the moral of the story—it wasn't about the treehouse at all; it was about being together.

The beautiful news is this also happens to be the moral of the Great Story.

Turns out it's so much easier than I thought in my younger days. It's never the work or the accomplishments. It's not even the destination or the journey. I find, happily, that all God really wants from me is me.

The answer isn't *no*. And it isn't *not yet*. The answer is always *yes*.

I just have to get the question right.

Heavenly Father, thank You for the weight of Your arm across my shoulder. You are the one and always constant. —Buck Storm

Digging Deeper: Genesis 5:34; Luke 10:40–42

Sunday, May 26

For I know the plans I have for you, declares the LORD, plans for welfare and not for evil, to give you a future and a hope. —Jeremiah 29:11 (ESV)

"I'm so mad at him. He's a jerk!" cried JoElla, my twelve-year-old daughter.

I felt so helpless. Logan broke her heart. Logan, a very independent horse, refused his jumps on the first day of the horse show. This refusal was personal for JoElla. My husband and I emphasized the positive aspects of the situation: she rode well and handled the refusal well in the ring.

After the first day of showing, we had a great dinner with other riders and her trainer. JoElla got to know her teammate Ginny, another twelve-year-old equestrian, and the day ended with smiles. However, the second show day was much like the first. Logan had moments of promise but still refused several jumps. An outpouring of support and encouragement did not console JoElla. "I did everything right, and it didn't make a difference." JoElla's lament echoed the ache in her heart.

When we got in the car to travel home, my husband handed JoElla one of the prizes Ginny won and said, "Ginny wanted you to have this. She said you worked really hard and deserve it."

JoElla smiled sweetly and said, "She didn't have to do that. Something good *did* happen this weekend." Our drive home was reassuring. JoElla spoke of how nice it is to win ribbons, but making friends and simply riding were more important.

Amen, I thought. Those beside us matter. God consistently places others around us, like Ginny, who lift us in the midst of hard life lessons.

Lord God, help me bring comfort and peace in times of uncertainty. —Jolynda Strandberg

Digging Deeper: Matthew 6:33–34; John 14:1–3; Philippians 1:6

Memorial Day, Monday, May 27

Remember [carefully] the former things. —Isaiah 46:9 (AMP)

Be careful," Randy says as we stand together by the flagpole in front of our house. He attaches the line to the grommets in the flag I hold. "Don't let it touch the ground when I raise it."

My husband served four years in the Air Force straight out of high school. Although it was wartime and Randy had a draft number, he joined before it was drawn. He patrolled military bases as a law enforcement specialist. He says he enlisted to find direction in his life. All these years later, he still removes his hat and stands taller whenever the national anthem is played. I've watched him blink back tears when the honor guard presented him with a folded flag for his father and his younger brother at their funerals.

I wasn't in the military. I don't have firsthand knowledge of what it takes to serve my country, to defend her principles and her resources. But as I observe the quiet reverence Randy continues to pay this nation in so many ways, I have grown to respect our veterans all the more.

The Red, White, and Blue ascends the pole. Together we watch the colors unfurl.

What began as Decoration Day in 1868 as a time for the nation to decorate the graves of war dead with flowers, Memorial Day today seems more about barbecues and less about honoring those who sacrificed for us. But this moment, standing beside him, my heart fills. This is a memory I'll never forget.

Thank You, Lord, for all of those willing to give of themselves, for those who sacrifice all or part of their lives so that we may live free. —Erika Bentsen

---

Tuesday, May 28

Therefore encourage one another and build each other up....—1 Thessalonians 5:11 (NIV)

I stared at the email, feeling my heart sink to my toes. My book proposal had been rejected. The negative thoughts started flying. *Who are you kidding? Why did you think they'd accept it? Why are you wasting your time? Your writing just isn't good enough.*

Each thought felt like a punch in the gut. Why had I hoped? Even though this same publisher had published my books before, there was no guarantee they would publish another one.

The rejection came on the heels of some other disappointing news, compounding the pain. There was no solution but to give up. Had I misunderstood what God said? After all, He was the one who gave me the idea for the book. And if He really wanted me to write the book, wouldn't He have made it possible? Had I been wrong to think God had gifted me to write?

I closed my eyes and prayed. *God, if You really want me to write, I need You to let me know. Show me so I'll believe, or I'll quit trying.*

The next day, there was a card in the mail from someone telling me how much they enjoyed my writing. OK, so one person liked it. The day after, I received an email from a reader who said how much they liked my last book. OK, then two people liked it.

At church Sunday, a lady stopped to tell me I'd kept her up at night because she couldn't put my book down. I smiled, remembering my prayer.

God had affirmed me with encouragement from others. Perhaps I could encourage someone else too.

Thank You, Lord, for encouraging me when I doubt. Show me who I can encourage. —Marilyn Turk

Digging Deeper: Psalm 10:17; 1 Thessalonians 5:14

Wednesday, May 29

Children's children are the crown of old men; and the glory of children are their fathers. —Proverbs 17:6 (KJV)

My friend Danny called me, seeking advice about his son. I assumed he meant Gabe, the youngest, who has dyslexia and—maybe as a result?—struggled with grades and with the social minefield known as high school. Nope, the issue was "J-Dan"— Daniel Jr., the oldest and everyone's idea of a golden boy. J-Dan had won a university scholarship but developed crippling depression that now threatened to derail his career.

"I should have seen this coming," Dan Sr. said. "This is my fault."

"*No*," I said firmly. "It isn't. Besides, you had your hands full with Gabe."

"Oh, Gabe's doing fine," Dan said. "Got into some great universities."

"Wait—what? Gabe is going to college?"

"Yep. Really applied himself."

"So you're responsible for J-Dan's issues," I said, "but take no credit for Gabe's success?"

Dan was quiet, then made an excuse and rang off. I hope he calls back, but I'll tell him the same thing again: our children are ours, and not ours. We guide them; we don't control them. We cannot save them from the world and certainly not from outrageous fortune. We try to help where we can, including savoring their successes, but we can only do so much. Then we do what parents have done since time began: we pray.

Lord, You love us as Your children; have mercy on us as parents—imperfect vessels of Your perfect love.
—Mark Collins

Digging Deeper: Hosea 11:1; Luke 18:16–17

Thursday, May 30

How great are his signs! —Daniel 4:3 (KJV)

My husband, David, and I were in Zimbabwe, trying to help a few hungry street kids. Yet, each morning when approaching our hotel's taxi queue, we always ended up in the same beat-up car.

A year later, with our daughter Keri joining us, there was that same taxi. When the driver,

Paddington, saw what we were trying to do, he wholeheartedly joined in. He had a deep love for his desperate country and longed to help the hordes of AIDS orphans. So, somehow, in the blink of an eye, we found ourselves partnering with this amazing man. By now, thanks primarily to Guideposts readers called to serve African children, we were compiling a list of donors who wanted to help.

As we rode through the dusty African bush in an un-air-conditioned taxi, God was weaving a beautiful tapestry of open hearts and pitiful needs. He was taking us to a rural community, where AIDS-broken families lived in hunger in mud huts. There, He visioned a farm where His hungry children were fed, taught new skills, and given animals to enhance their lives. He saw a school being built, and a library, and a home where countless orphans were taken in as family. And Paddington, who started by helping us check on the children and distribute food, eventually moved into the orphanage with his family and became a surrogate father to the children there.

If we had known what lofty plans He had for us, we would have run for the hills. Yet today, as we visit this amazing spot where children gladly walk miles to school and grandmothers are assured that there will always be food cooking over their fires, we are humbled.

To think, it all began with a taxi that He put in the right place at the right time.

Father, Your plans are incomprehensible. We are grateful to be included. —Pam Kidd

Friday, May 31

**Iron sharpens iron, and one man sharpens another.
—Proverbs 27:17** (ESV)

The wedding party is moving toward the dance floor,"
my friend Matt said. He pointed finger guns at me.

I laughed and shook my head. "I don't dance," I
said.

"It's my wedding," he said. "Five minutes." He
tapped on his watch as he disappeared into the crowd.

Matt and I had been friends since our first year
of college. Over the past decade, we had become
like brothers. Even so, our personalities were vastly
different. Matt was energetic and spontaneous. He
was easygoing and on the move. In contrast, I was
cautious and deliberate. I thought things through
before acting. I leaned back in my chair, wondering
how two people could be so different yet so close.

Soon, a hand clapped my shoulder from behind.
"Ready?" Matt asked.

"Matt," I said. "I don't dance."

"I know," he said. Matt looked toward the ground.
"But the truth is, I'm nervous. I'm not a good dancer,
and I don't know how to be a good husband." Matt
paused. "I need my best friend beside me."

Hearing Matt's words, I understood our
friendship. Our differences were complementary.

Matt moved me forward, and I kept him steady. He was the sails of this friendship, and I was the rudder. I was so thankful in that moment that God gifted me a friend like this.

I stood up. "I wouldn't do this for anybody else," I said.

Matt pumped his fists.

Then, together, we walked toward the dance floor.

Lord, thank You for providing friends who challenge and strengthen me. —Logan Eliasen

Digging Deeper: Proverbs 17:17; Ecclesiastes 4:9–10

YOU WERE CALLED TO PEACE

1 _____

2 _____

3 _____

4 _____

5 _____

6 _____

7 _____

8 _____

9 _____

10 _____

11 _____

12 _____

13 _____

14 _____

15 _____

16 _____

17 _____

18 _____

19 _____

20 _____

21 _____

22 _____

23 _____

24 _____

25 _____

26 _____

27 _____

28 _____

29 _____

30 _____

31 _____

JUNE

*You will keep in perfect peace
those whose minds are steadfast,
because they trust in you.*

—Isaiah 26:3 (NIV)

I... urge you to walk in a manner worthy of the calling to which you have been called, with all humility and gentleness, with patience, bearing with one another in love. —Ephesians 4:1–2 (ESV)

The wild turkeys that inhabit the landscape around my farm, Ploughshares, wandered across the yard this afternoon. There were four of them, as usual, doing their crazy turkey walk—heads bobbing and then pecking at things on the ground. They moved slowly, taking their time, even after I opened the front door and went out on the porch to watch them. They mostly ignored me, though the tom did ruffle his tail feathers in my direction. In no hurry, they were.

These big birds walk lightly upon the earth. On my treks around the farm, I often see tracks of deer, raccoons, coyotes, and other critters. But rarely turkey tracks.

As I watched them, I wondered what kind of footprints, both literal and figurative, I leave. Is it slight, like the turkeys, or more like a heavy human, sinking into soft mud? For the good of the earth, I hope it's slight. My faith calls me to earth stewardship—in particular to take care of this little plot of land that God has put in my charge for a little while.

What about in my interactions with my fellow humans, though? Am I kind and gentle and caring or heavy-handed (or footed, in this case)? Do I leave impressions in the heart or scars on the soul? Oh, how I pray that it's the former. That's because my faith calls me to human stewardship—taking care of my relationships and neighbors all around the world.

Loving Lord, teach me to walk easy with You and my fellow creatures. —J. Brent Bill

Digging Deeper: Luke 10:30–37

Sunday, June 2

Even so the body is not made up of one part but of many. —1 Corinthians 12:14 (NIV)

In my windows, I have hanging dozens of prisms. Little glass globes, cut with facets and hung, three to a string, where they can catch the light. Sometimes, when the sun's angle is just right, I will look up from my work to find I'm surrounded by hundreds of tiny rainbows, twirling and dancing about the room. It's a delightful surprise that never fails to bring a huge, happy smile to my face.

It occurred to me today when this happened that if it weren't for the prisms, I wouldn't have been able to see this lovely part of light's nature at all. How easy it would have been then to believe the single color I could see fully explained the light shining through my window. It's all my eyes can make out, after all, and it can be tempting to think that what I'm able to perceive is the way things really are.

But as I reveled in the merriment of the rainbows in my living room, I thought how wonderful it is that

God doesn't limit Himself to including only what I can comprehend. What a dull world it would be if He did. Because where I can see only one color, God has designed an entire vibrant spectrum. And I needed to look no further than the rainbows on my wall to know that it's a spectrum in which each color belongs. Where each is beautiful. And where each one is the good work of His hands.

Thank You, God, for sharing with me this glimpse of the miraculous depth and complexity of Your creation.
—Erin Janoso

Digging Deeper: Isaiah 55:9; Revelation 7:9–10

Monday, June 3

Therefore encourage one another and build one another up, just as you are doing.
—1 Thessalonians 5:11 (ESV)

Working from home means a lot of video calls. Can you relate? Most of my day is spent with my camera on, talking with coworkers across the country. Sure, that means sometimes a stuffed piggy or one of my kiddos makes a quick cameo in the corner of my screen, but mostly everyone understands that when Mom is in a meeting, you have to give me a little space.

One day was especially hard. After a six-hour, ten-person training session, I hung up at 5 p.m. feeling completely depleted. And yet, here were these three adorable people finally ready for me to play!

Beau, my youngest at age four, noticed my tired eyes and said, "Mama, I think we need a snack." He walked to the freezer and pulled out four individual ice cream cups. Now normally, this would feel like a ploy for treats, and certainly a terrible idea just before dinnertime, but today it felt so loving, so giving, that I gave in.

He carried his tower to the table while I grabbed the spoons and called the other two kids into the kitchen. Beau peeled the tops off each cup, passing them around, then opened mine last. "Look, Mom!" he said. "A heart!"

And there, pressed into the top of the ice cream, was a perfect heart. A perfect reminder from God that He loves me and wants me to care for myself. We ended up having a full ice cream party that night, passing sprinkles and whipped cream, while we talked about finding beauty, and God's love, in the things around us.

Lord, blessed am I to be surrounded by a loving family. Help me to never take them for granted.
—Ashley Kappel

Digging Deeper: Galatians 6:2; Philippians 2:4

Tuesday, June 4

Be careful that you do not forget the LORD....
—Deuteronomy 6:12 (NIV)

Mom fractured her pelvis and was stuck in bed at a rehabilitation facility. She received a bouquet and asked me to take a picture of it with her older-model iPhone. She wanted to thank the sender with a text and photo of the flowers.

I tried to take a screenshot of the text and photo to save it on her phone, but each time I pressed the sides of the phone to save the image as a screenshot, as I did on my iPhone 12, the screen darkened.

"Use the home button." Mom took her device and pressed the round button on the front in tandem with the button on the right side. *Of course!* Newer-model iPhones, like mine, had abolished the home button, but it was used for almost every function on the smartphones I'd had over the previous eight years. *How could I forget that useful and necessary action?*

Driving home, I remembered the day I upgraded. I was adamant I'd never adapt to not having a home button, but within the first twenty-four hours, I didn't miss it at all.

A knowing covered me. Mom in rehab had caused me to add daily hospital visits and tending her affairs to my already-busy life. In my rushing, I'd omitted my morning Bible reading. A habit I'd had for many decades, it, too, had been quickly and easily forgotten.

I placed my Bible and study material near my phone charger so I'd see it the next morning, lest I forget this useful and necessary action.

Dear Lord, You are my ultimate "home button." May I always remember and long for the vital function of starting my day with You and in Your Word.
—Stephanie Thompson

Wednesday, June 5

**Those who give to the poor will lack nothing,
but those who close their eyes to them receive many
curses. —Proverbs 28:27 (NIV)**

My husband, Jack, was a soft touch when it came to
charities. Every month in the mail, he received free
greeting cards, calendars, pens, notepads, address
labels, small fleece blankets, and dream catchers from
all the charities he sent checks to.

I've learned there are many ways to be a cheerful
giver. One friend donates her time to sit at the
reception desk at church so the secretary can go to
lunch. Another looks for people who need furniture
or clothing, then scours the neighborhood website
for people willing to part with such items. Then
she brings her own truck, picks up the goods, and
delivers them to those in need. Another friend
kept a watchful eye on her friend's house while he
recuperated from surgery in another state. One man
cooks a big dinner for anyone in the community of
any age or income every Tuesday at our church. For
a nominal fee, we get to meet new people in addition
to enjoying a terrific lunch, especially his chocolate-
chip-cookie cake.

These people have taught me that it doesn't
matter whether you give your time, talent, or

treasure. To be happy, you have something to give. And the thing about giving is that it's contagious. Whether I'm driving an elderly friend to a doctor's appointment or agreeing to be on the board of directors for my condo building, I find joy in giving my time. Giving keeps the world spinning on its axis.

Lord, let me reach out to more people more often and share some of the blessings You have showered on me.
—Patricia Lorenz

Digging Deeper: Psalm 146:5–9; Acts 3:6–10; Revelation 22:12–13

Thursday, June 6

Bear with each other and forgive one another.... Forgive as the Lord forgave you.
—Colossians 3:13 (NIV)

I felt a sense of dread while boarding the plane to Nashville. I was planning to see a friend with whom I'd had a friendship-destroying fight ten years earlier.

We pushed off for the runway, but there we sat for twenty minutes. The pilot came on to say that there was a slight delay and soon we'd be leaving. But then twenty minutes after that, she came on again to say a warning light remained on in the cockpit and we would have to return to the gate to fix it. By the time we returned to the gate, the pilot said the flight was canceled.

Thank God, I thought to myself. In fact, I then whisper-prayed out loud, "Thank You, God!" And when we deplaned minutes later, I walked down the concourse with a bounce in my step, grateful to avoid what was going to be a difficult meeting.

Just then, I received a text. "Am looking forward to seeing you. Are you still coming? I've been wanting to apologize for years, but didn't know how. So grateful that you're taking this first step. Inspiring me to do the same."

At the end of the concourse, I went straight to the airline rebooking desk and found the next available flight. Two hours after that, I was back in a cramped middle seat praising God with very different intentions.

I don't want to avoid You, Lord; I want to embrace what You show me as best for my life.
—Jon M. Sweeney

Digging Deeper: Ephesians 4:30–32

Friday, June 7

I remembered God, and was troubled.
—Psalm 77:3 (KJV)

Hey, Dad, come see the sunset," my youngest child, David, yells as he crashes into my study.

"David, use your inside voice," I reply, adding, "Can't you see I'm very busy? I have to get these emails out before the end of the day."

"But it's really bootiful," he finishes, as he leaves the room and heads for the kitchen.

I work on until the whoosh of the last email tells me I'm finished. Feeling a bit guilty, I look for David, but he's engrossed in one of his computer games now and doesn't even look up when I call his name. I gaze out the kitchen window. The last light of the sunset is long gone.

My work is through for the day, but contentment doesn't come. I am disappointed in myself, and surely God is disappointed in me as well.

Out on the porch, I breathe the cool evening air. I work hard, and my family certainly enjoys what's called the "fruit of my labor." But I wonder, where is the line between work and family?

One of my dad's old sermons floats through my head. I remember him saying that some of the greatest expressions of wisdom are the simplest. And sometimes, these expressions come, as Jesus said, out of the mouths of children.

"Oh, dear God," I said to the night sky, "I really blew this one. How about one more chance?"

I was back in the kitchen now. I closed the top on David's computer and smiled. "I'm sorry I missed the sunset," I said, "but if we hurry, we can watch the stars pop out." His grin was the only answer I needed.

Father, thank You for Your wisdom. I will do my best to put my family first. —Brock Kidd

Digging Deeper: Psalm 51:1; 1 John 3:20

Saturday, June 8

For he himself is our peace, who has made the two groups one and has destroyed the barrier, the dividing wall of hostility. —Ephesians 2:14 (NIV)

There's a saying that "time is the great equalizer," meaning that all of us—regardless of who we are, where we're from, or what we do—all have the same amount of time—twenty-four hours a day, 168 hours a week—to do what we may.

I learned another way that "time is the great equalizer" when I went to my fiftieth high school reunion. In my high school years, there were the popular kids and the not-so-popular kids, the bright and the not-so-bright kids, the athletes and the non-athletes. Cliques formed around those groups, and the groups didn't mingle.

What struck me at my reunion was the disappearance of all those classifications and the absence of cliques. Everyone was friendly toward and enthusiastically shaking hands with and/or hugging everyone. The former populars were having lively discussions with the former non-populars. Those who had been ignored now were indistinguishable from those who had been most sought-after. Many who had been considered the best-looking no longer were. Many who had not been seen as attractive now were.

No one seemed to care who had been who in high school. Time had taken away the importance of those petty distinctions and opened our eyes to the human dignity and worth that God has put in us all. That was worth waiting fifty years for.

Lord God, open the eyes of those who are currently experiencing the tumultuous high-school years. May they realize that we are all created equal.
—Kim Taylor Henry

Digging Deeper: Galatians 3:26–29; Ephesians 2:19–22

Sunday, June 9

May the favor of the Lord our God rest on us; establish the work of our hands for us—yes, establish the work of our hands. —Psalm 90:17 (NIV)

One of the best ways to find fulfillment at work is to serve and help others. No matter the career path or job, God can use us. Our availability to serve is more important than our job position and title. A staff member at church reminded me of the power of this principle.

One Sunday morning, a woman walked into the church building a few minutes after worship began. She sat at a bench in the narthex and didn't enter the sanctuary. John, the facility manager of the church, noticed she was alone and crying. He went to check on her and asked, "Is everything OK?" The woman said, "Today is the one-year anniversary of my daughter's memorial service." She was overwhelmed with grief.

John prayed for this woman. He asked God to comfort her and give her the strength to get through this difficult day. John's actions and prayer lifted me; knowing that church staff will go outside their job responsibilities to care for a person in need is powerful.

Weeks later, the woman sent a thank-you note to the church, not knowing who the person was that helped her. She wrote in her note, "The act of faith really helped me through that day and still consoles me." When we see our work as service, God uses us.

Lord, help us to see that we are called to not only work but also to serve and be used by You. —Pablo Diaz

Digging Deeper: Acts 3:4–7; Colossians 3:23–24

Monday, June 10

Why do you see the speck in your neighbor's eye but do not notice the log in your own eye? —Matthew 7:3 (NRSV)

Somehow these marital matters always seem to come up in the kitchen. I'll be loading the dishwasher and notice how my wife, Carol, has put the glasses on the wrong side. Or the soup bowls in a spot where they take up too much room. And why is the strainer there? Or I'll be putting away a pot and discover that the lid has been shelved in the wrong place. *Why doesn't she remember that?* I ask myself. *It was her idea in the first place.*

She's usually not in the kitchen when these moments occur, so I simply stew about them on my own. And if she were in the kitchen, wouldn't it be enough for her to see me rearranging things, with a few poignant sighs?

Just the other day, though, she and I were both there and she started rearranging spoons in the utensil drawer. *Maybe she's getting it now.* I looked over her shoulder and noticed that some of the salad forks were with the dinner forks and the dinner forks with the salad forks. How on earth did that happen? Who unloaded the dishwasher last time?

Me. I did it. Wrong. Completely wrong. "I'm sorry," I said. "That was me. I got them mixed up."

"I know," she said. That was it.

When it comes to forgiveness, it's not necessarily the big things that trip me up. It's the little things. The specks. Note to self: before you start complaining about somebody else, check on yourself first.

God, I beg Your forgiveness for all the wrongs I have committed. Help me see them and atone for them.
—Rick Hamlin

Digging Deeper: Proverbs 10:12; Matthew 6:15; Ephesians 4:32

Tuesday, June 11

So also you have sorrow now, but I will see you again, and your hearts will rejoice, and no one will take your joy from you. —John 16:22 (ESV)

"The grandkids will be here for the hottest week of June," I complained to my husband, Kevin, as I checked the seven-day weather forecast. "118 degrees!" I saw all my fun plans melting at the predicted high.

"We'll have to go outside early and then stay inside," Kevin advised.

With that in mind, I attached the hose to a Slip 'N Slide in the front yard at 7 a.m. on the first morning of Grandparent Camp. Micah, age nine, took a running leap as he body-planed down the neon orange and yellow plastic. Eager to copy his older brother, five-year-old Benjamin raced into his own watery adventure. More reserved, Madelyn, age seven, tiptoed through the arching spray, landing in the small pool at the end.

"What's that?" Micah asked, pointing to a crawling bug that had emerged from a flooded section of tall grass.

"A cockroach!" As I rushed to squash it, I sighed at one more thing gone wrong. Scorching weather and now cockroaches.

Rather than be disgusted, the kids grabbed their sandals and stomped the roaches with abandon as dozens more fled the soggy yard. Laughter filled the morning, dropping my angst by twenty degrees.

"What was your favorite activity?" their parents asked after the grandkids enjoyed four days of swimming, craft projects, and board games. The cockroaches received red-hot approval ratings.

"There were bugs everywhere," the kids exclaimed. "It was the best camp ever!"

Reflecting later on *my* favorite part of the week, I knew it was when I decided not to let any of my own grumblings or fears separate me from God's joy.

When my circumstances reach the boiling point, help me choose joy. —Lynne Hartke

Digging Deeper: Psalm 33:21; John 14:1

Wednesday, June 12

You will keep him in perfect peace, whose mind is stayed on You, because he trusts in You. —Isaiah 26:3 (NKJV)

I began reading my CAT scan results: "Large left renal mass, concerning for malignant tumor." I was shocked, stunned. I had been to my doctor about a symptom that started as a mild soreness.

My mind flooded with anxious thoughts. I didn't want to get entangled with fear. That dead-end road is too familiar. I told a friend about the tumor. "You cannot let negative thoughts into your mind," she said. But I was already thinking about many scary what-ifs—MRIs, cancer, surgery, general anesthesia—all new to me.

Because of the fearful thoughts, I became intentional about finding God's blessings in my situation—large or small. I would lose a kidney, but the other kidney is healthy. I thanked God! If the cancer was contained, the outlook was good. I praised God! Further scans revealed no spread. I thanked and praised God!

Whenever a fearful thought came, I praised Him from the list of blessings I had started. I made it a practice to fall asleep praising Him one by one from my growing list. In my morning prayer time, I did the same. From repetitively expressing praise for my blessings, I experienced a joy in God's presence that overpowered my fears. The practice of praise also brought deep gratitude along with peace and the trust to surrender everything I faced day by day to God. Ultimately, there came a successful surgery, a smooth recovery, and clear first round of follow-up scans.

Thank You, Lord, that by keeping my mind filled with Your blessings, my fears are replaced with Your peace!
—John Dilworth

Digging Deeper: Psalms 21:6, 103:1–2; Lamentations 3:22–23; Philippians 4:6

Thursday, June 13

But you, Lord, are a compassionate and gracious God, slow to anger, abounding in love and faithfulness. —Psalm 86:15 (NIV)

My seven-year-old son began to make groaning and banging sounds from behind his bedroom door one evening. He had already gone to bed for the night, and his door was shut. Yet, the rest of the family could clearly hear his frustration. Because he is on the autism spectrum, his big feelings can come out with yelling, tears, and stomping feet but not always with words.

I sat on the couch and sighed. I prayed for this to resolve quickly and calmly. I was already tired and in need of my own quiet time. Eventually, my son came out of his room to tell me that he was very upset because another child in Sunday school had bent the pages in his Bible. He was convinced it was ruined. I tried my best to express to him that God's love is much bigger than bent pages and that God would be very happy for him to keep reading regardless.

After some back and forth, he was ready to give going to bed another try. As I shut his door, I heard him call out and ask me, with great concern, if I still loved him. I reassured him that, of course, I did. It made me think of how God's love is also enough for me as His child. Like a good parent, God's patient ear is always open for me. His grace and love are sufficient, even on a night that I may have been struggling with the guilt of being impatient with my own son.

Thank You, Lord, that while I grow and make mistakes, You will always remind me that, of course, You still love me too. —Nicole Garcia

Digging Deeper: Psalms 136:26, 139:7–10; Jeremiah 31:3

Friday, June 14

I will perpetuate your memory through all generations; therefore the nations will praise you for ever and ever. —Psalm 45:17 (NIV)

Alzheimer's turned me into a New York Yankees baseball fan. Don't boo. Hear me out.

My mom was a fan of the Detroit Tigers, and I grew up rooting with her. She watched every game, yelling at the players through the TV screen, and not the least bit shy about praying. Her beloved Tigers needed all the help they could get.

As I moved around the country, Mom sent me the Detroit sports pages so I could keep up. One of the first signs of her Alzheimer's was that she would send me the wrong pages, the business section instead of sports.

Meanwhile, I was living in New York and becoming interested in an exciting young Yankees team. As my mother declined, I couldn't bear to follow the Tigers. Besides, New York was my hometown now.

Not long before Mom could no longer live on her own, I took her to a Tigers game. We sat in the hulking green ballpark on Trumbull Avenue. I don't know who the Tigers played or if they won that day. We left early because Mom was cold and having trouble following the game. So was I. I was thinking of the finality of life and the passion of a true fan and how it lives in the heart, nursed by unending hope.

As I helped Mom up the stairs to the concourse, she stopped and turned for one last look at the sun and the shadows and the impossibly green grass. I prayed it was a memory she would never lose.

Lord, I miss my mother and her unabashed passion, her faith in her team, and, most of all, her faith in You.
—Edward Grinnan

Saturday, June 15

**May the heavens be joyful, and may the earth
rejoice....—Psalm 96:11** (NASB)

My wife and daughter-in-law wanted to see sea turtles
and suggested a beach we hadn't been to before.
Personally, I liked the one close by. Sure, it might have
been light on turtles, but it had plenty of sand and ocean.
But, hey, who am I to argue? (Scratch that last question,
I can hear my family laughing even as I write it.)

And so we drove a few miles, walked down through
the trees, and emerged onto a white-sand strip of paradise.

*What do you think, Lord? Can you muster up a
couple turtles and make this worth it?* I thought, as I
lugged beach chairs and ice chest toward the water.

God, as He so often does, smiled.

He started with a massive monk seal sprawled
across the beach. Next came the whales, breaching
over and over in perfect tandem just off the coast,
the sound booming off the nearby cliffs.

All right, God, I get it.

Do you? A huge manta ray began kicking up spray
beyond the surf line.

I had to laugh.

So did He as a six-foot-long reef shark raced
through the foam not ten feet from the water's edge.

You think He was done?

"Look," my wife said, pointing. "Turtles!"

Isn't it wonderful how God works? Even in the little things?

A glorious sunset stretched the horizon as I packed my load back toward the car. "Thank You," I said.

And, as He so often does, God smiled.

Praise You, Lord! You are the fullness of joy!
—Buck Storm

Digging Deeper: Job 12:7–10; Psalm 96:11–12

Father's Day, Sunday, June 16

A good man brings good things out of the good stored up in him. —Matthew 12:35 (NIV)

When you think of a hero, do you think of a strong man with supernatural powers in a movie?

My hero wasn't like that. His strength was in his character and his power came from God.

As a young child, he contracted polio, resulting in one side of his body shrinking enough to put him off-balance and forcing him to walk with a limp. But that inconvenience never stopped him from doing anything he wanted to do. Today, he might be called "handicapped," but that word hadn't been invented yet, especially in his mind.

He rode a horse, then traded his horse for a car. He became an itinerant teacher in his county, sometimes traveling by boat to get to his students. When he left the country for the city, he became an accountant in the business office of a major university. As he grew older, he suffered the pain of arthritis but never complained. He loved going to work each day, thankful for the opportunity.

His wit attracted friends, and he made sure anyone he met left with a smile on their face. That's how he won my mother, with his sense of humor, solid character, and integrity.

To his children, he was the man who could fix anything, build birdhouses, and keep his yard and cars well maintained. Surprisingly, he taught many people how to waterski, even though he never waterskied in his life.

What gave him his positive outlook on life was his faith in God. In church every Sunday, he praised God with his baritone voice.

He was our father and our hero.

Lord, thank You for giving me a father who showed me a glimpse of You. —Marilyn Turk

Digging Deeper: Psalms 103:13, 111:10; Ephesians 6:4

Monday, June 17

A friend loves at all times. —Proverbs 17:17 (NIV)

We had just returned from a visit to our native New York State. While my husband, Dave, biked with his friends in the Empire State Ride, I had spent hours with my friends, two from my childhood and two from our kids' childhoods. It filled me up, in so many ways.

Back home, I finished unpacking. Each day, I planned to write thank-you notes to my friends. Each day, I never quite got around to it. I wanted to do it, so why was I procrastinating?

I talked it over with my friend Ginny, a professional violinist. When she's having trouble getting started practicing a new piece, she tells herself, "Just get out the music." Before she knows it, she is playing that piece!

I told myself, *Just get out the thank-you cards.* That was easy; I put them on my desk. It would only take a few more minutes to look up the four addresses. Then I found my roll of stamps. Next to that promising pile, I put my return labels. *Enough for today.*

The next day, my friend Kathy called. I told her about the notes I was working up to sending. She read me the sign on her desk: "Start slow and taper off!" After I stopped laughing, I decided to write one note, just one. The next day, I wrote two more. The following day, all of my notes were in the mail. And the best part of finishing this project was thanking God for each of the friends He's given me and the beauty they bring to my life.

Creator God, thank You for friends who love me through the years, inspire me today, and make me laugh. And for tasks that get done, one step at a time.
—Leanne Jackson

Digging Deeper: Proverbs 25:15; Colossians 3:12

*...*Make straight the way of the Lord, as said the prophet Esaias. —John 1:23 (KJV)

I sat quietly while an acquaintance took aim at me. I sensed I wasn't the true target, but my bruised feelings were saying, *I'm done with her.* Like the disorienting switchbacks I'd once experienced on the Mississippi River Road toward New Orleans, her sharp words pointed in the opposite direction from which I thought the relationship was headed.

Poised to end the conversation, I sensed an open door. The question was, could I accept the grace to walk through it? Would I "frustrate the grace of God" by clinging to my decision to be done with her, or would I seize the chance to demonstrate God's way?

I became excited. An opportunity to *live* John's words—to make straight the Lord's path—was staring me in the face. I began to "speak...comfortably" (Isaiah 40:2, KJV). No time for self-petting. The moment called for gentleness instead of pride; hope instead of self-defense; meekness instead of aggression. Jesus's mandate to forgive and the fact that the lady's faith was relatively new left no room for me to wallow in hurt. I must make His path as loving as I could.

That precious lady's true battle was with self-esteem. Perhaps, as a fellow believer, I was directed to absorb some of her pain, but whatever the case, the Lord helped me understand that rather than drawing the proverbial line in the sand, my assignment is always to make straight paths with a cool head and a kind heart.

Lord, help me not to simply describe the Highway of Holiness, but lay myself down as a paver of forgiveness and comfort. —Jacqueline F. Wheelock

Digging Deeper: Galatians 2:21; 1 Timothy 4:12

Juneteenth, Wednesday, June 19

But thanks be to God, who gives us the victory through our Lord Jesus Christ. —1 Corinthians 15:57 (NKJV)

As an African-American woman reared in a community and taught in a school system with very few people of color, I was in my early forties before I realized the historical importance of Juneteenth, the day when news of Abraham Lincoln's Emancipation Proclamation from January 1, 1863, finally reached the last group of slaves in 1865.

I attended my first Juneteenth celebration three years ago. My only regret is not bringing my children along; I want to educate them about how we as descendants can honor the lives and traditions of our ancestors.

Although Lincoln issued the Emancipation Proclamation in 1863, nearly 250,000 African-American slaves in the Union state of Texas were unaware that the government had granted them freedom. They continued to toil under the brutal hand of slavery, enduring not just the tortures of physical bondage but also the enslavement of the mind. Finally, on June 19, 1865—nearly two and a half years later—word arrived in Texas. The formal decree, named "General Order Number Three," enforced their liberation. Although there were attempts to keep the orders secret, by the next year, history would mark June 19 as Emancipation Day or Juneteenth.

Even more than 150 years later, it's still a cause for celebration. Juneteenth is an opportunity to educate, enlighten, and engage. Although Juneteenth reminds me of the struggle that African-Americans have faced, it also highlights progress toward racial equity and the work that remains. I praise God for the progress that's already been made, and I've committed my family to be part of that work.

Lord, You are the Great Emancipator. Thank You for my physical, mental, and spiritual freedom. I pray that You heal any racial divides and help me to continue to strive toward peace between all brethren.
—Tia McCollors

Digging Deeper: Psalm 119:45; John 8:36; 2 Corinthians 3:17

Thursday, June 20

And God created man in his own image. . . .
—Genesis 1:27 (ASV)

A group of about seventy of us, mostly strangers, bumped elbows, squashed in elevators, and climbed the stairs behind a tour guide in the state of Montana's Capitol building. When we filed into the room entitled the chamber of the House of Representatives, the guide swept her arm toward an enormous painting. "The state of Montana commissioned Charlie Russell to paint the story of Lewis and Clark meeting the Flathead Indians at Ross's Hole."

I gawked up at the scene of Native Americans mounted on horses, which towered above me. I listened to the guide share that in 1912, the twelve-foot-tall by twenty-five-foot-wide painting was transported to the Capitol in Helena, Montana—all in one piece—on horses. A feat in itself! Then she asked the question, "How much do you think this is worth?" A lot of us shrugged our shoulders and leaned toward her as she said, "This building is kept under guard at all times because this has been appraised at $94 million."

My heart skipped a beat. *Have I ever seen an artist's creation valued at $94 million?* As the group turned to leave the room, I heard a still, small voice, "Each of you is worth more than that to Me." I glanced at the painting, then around at the crowd. *A lifeless painting versus each one of us, priceless to God. No comparison. My God, the Artist, rocks!*

Lord, when we're lost in a sea of people, help us to remember that each one of us is a one-of-a-kind artwork created by You. Amen. —Rebecca Ondov

Digging Deeper: Isaiah 43:4; Matthew 10:29–31

If there is anything good and worth giving thanks for, think about these things. —Philippians 4:8 (NLV)

I'd been counting down the days to my vacation for months. Finally, all that stood between me and lazing by the pool with some of the people I love most in this world was one two-hour flight. At least, that was the plan.

Then came the airline update. My nonstop flight from Colorado to Arizona had been rescheduled. I'd now be enjoying a seven-hour layover in Las Vegas. My joyous anticipation began a downward slide into a mire of disappointment, frustration, and anger. I took a deep breath and did the only thing I could do, besides pray. I changed my T-shirt.

I have quite the collection of inspirational tees, sporting messages from "Make a difference today" to "She believed she could, but she needed a break, so she said, 'No.'" I don't wear them to inspire others but to challenge myself. After all, how can I give a fellow driver the stink eye if I'm wearing a tee that says, "Sprinkle kindness like confetti"?

Today, I chose "Life is good." Because, thanks to God, it is. Sometimes, it's hard, but it's still good. And spending several hours wandering through an airport isn't even "hard." It's just boring. Talk about a First World problem. When I finally made it to Phoenix and sat down to enjoy a ten o'clock dinner with friends, I arrived with both my luggage and my positive attitude intact. Life *is* good, when I keep my heart and mind focused on what matters most.

Lord, help me check my attitude, along with my to-do list, each morning. Keep my thoughts focused on all that is good in this life. —Vicki Kuyper

Digging Deeper: Psalm 27:13; Romans 12:2; Colossians 3:2

Saturday, June 22

Children are a gift from the LORD; they are a reward from him. —Psalm 127:3 (NLT)

We'd been invited to our daughter's home to celebrate her son's eighteenth birthday, but my heart clutched when I discovered her crying in the kitchen. "Honey, what's wrong?" I demanded, slipping my arm around her quaking shoulders.

She sniffed loudly. "I'm just sad that Wyatt grew up so quickly. Seems like only yesterday he was toddling around on chubby legs in a diaper, and now he's eighteen."

I felt my own eyes tear up. I'd felt exactly the same emotion when Bethany turned eighteen—overnight, it seemed—and joined the Army to become a linguist. I hugged her tighter, reminding her about one of Wyatt's silly baby antics. She laughed. Soon we were sharing happy memories of Wyatt's childhood days—much to my grandson's embarrassment when he joined us.

Several hours after the birthday party, I found myself wondering if Mary, the mother of Jesus, felt that same tug of regret when her precious Son left home to begin His ministry. I can't even imagine her grief as she watched Him die on the cross—for her sins and mine.

Being a parent isn't easy. It takes time and prayer to raise independent children who will turn their lives over to Christ. And no matter how old they are—whether six months or sixty—good parents still pray over their children. I do, constantly. And I always take the opportunity to say, "I love you." A parent—or a grandparent—can't say it too often.

Dear Lord, I thank You from the bottom of my heart for my children and grandchildren. The blessing of parenthood is incomparable.
—Shirley Raye Redmond

Digging Deeper: Proverbs 17:6; Matthew 18:1–3

Sunday, June 23

STAR WORDS: Surprise—Flatware
Then he said to them, "Watch out! Be on your guard against all kinds of greed; life does not consist in an abundance of possessions." —Luke 12:15 (NIV)

When I moved from Wyoming to New Hampshire to help my ailing parents, I had planned to stay one year, then return to Big Sky. I shoved most of my possessions into storage—where they languished for fifteen years. No, I never returned "home." One casualty of the move was flatware I had scrimped to purchase. Nothing special, except the pieces matched. By the time I cleared out the storage unit,

I figured it would cost more to ship it than buy new back East. I gave it away.

God provided generously when I furnished my new apartment: sofa, chairs, dining set, bookcases came my way. Even flatware. Cheap and mismatched but serviceable. Other yard sale finds like dishes and glassware complemented my eclectic, Boho décor.

Still, I rankled at the flimsy flatware, perhaps because I missed my hard-earned set. When I reflected that much of the world needed food, never mind fancy eating utensils, I talked myself out of buying more. I didn't want to forget world hunger. Then, I'd flip and wish again for a matched set. This continued for six years! Finally, I bought a simple service for four for $25.

I didn't open the box for weeks; feelings of guilt ambushed me. Eventually, I stored the new stainless with the old pieces and used both. Then another surprise caught me off guard. Instead of forgetting the hungry, the old, flimsy pieces remind me to share with the local food pantry, the vibrant Friendly Kitchen— where the "chandelier" features dangling flatware.

Creator God, may possessions never control my life. Amen. —Gail Thorell Schilling

Digging Deeper: Ecclesiastes 6:2; Matthew 19:21

Monday, June 24

My voice You shall hear in the morning, O LORD; in the morning I will direct it to You, and I will look up. —Psalm 5:3 (NKJV)

I checked my phone this morning before I got out of bed. In my social media stream was a video of a goldfish driving a little car that scientists had developed, essentially a rectangular fish tank set on top of four motorized wheels with a bunch of sensors in the front that controlled the steering.

The scientists in the experiment were surprised that the goldfish mastered the technique of controlling the tank and driving the car in fewer than ten practice sessions through reward reinforcement. But the real message they wanted to get out is not that fish can drive but that they are more complicated than we once thought.

When I was growing up, I had a brilliant goldfish that I won at a carnival. The night I brought him home, my mom prepared me for the hard truth that he probably would not last. I named him Butch, thinking a strong moniker might help him survive. Perhaps it helped because he grew into the most majestic goldfish, with a goofy and friendly way of greeting me every time I entered the room.

One of the scientists said that the amazing thing she learned is not that fish can learn to drive but that each one had a unique personality. Some loved the exercises, while others seemed to grudgingly resist. "They really are amazing," she said.

Of course, I already knew that God makes everything special. The truly amazing thing is how wonderful it is to live in a world where we discover marvelous things—like goldfish driving cars—before the day even begins.

Lord, what other wonders will I discover on this brand-new, beautiful day? —Sabra Ciancanelli

Digging Deeper: Psalms 118:24, 145:2

Tuesday, June 25

SEEKING CONNECTION IN THE BIBLE'S STORIES: God Seeks Me

The LORD has looked down from heaven... to see if there are any who understand, who seek God. —Psalm 14:2 (NASB)

When a missionary friend introduced me to "Bible storying" as a way to more personally connect with biblical text, I fell in love with it. Five questions are asked at the close of each story: What did I like? What didn't I like? With which character do I identify? What did I learn about God? How can I apply this story in my life? These questions have shown me that the Bible holds the story of every person—a truth both challenging and comforting.

Jesus engages a woman—alone at the well—in conversation. She has not lived an exemplary life. He respectfully tells her details of her life impossible for Him to know unless He is sent from God.

She desires the "living water" Jesus offers her. She listens when He says God seeks those who will worship Him in "spirit and truth" (John 4:23, NASB). This means believing in Him as Messiah and living God's way.

The woman embraces Jesus as the truth and joyfully invites her whole village to come seek

Him—and they do. How glorious to know in this story that God is seeking me to seek after Him!

I wish I knew the name of the "well woman." I'd like her for a friend. We could have a long conversation about making changes to honor the One who gave His life for us. In my life, I've had to become less selfish and more wholesome in thought, let go of habits, stop judging, and learn to allow God's Spirit to speak into mine.

Just to know I'm sought after keeps me seeking Jesus more.

Savior, in every good change I make, I worship You.
—Carol Knapp

Digging Deeper: Psalm 63:1; Luke 19:10;
John 4:7–26; Hebrews 11:6

Wednesday, June 26

... Watch. —Mark 13:37 (KJV)

When Brock was a toddler, my mother shared a poem written by a woman who regretted ignoring her children when they called out, "Watch, Mamma."

The poem made me sad. It also emboldened me to never make this awful mistake, and so, when it came to our children, Brock and Keri, I tried to always "watch," and my regrets are few.

Unfortunately, my commitment went by the wayside in other areas. How many times have I chastised myself for letting a season pass without really seeing its glory or stayed all snug inside after a soft snowfall?

Still, in many ways, the year of Covid-19 brought unexpected "watching" benefits.

Isolated for months, David and I created a sort of grotto on our back deck. Surrounded by nature, we suddenly had time to watch flowers bloom. We took time to identify the birds that came to our feeder. We became still for sunsets. We sat on our covered porch and watched the rain. We saw the moon waxing and waning through the trees.

We watched as the days slipped by and our lives became simpler, calmer, more peaceful.

Recent studies claim that watching nature decreases stress and makes one happier. The same is true for not only watching our children but also watching those we happen to pass every day. When we look into another's eyes, acknowledge their worth, and show our love, happiness lingers. And remembering the wonderful words in the finale of *Les Miserables*, "To love another person [or sunrise, or greening leaf] is to see the face of God," I think He must be pleased when we watch.

Father, watch us, Your children, as we pause and watch the amazing universe that You lay out for us.
—Pam Kidd

Digging Deeper: Proverbs 8:34; Habakkuk 2:1

> Out of the ground the LORD God formed every beast of the field and every bird of the air, and brought them to Adam to see what he would call them. And whatever Adam called each living creature, that was its name. —Genesis 2:19 (NKJV)

As I write this afternoon, our golden retriever, Lexi, is asleep on the porch next to the table where I am working. She is the seventh golden retriever that Beth and I have raised in our forty-five years of marriage. Often we have raised our dogs as "pairs." We have watched these gentle dogs have litters of puppies and found good homes for each of them.

A year ago, our last golden retriever, Buddy, passed away in old age. Our grief was intense. Buddy had moved with us from Texas to Georgia and had softened our transition with his familiar presence. After his death, we were without a dog for a year. Then Beth contacted a golden retriever adoption and rescue center. They had a puppy they wanted us to adopt. We named her Lexi, and now she is a part of our family.

In Genesis, we read that Adam and Eve gave animals their names. To give an animal a name is to recognize our personal responsibility for them. Once we named Lexi, we knew that we were in a relationship with her for as long as she lived. Even if she should later be adopted by another owner, we would remain in relationship by memories, prayers, and lifelong gratitude for her. May we not forget that our responsibility for animals is a sacred trust.

Dear God, may I gratefully accept my responsibility to love and support all living creatures. Amen.
—Scott Walker

Digging Deeper: Job 35:11; Psalm 145:9; Matthew 6:26

Friday, June 28

Ah, Sovereign LORD, you have made the heavens and the earth by your great power and outstretched arm. Nothing is too hard for you. —Jeremiah 32:17 (NIV)

Every few years, I order truckloads of hardwood mulch in the spring to spread on my garden beds. But last year, my busy schedule delayed the delivery until early summer. With hotter temperatures on the way, I shoveled and distributed the mulch with intense motivation for several days until my muscles revolted. How would I complete the job before the next rain?

Thankfully, my husband fired up our ancient riding lawnmower, attached our little yellow wagon, and transported buckets of mulch where needed. All I had to do was scatter the shredded bark around the trees and bushes. After hours of sweating and multiple water breaks, we accomplished the mission and admired the finished product as raindrops began to fall.

When the downpour ended, I realized completing the job without my husband's help would have been difficult, if not impossible. Shoveling large amounts of rain-soaked mulch would have required more strength than I have and produced messy results. Just thinking about the struggle reminded me of a painful project I attempted years ago—pushing God aside, thinking I could handle everything myself. Fortunately, the Lord is compassionate and long on patience. He waited on the sidelines until I asked for help from the One who finds nothing impossible and makes no mistakes.

God, thank You for being the creator and master of the universe, the only One who can do the impossible. Give me the wisdom to ask You for help in everything I do. Open my eyes to Your outstretched hand and willing offer to help at all times. —Jenny Lynn Keller

Digging Deeper: Mark 10:24–27;
Luke 1:35–37; John 15:5

Saturday, June 29

The knowledgeable among the people will make the many understand. —Daniel 11:33 (JPS)

"God wants us to be perfect," said one of the other members of the Ritual Committee. I disagreed, and said so: "Well, the original sacrifices had to be unblemished, but God never said that about the people bringing the sacrifices—and God knows even our ancestors were deeply flawed."

By and large, perfection is not a Jewish value—except in one case. A Torah has to be pristine (*kosher*): not even a single letter can be broken or chipped. My congregation had been a bit neglectful about that.

By the time we sent for the *sofer* (scribe) who had done the last repair years before, three of our four Torahs were *pasul* (imperfect for ritual purposes). That was cutting it a little close! When he examined the Torahs, he told us that two could be repaired but that it would not be possible to fix the oldest one.

"Do we just bury it?" I asked him, since burial is the only accepted way of retiring a Torah.

"Well, of course you can, but you don't have to," the *sofer* answered. "You can use it to show people what the words look like and explain how it's made and why it takes a year to write one. You can help people see how precious it really is, even though it's *pasul*."

We gave the 120-year-old Torah pride of place in the Hebrew school classrooms, on a display stand, open to the Song of the Sea. It fascinated and awed the kids, the teachers, and the congregants who came to see an open Torah close up for perhaps the very first time.

Thank You, God of All, for a lesson in the undeniable worth of the imperfect. —Rhoda Blecker

Digging Deeper: Leviticus 18:14; Deuteronomy 27:18

You are precious in my eyes, and honored, and I love you. —Isaiah 43:4 (ESV)

When our church introduced a new hymnal, the worship committee invited us to purchase copies and suggest names for individual bookplates.

My wife, Kate, and I enthusiastically joined in, giving respect to our parents, David and Birdie Boyce and Glenn and Rosetta Sampson. I then identified my high school coach and English teacher, Will Byker, who along with his wife, Janie, became like second parents. I paid tribute to college choir director John Lundberg and mentor/musician Dave Talbott and his wife, Carla.

Our daughter Jenn, just home after schooling in Taiwan and Australia, did the calligraphy. Opening up a hymnal in the choir loft and seeing the inscriptions to these relatives and friends always warms my heart. With the pandemic, choir singing stopped. We moved to sanctuary pews, usually sitting in the middle, left-side section.

One Sunday, opening the closest hymnal for our morning song of praise, I read the bookplate: "Presented in honor of family, friends, and all who read this book by Dave and Becca Kashinski."

Whoa! went my spirit. Here was a generous, grace-filled inscription. It bestowed respect upon me. The esteem given to me by the Kashinskis mirrored that of our God. In applauding my unique identity as one who "read this book," the plate also reflected an expanded recognition, celebrating the value of each one of us, created in the image of God. We all are cherished by God.

I continued worship, energized by the recognition awarded in the hymnal. And I remain animated still, inspired by the well-chosen inscription.

Creator God, You "call us by name, and we are Yours." May we embrace Your calling, along with all Your children. Amen. —Ken Sampson

Digging Deeper: Psalm 73:28; Philippians 4:7

YOU WERE CALLED TO PEACE

1 _____

2 _____

3 _____

4 _____

5 _____

6 _____

7 _____

8 _____

9 _____

10 _____

11 _____

12 _____

13 _____

14 _____

15 _____

16 _____

17 _____

18 _____

19 _____

20 _____

21 _____

22 _____

23 _____

24 _____

25 _____

26 _____

27 _____

28 _____

29 _____

30 _____

JULY

Grace, mercy and peace from God the Father
and from Jesus Christ, the Father's Son,
will be with us in truth and love.

—2 John 1:3 (NIV)

SEEKING CONNECTION IN THE BIBLE'S STORIES: Jesus Reveals Himself

Your word is a lamp to my feet and a light to my path. —Psalm 119:105 (NASB)

One of my favorite Bible stories happens shortly after Jesus's resurrection. Two of Jesus's followers arc trekking the seven miles to the village of Emmaus, trying to make sense of the recent events in Jerusalem. Unrecognized by them, Jesus approaches as a fellow traveler and joins their discussion.

When they explain to Him their confusion at all that has happened, Jesus immediately opens the Scriptures to them about "all the things concerning Himself" (Luke 24:27, NASB1995), going clear back to Moses. It is not until they reach Emmaus and invite Jesus to stay over with them that they know who He is when He blesses and breaks the bread in their evening meal.

Just as astonishing, He then vanishes. The two men are so excited to see for themselves that Jesus has really risen they turn around and make the return trip to Jerusalem that same night—eager to tell the others. They say to each other, "Were not our hearts burning within us while He was speaking to us on the road?" (Luke 24:32, NASB1995).

I love a walk on a gravel country road. I often imagine that journey to Emmaus and picture Jesus traveling companionably beside me, bringing His words to life. When my daughter-in-law and I had a misunderstanding, it was on "our" walk that Jesus urged me to show compassion—to go to her and make things right. My heart, too, "burned within me" as He opened the way for reconciliation. There are no words like His words!

> **Life-speaking Savior—walk with me—encourage me—teach me!** —Carol Knapp

> **Digging Deeper:** Jeremiah 15:16; Luke 24:13–35; John 1:14, 6:68–69

Tuesday, July 2

Do not boast about tomorrow, for you do not know what a day may bring. —Proverbs 27:1 (NIV)

My father sang an old Puerto Rican folk song as he wiped tears from his eyes. I've heard him sing this song my whole life, but in that moment the words cut deep.

It had been a few weeks since my parents moved in with me. My eighty-eight-year-old father's dementia kept progressing. More than ever, I envisioned him as the old man in the song, lamenting being so far away from his homeland as his life approached its end.

That day, I booked two tickets to the island. For two months, I told him every day about our upcoming trip. It was a surprise to him each time. On the airplane, he wanted to know where "this bus" was taking us. As we opened the door to our hotel room, he wanted to know how long he needed to stay there. Maybe this trip wasn't going to be as significant as I'd imagined.

The next day, we went to the Spanish Fort in San Juan, a historic landmark on the island. My father lit up as he saw the structure and the crystal ocean behind it. "Puerto Rico is so beautiful," he said, coming to life as I'd hoped he would.

I reveled in his joy as we toured the fort, despite the knowledge he'd retain no memory of it. The moment was enough. I didn't know what each day in the future held, but I knew God would take care of us through every moment.

As my father looked out to the horizon, he sang the old folk song once again. This time there were no tears.

Lord, teach me to live in the present every day and cherish every moment I'm given. —Karen Valentin

Digging Deeper: Psalm 31:14–15; Ecclesiastes 3:1

Wednesday, July 3

This is what the LORD, the God of your father David, says: I have heard your prayer and seen your tears. —Isaiah 38:5 (NIV)

I was looking through past prayer requests in my daily journal when one entry stood out: *Please, Lord, give our family a brighter future!* I'd prayed that prayer for twelve straight years, years when we'd experienced one dark time after another. A marriage dissolved. Two grandchildren lost their father to a heart attack. Someone stopped communicating with other family members. Chronic health problems made life difficult for a young adult. Then Covid-19 hit, causing illness, lost work, and periods of isolation. Finances were uncertain. My husband, Don, died, and my time and energy were consumed with managing a rental property, farm, and finances.

As I read further into the journal, though, I made an amazing discovery. Many of my frantic prayers had already been answered. The sharp grief over separation and deaths eased. Family members affected by Covid-19 recovered and some jobs returned. My farm had an excellent corn crop. And there were blessings I hadn't asked for or anticipated. Son Patrick; his wife, Patricia; daughter Rebecca; and grandson Mark moved back to southwest Kansas, and having them close has kept me from being lonely. Grandson Caden won his county's 4-H Club pig show. Proceeds from selling the animal are helping with college expenses.

Our life circumstances aren't perfect. Health, work, and communication issues remain. But I'm thankful to God for giving us a brighter future on earth and a glimpse of the glories that await in heaven.

Thank You, blessed Lord, for hearing and answering my prayers. —Penney Schwab

Digging Deeper: Jeremiah 29:11–13; Romans 12:12; Philippians 4:6–7

Independence Day, Thursday, July 4

Greater love has no one than this: to lay down one's life for one's friends. —John 15:13 (NIV)

When I think about the Fourth of July and the celebration of freedom that Americans enjoy, I can't help but remember my dad. I didn't know he'd been a POW in WWII until I was in my fifties. Our son, serving as an airborne ranger, was home for Thanksgiving. As we sat around the table, Dad calmly said, "We were rescued by airborne rangers."

"Rescued from where?" I asked.

"The POW camp."

I literally could have fallen off my chair. I had no idea my father had been captured and taken into Germany as a prisoner of war. He told me the most frightening moment of his ordeal happened shortly before his rescue, when the German guards could see the American paratroopers coming down from the sky, landing close to the camp. The biggest fear among those captured was that Germans would kill them rather than let the rescuers see the conditions under which the prisoners had been forced to live.

"What happened?" I asked, anxious to hear each word.

He gave me a half smile, and tears filled his eyes as he spoke. "They were young men like us. All they wanted was to go home to their families, the same as we did. When they realized there was no hope, they laid aside their guns and ran."

As I gather with my family for a huge barbecue and eagerly await the fireworks display, I thank God for those who have gone before and are currently serving our country. I want to live my life worthy of their sacrifice.

Jesus, help me to never take for granted the sacrifices that have been made for our country's freedom.
—Debbie Macomber

Digging Deeper: Ephesians 4:1; 1 Peter 2:16–17

Friday, July 5

Behold, God is my salvation; I will trust, and not be afraid: for the Lord Jehovah is my strength and my song; he also is become my salvation.
—Isaiah 12:2 (KJV)

Joy was the last thing on my mind when I inched forward and peered into an unfamiliar abyss called a well. I was a child who knew only hand-pumped water, so if that dark, mysterious column started to produce evidence of the amorphous threats spinning up in my mind, I was perched to flee.

But now, as an adult reading Isaiah's promise that "with joy shall ye draw water out of the wells of salvation" (Isaiah 12:3, KJV), I see my childhood experience in a different way. The spiritual wells of which Isaiah speaks do not cause the same angst as the physical well of my childhood. Rather, they offer the mystery of God's endless love, one into which His repentant followers—no matter the scope of their sins—would be able to let down their depleted souls and come up with hope in the face of life's trials.

Water produced from a man-made well is not without limits, but Isaiah's wells of salvation never run dry. Though God's children must draw from His strength while shouldering the weight of bereavement, poverty, health challenges, and more, hope and joy are staples within His wells if we can but remember their constant availability.

The joy of salvation is not a quick burst of the type of holiday hype for which we have acquired a taste (might it be that joy is too much equated with spontaneity?) but a steady heartbeat, a step-by-step sanctifying relationship with Jesus—an expanding reservoir of assurance through the perseverance of life's trials, yielding the beauty of faith in the Lord Christ.

Help me, Lord, to daily draw upon the joy freely provided in salvation alone. —Jacqueline F. Wheelock

Digging Deeper: Isaiah 55:1; John 4:14

Saturday, July 6

Rejoice always, pray continually, give thanks in all circumstances; for this is God's will for you in Christ Jesus. —1 Thessalonians 5:16–18 (NIV)

This morning as I vacuumed the stairs, I grumbled. Of all the household chores, vacuuming the stairs is my least favorite. I hate the balancing of the hose and the vigorous scrubbing to clear away matted pet hair.

When we first moved into our house, before we had a dog, we didn't have a carpet runner, and keeping the stairs clean was easy. But once we got Soda, we noticed that the stairs were too slippery, and after a scary tumble, we put the carpet runner down for his safety.

As I cleared the top stair, I thought about a worse job that I no longer have—changing the sheets on the top tier of bunkbeds. Back when the boys were young, I had to climb up to the top bunk, hunch over, and stretch beyond my limits to change the bedding. Often, I pulled my neck or back muscles, and many times I searched online for an easier solution. But now that the boys are grown, I miss the sight of Henry in his top bunk, surrounded by dozens of stuffed animals.

I once read that the best way to approach a chore is to change "have to" to "get to"—to be grateful for the circumstance. So as I go about vacuuming the stairs—step by step—I think of blessings that have led me here, beginning with the most obvious of having a home I love, and sons and five cats, and ending with the reason for the carpet in the first place: the rescue dog that stole my heart.

Lord, thank You for reminding me that showing gratitude is at the core of every responsibility.
—Sabra Ciancanelli

Digging Deeper: Colossians 3:23; 1 Timothy 5:8

Everyone then who hears these words of mine and does them will be like a wise man who built his house on the rock. —Matthew 7:24 (ESV)

It didn't look hard. I'd watched a hundred guys hop on a paddle board, bob out through the surf, and soar. So, when I had the chance to give it a whirl, I was all in. I was a little disappointed my first experience was on a lake rather than the ocean, but, hey, you've got to start somewhere.

Now everybody knows the idea of paddle boarding is to stand on the thing and paddle around. Simple. The thing is, I don't think anyone had ever told that paddleboard. I went one way, and the board went another.

No prob. If at first you don't succeed...

"Keep your eyes on the horizon," someone said.

The horizon wasn't the problem, the water was.

"You want someone to hold it for you?" my ever-helpful wife suggested.

Yeah, right. *Splash.* If an inanimate object could laugh, that board would have been rolling. I know my wife was.

You know, I've found life to be the same way. Just when I think I've got it figured out, the planet goes spinning off in one direction and I go the other. God picks me up and dusts me off. *You want Me to hold it for you?*

Believe me when I tell you it's taken a lot of splashes—and some near drownings—but I'm finally learning to say *yes, please.*

I might not be out on the ocean yet, but, hey, at least I'm on the right side of the board.

I'm trying not to look at the water.

The horizon looks beautiful.

Lord, You are the God that calms the waves. Thank You for Your endless patience! —Buck Storm

Digging Deeper: Psalms 25:4–5, 62:5–8

Monday, July 8

SEEKING CONNECTION IN THE BIBLE'S STORIES: Mary's Trust

And Mary said, "... may it be done to me according to your word." —Luke 1:38 (NASB)

Isn't that typical of me," I muttered, "comparing myself with another woman?" I'd been thinking about Mary, mother of Jesus, and wondering if I had what God was looking for when He chose her to birth and raise His Son. Aware that both "glitches and glories" are revealed in the people of the Bible, I believed God was fashioning me, too, for His good purpose.

Mary is a teen when the angel Gabriel appears to her. She is puzzled, yet accepting, of Gabriel's startling proclamation. She has "found favor with God" (Luke 1:30, NASB1995) and will "bear a son" and "name Him Jesus" (Luke 1:31, NASB1995). Mary unflinchingly offers herself to God's plan.

From her song of praise, known as the Magnificat (Luke 1:46–56), I learn Mary's love for God runs deep. She desires to serve Him with her whole heart. She is humble and thankful.

When Jesus is born and shepherds visit with their own story of angelic proclamation, she "treasured all these things, pondering them in her heart" (Luke 2:19, NASB). Mary is contemplative.

I'd have questioned Gabriel nonstop, just needing to figure it out—to be sure. I, too, want to serve God—but there's hesitancy when it means taking on something new. I'm relieved to know humility means more to me than it used to. Gratitude is essential. I also am a ponderer.

In Mary's story, I discover I have places to grow more faithful to God—and I'm encouraged in ways I continue to please Him. Mary's ready "yes" to God shows me faith is a journey of both anticipation and participation.

Thank You, Father, for Mary's eager trust in accepting Your calling for her. —Carol Knapp

Digging Deeper: Matthew 12:46–50; Luke 1:26–56, 2:48–51; John 19:26–27

Tuesday, July 9

Therefore encourage one another and build each other up....—1 Thessalonians 5:11 (NIV)

I thought it would be a snap to make my dad an ice cream cake for his birthday. According to Internet recipes (what could go wrong?), all I had to do was bake a chocolate sheet cake, cut it into three segments, and put his favorite ice cream flavor—black walnut—in between the layers.

My first hint that I was going to have trouble came when the sheet cake partially stuck to the pan. Then I realized the cake was so thin that I wouldn't be able to manage more than two layers from it. Ah, well! Undaunted, on I continued.

But as it turned out, spreading softened ice cream across an even softer cake is, well, no piece of cake. My end result looked like a giant, pathetic ice cream sandwich.

I was so amused by my kitchen failure that I decided to post a photo to social media. Many of my friends are master bakers, so I thought they'd get a kick out of my disaster. At least my efforts could provide a chuckle or two.

I was so touched when dozens of friends commented with notes of encouragement: "Your dad will love it anyway!" … "I bet it's delicious!" … or even, "Hey, I'd eat it!" Some offered tips for the future or methods to salvage my mess. "Just freeze the cake layers first next time," a caterer friend from my college years suggested. "Whipped topping and a chocolate drizzle on top will disguise a lot of mistakes!" wrote my preacher's wife.

My friends were right: the taste didn't suffer a bit. And Daddy loved his ugly but delicious cake.

As for me, the unexpected encouragement from God-given friends? That was the sweetest part of all.

Dear Lord, thank You for the encouraging friends and family who surround me and lift me up.
—Ginger Rue

Digging Deeper: Romans 14:19; Ephesians 4:29

Wednesday, July 10

You must understand this, my beloved brothers and sisters: let everyone be quick to listen, slow to speak, slow to anger. —James 1:19 (NRSVUE)

I might seem like an even-tempered guy, never raising my voice. Alas, get me behind the wheel of a car and I surprise myself. Someone cuts me off, say, and the words that come out of my mouth...well, you don't want to hear them. *I* don't want to hear them. I reassure myself that the other driver can't hear me through the closed windows.

The thing is, God can hear me. Even if there's no one else in my car. Even if I mutter the imprecations under my breath.

What to do about these unspeakable outbursts? How to control my anger?

One day, a good colleague offered some priceless advice. No, I don't think she was a passenger when I burst out at some driver. (At least that's what I tell myself.) Instead of saying what I should do, she managed to couch it as an example of what *she* does. "I always try to imagine what kind of day that person might have had. And why they needed to cut into my lane."

Maybe that wayward driver just got some bad news. Maybe he is cutting in front of me because he's rushing home to comfort a grieving wife or suffering kid. Maybe his boss just unloaded on him, and he's not feeling so hot. Can't I cut him some slack? Can I?

Yes, I can. You can too.

Jesus told us to love our neighbors as ourselves. I'm trying to put that precious advice into practice on the road. Not just for my neighbors but for myself.

Forgive me for my outbursts of anger, Lord, and help me control my words and thoughts.
—Rick Hamlin

Digging Deeper: Proverbs 15:18; Ecclesiastes 7:9; Ephesians 4:26–27

Thursday, July 11

And the peace of God, which surpasses all understanding, will guard your hearts and your minds in Christ Jesus. —Philippians 4:7 (ESV)

There are birds that like to nest on our roof. Medium sized, black. They are probably crows, not that I know anything about birds, but, regardless, they are (moderately) quiet and completely harmless.

I wouldn't even notice them, except for my hundred-pound, strong golden retriever, Zeke.

Every time Zeke catches a glimpse of one of the birds on the roof, he absolutely melts into a puddle of fear. He hides behind the door, whimpers, and refuses to go outside. It got to the point where he refused to step off the porch to use the bathroom if one of us didn't check the roof first.

We started doing a little pet therapy with him. When he becomes anxious, we sit by him and talk soothingly. We snuggle him and remind him that we are right there, and we will protect him from the big, bad birds. Then we slowly take a step forward, hands on his back, until he is off the porch.

He still refuses to look up at the birds—that might take years of "pet therapy"—but he is willing to step off the porch now and onto the lawn.

Like the birds, there are things in life that feel a bit scary—circumstances that are confusing or unknown. But our God is always there to do a little "pet therapy" if you will. When we are fearful, He is there to give us peace—a peace that goes beyond understanding.

A peace that centers us in Jesus and protects us from even the scariest things.

Like black birds on the roof.

Jesus, thank You for using my sweet dog, Zeke, to remind me that Your peace is always available to me.
—Erin MacPherson

Digging Deeper: Psalms 34:4, 56:3

Friday, July 12

Let your steadfast love, O LORD, be upon us, even as we hope in you. —Psalm 33:22 (ESV)

On a warm July afternoon, I heard Boris Karloff's voice in *How the Grinch Stole Christmas* echoing from our living area. My seven-year-old son, Jacques, seemed to have an increasing affinity for the Grinch. He enjoyed all things Grinch. I didn't exactly understand his preference and was intrigued by Jacques's interest. So I asked him, "Why do you like the Grinch so very much? It's not even Christmas." Wisdom often trickles from the mouths of children, so I wasn't surprised at his answer. He said exasperatedly, as if I should already know, "Mommy, because he changes. His heart grows bigger."

For me, Jacques's response articulated hope and transformation—the hope for change, the hope for love. The Grinch transformed into someone filled with joy and love in *How the Grinch Stole Christmas*. These characteristics drew Jacques toward the Grinch. As Jacques continued to watch the movie, my thoughts meandered toward Christmas.

Christmas is all about Jesus—God's masterful act of love and hope. Jesus transforms me as only He can. As I know Him, my heart, too, grows in love. Sound familiar? I suppose the Grinch and I have more in common than I thought. Thanks to my Grinch-loving seven-year-old, this humid July afternoon feels like Christmas!

Dear Lord, may the love and hope of Christmas be exemplified in all my deeds and thoughts. Amen.
—Jolynda Strandberg

Digging Deeper: John 1:1–5; Romans 12:1–3; 2 Corinthians 3:17–18

Each of you should use whatever gift you have received to serve others, as faithful stewards of God's grace. —1 Peter 4:10 (NIV)

At the end of baseball season, postseason play begins. For us and our crew of six-year-olds, that means evaluations for the postseason teams. Our town had three teams per age group, and when I tell you that these six-year-olds can play, I mean it. They throw outs at first, hit without a tee, and swing for the fences.

When we saw the lists come out, we realized that James hadn't made the top three teams. Then, something caught Brian's eye: none of James's buddies had made the teams either. He called a fellow coach and shared his idea: what if we took this crew and made a team?

That first practice, as the team gathered, was holy ground. These boys love each other, love baseball, and love a good time, so day after day they played, got better, and had a blast doing it.

Our first game was against one of the town's best teams, and the air just felt different. Their boys were frustrated, struggling to work as a team after a season of being the best at every game.

Our boys, on the other hand, were used to doing their best, falling short, and cheering each other on. We watched as they came together, had a ball, got better, and won!

On the way home, James couldn't believe they had done it, and we reminded him of the Bible story of the talents. When each brings what he has, God will bless it. And that day, He did.

Lord, thank You for allowing us each to bring our own strengths to Your table. Help us use them to encourage others, always. —Ashley Kappel

Digging Deeper: Romans 12:6; James 1:17

Sunday, July 14

And He has said to me, "My grace is sufficient for you, for power is perfected in weakness." —2 Corinthians 12:9 (NASB)

My phone rang. The assistant pastor was calling to ask if I would be willing to speak one Sunday for a special series. My son, who is on staff at the church, thought I should do it. So did my wife. And why not serve here at home? After all, I'd done the same around the world. Except somehow it felt wrong.

At the time, I was on a writing sabbatical. A time to question and rediscover my faith with unvarnished honesty. I needed space. To set all the work aside—the music, the writing—and just *be*. I was tired, bruised. I wanted God, one on one, with nothing in between. Bottom line—I wasn't in the mental or spiritual state to teach anyone anything. I should have said no.

But, in my pride, I didn't.

A few weeks later, I found myself standing in front of my own church struggling through a disjointed message. I felt embarrassed. A sham. Here

I was striving for honesty with God, masking my weakness before people.

Looking back, it's clear to me I put reputation before relationship. Did God use me that morning? Absolutely. He used it to teach *me*. He answered my question. Am I enough? No, I am not. But He is. In the depths of my weakness and my *wrong-ness*, I crashed into His strength and acceptance.

God isn't about our history. In fact, He knocks our carefully built towers away with a swipe of His hand.

He wants our *now*. *Now* overflows with His love. And now never ends.

Little ones to Him belong, I am weak but He is strong. Yes, Jesus loves me! Just as I am. And I am overwhelmed. —Buck Storm

Digging Deeper: Psalm 34:18; Matthew 11:28

Monday, July 15

SEEKING CONNECTION IN THE BIBLE'S STORIES: The Servant Girl's Courage

Naaman went in and told his master, saying, "Thus and thus spoke the girl who is from the land of Israel." —2 Kings 5:4 (NASB1995)

When Terry and I returned to our "hometown" ten years ago, I wanted to utilize my gift of writing to encourage our community. I began a newspaper column titled "Preacher's Kid." After our century-old town paper folded, I thought I was done. Then the larger county paper invited me to continue.

Looking at the story of Naaman—captain of the king of Aram's army—I identify my "newspaper voice" in that of a young maid. She's been captured and brought from Israel. Yet she boldly speaks up, telling Naaman's wife there is a prophet in her country who can cure Naaman of his leprosy.

Naaman sets off with many riches to bestow upon Elisha. He is not happy Elisha tells him to dip seven times in the Jordan River. He's expecting something more dramatic. At first he refuses, but his servant implores him to try it. And he does.

When he rises from the water the seventh time, his leprosy is gone. He returns to Elisha, acknowledging Israel's God is the true God.

It took courage for a servant girl to offer a healing solution for the captain of the king's army. What if she was rejected? What if God didn't come through? Her faith told her she had to try.

I don't know what disagreements or prejudices those who read my column might have when I speak for Christ or how they will regard me. I only know God inspired the idea and title and provided the platform. I can't be afraid to make Him known. He'll do the rest.

Lord, my voice is small, but it speaks big when it tells others of You. —Carol Knapp

Digging Deeper: 2 Kings 5; Matthew 28:19–20; 2 Timothy 1:7

But a Samaritan, as he traveled, came where the
man was; and when he saw him, he took pity
on him. —Luke 10:33 (NIV)

Have you ever wished you could replay an event and
act differently? I do. Something that happened ten
years ago often replays in my mind when talk turns
to courage and Christian responsibility.

My young granddaughter, age thirteen, and I had
just arrived at South Station in Boston and stood in
the ladies' room line waiting for stalls. A disheveled,
elderly woman emerged from the far end pushing a
walker. A six-foot-long trail of toilet tissue followed
her, apparently caught in her baggy pants. No one
paid attention.

"Nana! Do something!" hissed my granddaughter.
But I froze. Before I could rally the courage to speak
to her, she had shuffled off. At my core, I found that
I was not as courageous as I wished.

Perhaps I froze because days earlier I had heard
a story of an elderly man attacking his would-be
rescuer. Perhaps I froze because I wanted to protect
my granddaughter. Perhaps I expected someone
else to assist the woman. I've posed this dilemma in
several discussion groups. Most women agree that
I was protecting a child by not getting involved.
Was I?

If God gives me another chance to be helpful—
and I hope He does—I know what I'd do differently.
So does my granddaughter.

Lord of All, You promise that perfect love that casts out fear. I need more practice. Amen.
—Gail Thorell Schilling

Digging Deeper: Job 29:16; Hebrews 13:2; 3 John 1:5

Wednesday, July 17

I have filled him with the Spirit of God, with wisdom, with understanding, with knowledge and with all kinds of skills. —Exodus 31:3 (NIV)

People say my handwriting is hard to decipher, and I admit it's probably gotten worse through the years. But compared to the great novelist Charles Dickens, my scrawl looks like calligraphy. That's because Dickens wrote many of his notes in a personal shorthand based on an obscure eighteenth-century style of stenography he learned as a young court reporter and then modified over the years.

One of his notes for a letter he sent to a newspaper publisher—the letter itself has been lost—had famously remained undeciphered by intrepid but baffled Dickens scholars for 163 years until the University of Leicester posted it online recently and offered a small cash prize for anyone who could make sense of it.

Someone did. Not a scholar. Not a linguist. Not even an amateur Dickens buff. No, the man who broke the cipher had never read a Dickens novel in his life and had only made Cs in literature. He was a computer technical support specialist from California. The runner-up was a twenty-year-old cognitive science major at the University of Virginia.

The subject matter of the note was mundane—Dickens protesting the newspaper publisher's refusal to run an ad. But these non-literati types cracking the code was rich with irony...until I thought about it. Wasn't it more about the different gifts God gives people? This time they were used to decipher an obscure note from a famous author. But imagine the problems we can solve when we all share our unique talents and work together.

Thank You, Father, for the gifts You give us.
Let us be generous enough to share them.
—Edward Grinnan

Digging Deeper: 1 Chronicles 22:14–16;
Proverbs 22:29

Thursday, July 18

For you have been given not only the privilege of trusting in Christ but also the privilege of suffering for him. —Philippians 1:29 (NLT)

When you have been married for a while, you earn certain "privileges." I know when one of these privileges is coming because it is always preceded by the word "let."

My wife says, "Danny, I'm going to *let* you take out the kitchen trash because it's too heavy for me. And, then, if you could clean the toilets, please?"

I don't mind most of these privileges, but I cringe when Sharon says, "Honey, I want to mail this book to Carolyn, so I'm going to *let* you prepare it for mailing."

Arrrggh, I say to myself. *This means stumbling around in a hot, stuffy attic, looking for the perfect box, then wrestling with a stubborn tape dispenser, and, finally, trying to write on rough cardboard with a dried-out marker. I would rather eat dirt.*

I like to play fair, so I sometimes extend privileges to Sharon. "Sweetheart, I'm going to *let* you call the police station about all the noise in our neighborhood last night."

"Well, OK, I'll take care of it."

What makes these privileges bearable is that we are doing them for someone we love.

When God gives me a job to do today, it might be easy, like taking cookies to our new neighbors. Or hard, like counseling a couple on the verge of divorce. But there is fulfillment in these tasks because I am doing them for the God I love.

Thank You, Lord, for "letting" me serve You, even if it means suffering. —Daniel Schantz

Digging Deeper: Romans 8:18; Revelation 2:10

Friday, July 19

A gift is as a precious stone. —**Proverbs 17:8** (KJV)

Gifts. Thinking back, like you, I have some favorites.

I once told my son, Brock, that the piano piece "Doe Eyes" was a favorite of mine. On the sly, he began taking piano lessons, and on Christmas Day, he played the entire composition as my gift.

My heart was heavy for a boy named Prince in Zimbabwe. Dying with AIDS, he had dreams of going to school and seeing the world. Yet, he had never left the village where he lived in great poverty. On Christmas Day, Keri presented me with a portfolio of photos: Prince on a playground in the city; Prince at a pizza restaurant surrounded by Village Hope children; and Prince back home, surrounded by books, gifts, and food. For my present, Keri had sent money to my friend Paddington, who also lived in Zimbabwe. "Make Prince's dreams come true as best you can," she directed.

Recently, my husband, David, gave me a necklace fitted with one of those "precious stones" as mentioned above. But it was a gift with a twist. The back of the necklace is a genuine widow's mite—maybe the same one as in Jesus's great story (Mark 12:41–44; Luke 21:1–4)?

Hoping that similar offerings from family or friends have come to you, I suddenly realize there's another layer to all of this.

When others love you, they offer you their best, and isn't God, our Father, the same? Consider the redbird outside your window, tilting his head before he stretches his wings in flight, or the stunning sunrise that flashes across the sky, outclassing any jewel. He scatters countless reminders of His loving care through our days. His gifts are always near, waiting for our notice.

**Father God, how precious are the gifts You give...
our thank-yous are unending. —Pam Kidd**

Digging Deeper: Romans 12:18;
2 Corinthians 9:7

Saturday, July 20

**[There is] a right time to rip out and another
to mend. —Ecclesiastes 3:7 (MSG)**

Last summer, my brother came to visit. I noticed that he hadn't slept on the futon but, rather, wrapped in a blanket on the rug. So the next night I pulled out a ratty old quilt to cushion his bones. "Oh, I recognize this," he said. "It's seen better days. 'Change and decay,'" as the hymn line laments.

The quilt was made by our aunt, an expert quilter who took pride in counting stitches per inch. In our teen years, the bed covering provided warmth and beauty, all in one piece. I inherited it, already worn from decades of use. In repair mode, I replaced the binding. After more years on my bed, the pastel quilt fared so badly—cotton disintegrating around the perimeter—that I trimmed two inches off each edge and stitched on a new border. Though diminished, what remained could still envelop body and spirit.

More years, more tumbled washings. When numerous gaping tears pocked the batting, I relegated the quilt to a closet floor. When I pulled it out for my brother, it so embarrassed me that I marked it for trash. But I nostalgically assessed it one more time. Did I have another chance to embrace change and excise decay? I found a way. I cut out and finished off three yard-square lap robes: one for myself, one for a neighbor girl's dolls, and one I mailed to my brother—with a prayer for God's comfort and best wishes for warm feet.

Lord, show me ways to mend and salvage what is useful and good. —Evelyn Bence

Digging Deeper: 2 Corinthians 13:9, 11–14

Sunday, July 21

SEEKING CONNECTION IN THE BIBLE'S STORIES: Two Spies Believe
And the LORD said to Moses, "How long will this people be disrespectful to Me?"
—Numbers 14:11 (NASB)

God had promised Abraham his descendants would have their own land; instead, hundreds of years later, they found themselves in captivity in Egypt. Then, through a series of God's miracles, they were freed and placed under the leadership of Moses. The wilderness became their new dwelling as they traveled toward this land of promise.

When they neared the place, God directed Moses to send a dozen men to spy out the territory and bring back a report. Ten spies gave a discouraging report. They could not hope to possess the land—its occupants were too big and strong.

Two of the men clung to their faith in God's promises and insisted, "He will bring us into this land and give it to us" (Numbers 14:8, NASB). But the rest of the Israelites would not listen. God withheld the "land of milk and honey," and they wandered the wilderness forty more years.

I found myself in this story in the spring of 2020, when the Covid-19 pandemic caused a lockdown across our country. I felt paralyzed—afraid even to go to the grocery store. All activity outside home— and with others—stopped. It was a dry and barren time.

One morning, in my heart I heard God ask, "How long will you wander in the wilderness because you refused to live in the promise?" I understood immediately. My fear had imagined the virus greater than the God who promises to be with me—who holds my days in His hand.

From that moment forward, while still taking sensible safeguards, I reached confidently for life— secure that my God is with me every day.

I get scared, Lord, and forget You are able to do "far more abundantly beyond all that we ask or think..." (Ephesians 3:20, NASB). —Carol Knapp

Digging Deeper: Joshua 1:1–9;
Psalm 4:8; Mark 6:45–52

If I have the gift of prophecy and know all mysteries and all knowledge, and if I have all faith so as to remove mountains, but do not have love, I am nothing. —1 Corinthians 13:2 (NASB)

I'm a compulsive researcher. Give me a problem, and I'm online till I solve it. Medical issues are especially enticing. If someone reports mysterious symptoms or an intractable-seeming malady, I read every scholarly article my cursor can find, cram weird medical vocabulary, and study online X-rays, diagrams, and procedures till I know—or *believe* I know—exactly what's wrong and how to fix it.

So, when my sister, a retired nurse, reported her husband's prostate cancer recurrence, I was on it. Sharon was steadfastly hopeful—citing her nursing experience, amazing advances in cancer management, and acquaintances' long survival with the same cancer—but my research made me less optimistic.

Months later, my sister reported she, too, was struggling to stay positive. "I have to be, though, or I'll fall apart," she said sadly.

She worried she was in denial, like many patients and spouses she'd met as a nurse. Their unrealistic positivity infuriated her. Now, people's similar response to her own optimism compounded her suffering. Recently, after she reported that her husband was "doing great," a friend, unaware Sharon saw her, turned to another friend and rolled her eyes.

I felt so bad for my sister—and so mortified by my own secret pessimism. I prayed a retroactive prayer that I hadn't hurt her, too, as her self-appointed armchair physician. Instead of trying to know better, I should've devoted myself to loving better.

When I die, Father, I want others to say, "She loved well," not "She was smart." Help me get there.
—Patty Kirk

Digging Deeper: Proverbs 17:17–22; 1 John 4:7–21

Tuesday, July 23

REMEMBERING GRATITUDE:
Standing on the Promises
The Lord is trustworthy in all he promises and faithful in all he does. —Psalm 145:13 (NIV)

Whenever I look at my gray stoneware crock, I remember my designer-friend David bringing it to me. I'd moved to a tumbledown log cabin after my marriage ended, balancing parental caregiving with a full-time nursing job while dealing with pain from neurofibromatosis.

David appeared at my door in the midst of my cabin repairs with his latest creation. In raised cobalt blue was the outline of Noah's ark and the words: "God keeps all promises." I rearranged paint cans, steel wool, and tack cloths to make a place of honor for the crock on my living room mantel.

For over two decades, those words have proven true. I wanted to thank my friend, but I couldn't locate him. Then a letter from a *Walking in Grace (Daily Guideposts)* reader arrived. Her family lived with my same condition, the same horrendous nerve pain, surely some of the same doubts. I awakened at 3 a.m. with an urge to pray for them. While my words failed me, the ones on my crock did not. David's gift was a passing moment for him, but for me it was a defining moment. With keystrokes on my laptop, my heart thanked David and God, at the same time reaching a dear reader:

I'm so sorry your family has to live with neurofibromatosis. But I'm grateful they have you *to lean on. Chronic pain is so hard to cope with. I would not—could not—have made it through without God and those who've been there for me. If I'm sure of anything, it's that He never leaves us or forsakes us. That's a promise. And He's a promise-keeper.*

Love,
Roberta Messner

Your promises are sweet and sure, Lord. Thank You.
—Roberta Messner

Digging Deeper: Deuteronomy 31:8;
Isaiah 40:29, 41:10

CELEBRATE!! A Miracle
The joy of the LORD is your strength.
—Nehemiah 8:10 (NIV)

At our Bible study, we were asked to describe an experience when we felt supernatural peace that did not fit the situation. Immediately, I knew mine.

My husband, Lynn, and I, along with our son Derek and his wife, were leaving a mountain town to head home. Suddenly Lynn said, "I have a terrible headache." I knew immediately this was an emergency, so we quickly found our way to a small hospital, where we learned that Lynn had a brain hemorrhage and his life depended on quickly getting to a brain surgeon on the other side of the mountain. Lynn was losing consciousness as a small plane appeared at the hospital. The nurse told Derek, "Tell your dad anything you want him to know."

Soon I was scrunched next to the pilot. Lynn was on a gurney behind me with a medic on each side. I saw only one monitor—which flatlined several minutes into the flight. The medics would not make eye contact with me. The engine was too loud for conversation, so I looked out the window, suddenly awed by the beauty of the mountains below and the blue sky above. I felt a wave of peace. "Lord, if You have chosen to take Lynn, thank You for this setting." In that moment, I was filled with peace that passed any understanding.

When we finally landed, a medic gave me a thumbs-up. Lynn survived the flight and critical brain surgery and is with me today, almost twenty years later, as I remember the day I touched the face of God.

Lord, remembering precious moments of Your presence strengthens my faith. Thank You.
—Carol Kuykendall

Thursday, July 25

**A new command I give you: Love one another.
As I have loved you, so you must love one another.
—John 13:34 (NIV)**

My wife, Pat, and I took a European tour. Our last stop was Paris, where we spent the final day of our trip at the Palace of Versailles. There was a fellow on the tour who I found annoying. I remembered him from the bus ride from the airport to the hotel the very first day. Sitting behind me, he seemed loudly outspoken on a variety of topics. I found some of his opinions lacking compassion. I had a couple of brief encounters with him during the trip and they were fine. But that first annoying impression never went away.

It was a tiring day at the palace. Shoulder-to-shoulder crowds, hot temperatures, and a lot of walking and stair climbing made it a draining day.

After touring the palace, Pat and I walked around the gardens, enjoyed a cold soda in the snack bar, and returned to the bus. I saw in the distance a man helping a tired traveler coming toward the bus. Their silhouette resembled the image of a soldier carrying a fallen comrade to safety. As they got closer, I recognized the man helping his weary friend: the man I had dismissed as annoying. Yet he was the compassionate one who put his kindness into action being the hands and feet of Jesus. I felt ashamed and remorseful for my judgmental attitude. I asked for God's forgiveness.

Thank You, God, for examining our hearts and letting us know things we do—or don't do—that are offensive to You. Amen. —John Dilworth

Digging Deeper: Psalm 139:23–24; Proverbs 3:5; Luke 6:37

Friday, July 26

The LORD will guide you always; he will satisfy your needs in a sun-scorched land and will strengthen your frame. You will be like a well-watered garden, like a spring whose waters never fail. —Isaiah 58:11 (NIV)

Summer in the southern United States tests your endurance and air-conditioning system. If the heat fails to wilt you, the humidity will be more than glad to try harder—draining your energy and dampening your clothes. Nothing survives for long without water and shade, especially my garden. No way I can relax in my air-conditioned house while my vegetables and flowers endure scorching sun and long periods of drought.

One solution is installing an irrigation system, but it's not my style. I prefer to get up early in the morning, drag out the garden hose, and water my plants every few days unless it rains. Giving each one personal attention and encouragement has produced abundant results.

Yes, I talk to my plants. I also talk to God as I water the delightful piece of earth He's given me, thanking Him for showering me every day with blessings galore. Years ago, during one of my early-morning watering sessions, I realized God provides me the same individual care and inspiration by supplying food, water, and shelter for my body and soul. An added bonus is He talks to me. Through His Holy Spirit and written word, I'm lavished with abundant love and instructions for how to live and glorify Him.

Lord, thank You for being the perfect gardener. Your living water is the greatest gift ever offered. May we accept it and live the life You intended for each of us— one filled with Your everlasting love, mercy, and grace.
—Jenny Lynn Keller

Digging Deeper: Psalm 1:1–3; Jeremiah 17:7–8; John 4:7–14

Saturday, July 27

For I have had great joy and comfort in your love, because the hearts of the saints have been refreshed through you, brother. —Philemon 1:7 (NASB)

My grandpa shaded his eyes from the glare of the pool. He sat in a folding chair. I sat on the pool's edge, my feet in the clear water.

"Did you know this pool is nearly fifty years old?" my grandpa asked.

I looked down. The floor of the pool was a bit uneven from years of settling. But the pool was in remarkable condition for its age. It had been well cared for. Years ago, my mom and her sisters swam in this pool. I had spent a number of summer days in the pool myself. I remembered swimming with my brothers, cousins, and friends.

Oddly, I had no memories of my grandpa in the pool.

"When was the last time you went swimming?" I asked.

My grandpa leaned back in thought.

"Probably twenty years ago," he said.

I thought of all the times I had watched my grandpa skim leaves off the water's surface and check chlorine content. I didn't understand why he had spent years caring for a pool he didn't even use.

"How does the water feel?" my grandpa asked.

I moved my feet in the cool water.

"Refreshing," I said.

And I began to understand. My grandpa maintained this pool because it brought refreshment to others. Every person who swam in that pool was a recipient of that blessing. And providing that blessing brought my grandpa joy.

I looked up at the man who had provided half a century of refreshment for others. And I desired to be a giver of blessings like him.

Father, help me be a source of refreshment to the people in my life. —Logan Eliasen

Digging Deeper: 1 Corinthians 16:17–18; 2 Timothy 1:16

SEEKING CONNECTION IN THE BIBLE'S STORIES:
The Lawyer Learns Mercy

But wanting to justify himself, he said to Jesus, "And who is my neighbor?" —Luke 10:29 (NASB)

The lawyer's question about inheriting eternal life is answered in a way he is not expecting. Besides loving God with all his heart, soul, strength, and mind, Jesus tells him he must love his neighbor as much as he loves himself. The lawyer asks Jesus to define neighbor. There follows the well-known story of the Good Samaritan.

Jesus then asks the lawyer to state who was the neighbor in the story. He answers, "The one who showed mercy toward him" (Luke 10:37, NASB).

I'm like that lawyer in accepting the loving God part—but sometimes reluctant on the neighbor end. One incident stands out with our only close neighbor. His daffodil bed was stunning—dozens of blooms opening each year to the spring sun. A scattered few had popped up on our side of the fence. One day, he saw me snipping a daffodil bouquet for my kitchen table. He felt they were his, and I should not be taking any.

I firmly—yet kindly—defended my action as I continued cutting and walked back to the house. After the blossoming season was over, something seemed different as I passed the flower bed. All the daffodil plants were gone. In their place grew clusters of decorative grasses.

I was stunned. Obviously my cutting the flowers had been an affront to him. I may not have understood, or agreed with, his reasoning—but the loving thing to do would have been to stop clipping when he became upset.

When I insist on going for what I want—and lack consideration toward others—I fail to love my neighbor.

Jesus, You have shown loving You and loving my neighbor go together—like daffodils and spring.
—Carol Knapp

Digging Deeper: Luke 10:25–37; Galatians 5:13–15; Colossians 3:12–14

Monday, July 29

Wherever your treasure is, there the desires of your heart will also be. —Matthew 6:21 (NLT)

Choking smoke filled the summer skies. The air was thick, gray. Like filthy skiffs of snow, the ash coated vehicles, animals, everything throughout the day and night. I put a scarf over my nose and mouth to check our cattle, wishing they could find relief from the smoke. Even the grass seemed to stop growing in the prolonged gloom.

We'd already experienced eleven forest fires of various sizes within a few miles of our home even before the massive Bootleg wildfire boiled up in July. Ranchers and volunteers came out in droves to push livestock away from the path of the inferno. In spite of everyone's best efforts, the losses to wildlife and livestock were staggering.

Long before we were added to the evacuation area, I packed a "go-box." Important documents, computer files on drives, a change of clothes, dog food. I prepared early so that when the time came, we could focus on getting the animals out, not worrying about the house.

I snapped photos in each room as I catalogued our home. The antique rocker. Cherished books. Framed art. But when it all came down to what's important, these wonderful treasures suddenly became stuff.

Years ago, I'd lost nearly everything I owned in a house fire. One unexpected reaction was relief of being free of belongings. The things I truly missed were surprisingly minimal.

Mercifully, the wildfire shifted away from us before we had to evacuate. But the reminder of what is truly precious—life, limb, and love—was a blessing in the blaze.

Lord, true riches are in heaven, not in our house. Praise Your name! —Erika Bentsen

---

Tuesday, July 30

**Do nothing out of selfish ambition or vain
conceit. Rather, in humility value others above
yourselves, not looking to your own interests
but each of you to the interests of the others.
—Philippians 2:3–4 (NIV)**

Sharing God with others is something that I aspire
to do but am somewhat shy about actually doing.

For about three months, my ninety-three-year-
old dad was in a rehab facility, recuperating from a
hospital stay. On weekend nights when I came to
visit him, Gloria, the security guard, administered the
required Covid-19 test to all visitors. While we waited
fifteen minutes for the results of the rapid tests, Gloria
and I would chat, as she did with many others. She
asked about the patients we were visiting and wished
them well.

It was a shock to me when one night, Gloria
shared her own story: Her mother had just returned
home from a hospital stay after contracting Covid-
19. Gloria had little local family support and
was plenty worried about her mother's long-term
prognosis—how she would care for her and to
whom she could turn to assist her.

I followed the Holy Spirit and without even
debating it in my mind, I invited Gloria to my

church. The next Sunday, Gloria was there! I was so happy to see her and introduced her to many other members. A minister prayed with Gloria, and several others offered her socially distant greetings. Even in these Covid-19 times, I was grateful for the opportunity for my church to show Gloria some love. And even more, I was thankful to be able to shed my fear and share my faith, which manifested in mercy, just when Gloria needed it.

Lord, help me to be attuned to the many ways that I can share You with others.
—Gayle T. Williams

Digging Deeper: Hebrews 13:16; 1 John 3:16

Wednesday, July 31

Now to him who is able to do immeasurably more than all we ask or imagine, according to his power that is at work within us. —Ephesians 3:20 (NIV)

While attending a Philadelphia writers' workshop, I was excited to take in the city's sights—the Liberty Bell, Independence Hall, countless museums, and the Rocky statue.

History is interesting, but I'm a big Sylvester Stallone fan. The *Rocky* movies inspired me, and I had a huge crush on the hulky heartthrob. Despite being athletically challenged myself, my dream was to run up the steps of the Philadelphia Museum of

Art (just like in the movie) while humming the *Rocky* theme song. I couldn't wait to stand next to the fictional boxer's statue and have my picture taken.

That Friday, I met a colleague, Susan, at the airport. I hesitantly confided my Rocky dream as we Ubered past centuries-old architecture. Sue chuckled when she learned of my love for Rocky.

We checked in to our hotel on Logan Square, dropped our bags in our rooms, and met back in the lobby. As the two of us waited in the empty foyer for others at the workshop, the elevator doors opened. Out stepped Sylvester Stallone, in the flesh.

Oh my gosh! That's him! Don't look! Tongue-tied and flustered, I stared at my shoes as the superstar approached.

"Well, hello," Sue coyly called.

I glanced up. Sly and I were face-to-face. He smiled, nodded, and answered, "Hello."

God knows the desires of our hearts, however small. The irony was not lost on me. I longed to get a picture with a bronze statue; instead, I encountered the real thing.

Dear God, thank You for gifting me with immeasurably more than I asked for, even something seemingly trivial. —Stephanie Thompson

Digging Deeper: Psalm 38:9; 1 Corinthians 2:9; James 1:17

YOU WERE CALLED TO PEACE

1 _____

2 _____

3 _____

4 _____

5 _____

6 _____

7 _____

8 _____

9 _____

10 _____

11 _____

12 _____

13 _____

14 _____

15 _____

16 _____

17 _____

18 _____

19 _____

20 _____

21 _____

22 _____

23 _____

24 _____

25 _____

26 _____

27 _____

28 _____

29 _____

30 _____

31 _____

AUGUST

*Blessed are the peacemakers, for
they shall be called sons of God.*

—Matthew 5:9 (NKJV)

Thursday, August 1

Everyone should be quick to listen, slow to speak and slow to become angry. —James 1:19 (NIV)

Gotta go. I'm back home now, and Chuck expects dinner," I said to my friend Rosemary on the phone.

She laughed. "OK then, goodbye. Love you."

"Love you too."

I disconnected the call, glad for a chance to talk to my lifelong friend, taking the opportunity to call her while walking in the neighborhood. Multitasking, you know. It was important for us to stay in touch, even though our conversations were infrequent. I stayed busy, but Rosemary always had time to talk, encourage, and laugh with me.

She's always been a steadfast, loyal friend, the person I could talk to about anything. Being a good listener is one of her strengths, plus she understands me and never criticizes. Sometimes she offers suggestions but not in a judgmental way. I always feel better after our conversations.

When I told my husband, Chuck, I had talked to her, he asked me how she was and how her family was doing. I froze because I didn't know how to answer him. With a sickening, sinking weight in my heart, I realized I didn't know because I never asked her. I was the talker. She was the listener. Our conversations weren't really conversations because I was the only one talking. As this truth settled into my mind, I wondered how she had tolerated me and my selfishness so long. I determined right then to make a concentrated effort to talk less in our future conversations. To do so, I would ask about her family, then really listen to her answers instead of trying to think of the next thing I would say.

Lord, please help me listen to others the way You always listen to me. —Marilyn Turk

Digging Deeper: Psalm 66:19; Proverbs 18:13

Friday, August 2

...hold fast that which is good.
—1 Thessalonians 5:21 (KJV)

It's a time I will never grow tired of talking about. Imagine a late summer afternoon. A calm lake. A small red boat, twelve feet long from stem to stern, just right for two people.

My mother bought the boat for $100 from an old man's yard. In better days, it must have been shiny. It had a glass bottom in the middle of the hull, thoroughly scratched and impossible to see through. My dad named him *Thunder*, and for many a season he was our only boat. I see us there, my dad and me, squeezed in *Thunder*, bouncing across the water in sight of the little cabin my grandfather had built.

I planned to buy a big, fancy fishing boat one day. But now, as the sun headed west, we were out in *Thunder*. We cast our lines, we talked, we laughed. And when the sun got serious about setting, we simply watched. My sister, Keri, and my mom would have dinner waiting for us at the cabin. Later, we would take our usual night walk, soaking in the brilliance of the rural sky, the curtains of lightning bugs, the songs of frogs.

And so our summers went. My dad was a minister, and there was not a lot of spare money for beaches and big cities, just the cabin, our little family, and *Thunder*.

God is good. He gives us each other; He gives us night skies and lightning bugs in summer. In the end, He gave me success in a career I love. And, yes, finally, I did buy that big, shiny boat.

But *Thunder*, ahhh *Thunder*. There will never be another *Thunder*.

Father, thank You for the simple times. Life as You give it is good. —Brock Kidd

Digging Deeper: Psalm 33:5; Philippians 4:8

Saturday, August 3

He performs wonders that cannot be fathomed, miracles that cannot be counted. He provides rain for the earth; he sends water on the countryside. —Job 5:9–10 (NIV)

I looked out at my market garden in despair. The thermometer was reading 108, and my squash plants' leaves were wilted to the ground. The broccoli and cauliflower were looking no better. I'd given up on my herb beds weeks ago. Crispy brown twigs were all that was left of the thyme, rosemary, and basil I'd started from seed and tended so carefully for months. The heat was brutal and relentless.

To make matters much worse, our garden well wasn't keeping up with the demand, so I'd been hauling water from our house, a mile up the road, and dumping it into a large holding tank. From there, it got pumped into drip hoses that delivered the water to the plants. But no matter how hard I worked, there just wasn't enough to go around. The plants were on their last legs. I was losing this fight.

Until the following morning. Stepping out into the day, braced for more wind and heat, I was shocked to find the air fresh and clean. And there were...puddles. It had rained! I dashed to the garden and dug my fingers into its soil. Even inches down, it was saturated.

I sank down onto the path, humbled to my core, and acutely aware of the enormous amount of energy it would have taken me to bring this volume of water down onto my garden. In one night, with a singular small storm system, God had accomplished what I'd not been able to in weeks of backbreaking work.

Thank You, God, for water. And for the profound, life-giving power You've breathed into every part of Your beautiful creation. —Erin Janoso

Digging Deeper: Deuteronomy 11:10–12; Job 40:4–5; Isaiah 55:9–10

Sunday, August 4

There are "friends" who pretend to be friends, but there is a friend who sticks closer than a brother.
—Proverbs 18:24 (TLB)

Twice a year, my neighborhood hosts the ABC Fair (Art, Books, Crafts) in our community clubhouse. Local artists, writers, and crafters bring their creations to display and sell. One year, I decided to haul suitcases full of my painted jars, alcohol ink paintings, and books I've written to sell at the ABC event. It was a lot of work, and because I priced my jars and paintings so low, I only made a little over $100 for all my time and trouble. But I learned that it isn't really about the money. It's about the people I meet. And at my age, meeting new people is critical.

One year at the ABC Fair, I met Bruce and his wife, Melissa, who had just moved into our neighborhood. I met Jonathan, a retired middle-school principal who I didn't even realize was on my neighborhood community's board of directors until that day. I met Mary Fran, who only lives a block from me. I talked to dozens of people, many of whom I'd never met before but since have become friends.

Three weeks later, my church had a similar event and, in the spirit of making more new friends, I lugged all my wares to church and set up my table. And wouldn't you know, the people I met there are now friends I chat with after mass on Sundays. I learned that if I put myself in places where there are lots of strangers and then work up the courage to open my mouth and start conversations with them, I just might end up with a new group of friends.

Father, thank You for the courage to start conversations with strangers and the wisdom to keep the friendship going. —Patricia Lorenz

Digging Deeper: 1 Samuel 18:1–3; Proverbs 18:24

SEEKING CONNECTION IN THE BIBLE'S STORIES: Paul's Forward Focus

...so that He may establish your hearts blameless....—1 Thessalonians 3:13 (NASB)

For an entire decade in midlife, I discarded what God was telling me. I dug myself in deeper and deeper in wrongdoing. My family suffered from it—I suffered from it—and God suffered for it. Jesus died to forgive sin.

Years later, I find comfort in the words of the Apostle Paul, "...forgetting what lies behind and reaching forward to what lies ahead" (Philippians 3:13, NASB). Paul was a fanatical persecutor of believers in Christ—until Jesus intervened in his life in a blaze of light as he traveled to Damascus.

Paul had every reason to wallow in regret. The faith he was now following he once tried to destroy. Instead Paul loved and served His Savior—and his brothers and sisters in Christ—the more vigorously.

I'm not supposed to look back, I tell myself. *At least not in ways that pull me from God.*

There is a remembering God encourages. And that is to recall the great things He has done in my life. Moses told the Israelites in their escape from captivity in Egypt, "He is your God, who has done these great and awesome things for you which your eyes have seen" (Deuteronomy 10:21, NASB).

This kind of looking back draws me to God. He is my focus. Praising Him for what He has done strengthens my faith. Continuing to bring up past regret focuses on me. What I did wrong—not what God did right.

There are two ways to remember—but only one moves me next to God. I want to stay glued to His side in praise, recounting His rescues and goodness.

**Jesus, Your side, scarred for me, is the very place
I find refuge.** —Carol Knapp

Digging Deeper: 1 Chronicles 16:8–12;
Romans 8:31–34; Hebrews 7:25

Tuesday, August 6

STAR WORDS: Surprise—Gifts of Grace
**Each of you should use whatever gift you have
received to serve others, as faithful stewards of God's
grace in its various forms. —1 Peter 4:10 (NIV)**

In late summer, my pastor invited my friend
Mary and me to head Faith Formation at our

church. I eagerly embraced the opportunity to create meaningful curricula for study groups. By September, we had assembled books and videos ranging from learning about God's love through pets to contemporary titles on joy and the book of Ruth, as well as Advent and Lenten programs.

Though we were not expected to lead each session as well, by February no one else had volunteered. Worse yet, my coleader preferred the role of administrator. "I just don't know how to ask questions, Gail. And you're so good at it!" *Why me? Sigh.* I resigned myself to lead "Contemplative Knitting."

Despite my low energy and resentful attitude, I prepped for the hour-long meeting. Only one woman showed up in person; three more appeared online. We opened with a prayer, "...wherever two or three are gathered in Your name..." After a brief video, the ladies began to share both their fiber arts and their prayer practices.

Their stories touched me. One woman, a new American, described meeting a homeless man who needed a blanket. She began to crochet. Over the next few weeks, coworkers offered her yarn for her prayerful project. Eventually, she draped her crocheted afghan over the chilled man's shoulders. Her story made my eyes prickle with tears. Only then did I realize that I "led" this group not to teach, but to learn more love from these grace-filled women.

Divine Teacher, grant me the grace to learn from others, especially when I'm leading.
—Gail Thorell Schilling

Wednesday, August 7

Love is patient....—1 Corinthians 13:4 (NIV)

My friend's new puppy, Luna, ran to me as I walked through the door, excitedly jumping about my legs.

"OK, Luna," I said, not petting her. I'm allergic to dogs, so touching her would result in red, itchy blotches. I was also not in the mood for anyone's affection. The news and general condition of the world weighed heavily on me that week and I just wanted to be left alone.

My boys and I were staying in our friend's summer house for a few weeks, and this new little puppy obsessed over me despite my coldness.

"Go play with the boys," I said as I closed the bedroom door, leaving her whimpering outside. I lay on the bed, covered in blankets and anxiety. I couldn't even pray. Recent events had turned me off to the very word of Christianity. Even people I used to admire spiritually were a disappointment.

I understood that God's love could not be measured by the actions of human beings, but I still could feel myself pushing away from Him anyway.

My son opened the door, and Luna ran inside and jumped on my bed.

"Luna, get down," I yelled.

She just looked back at me with her big brown eyes. They were filled with love, unfazed by my shouting. She rested on my legs, and I finally just let her. Luna inched closer to my chest, and I wrapped my arms around her. I didn't even care about my allergies. In that moment, I was thankful for her unrelenting love and reminded of God's unrelenting love for me. As I felt my anxiety melt away, I knew that love was exactly what I needed.

Lord, thank You for Your unrelenting love, even when we don't recognize or appreciate it. —Karen Valentin

Digging Deeper: Genesis 28:15; 1 John 4:10

Thursday, August 8

For I am the LORD your God who takes hold of your right hand and says to you, Do not fear; I will help you. —Isaiah 41:13 (NIV)

I was sipping tea and enjoying a chocolate chip cookie before bedtime when it happened. I heard the crack and then felt the jagged edge of my molar. Years ago, when I had what I call my "monster filling" put in, the dentist said, "If you ever feel even a hint of pain here, don't hesitate. Come in immediately."

Broken teeth and fillings terrify me, so I felt faint as I ran to the bathroom mirror. My hand was shaking as I contorted my mouth to get a better look. My husband confirmed my fear. I'd broken the edge of my molar.

I Googled the problem, which was probably the worst thing I could have done. I tried to go to bed but spent the night worrying and praying. The next morning, I waited for hours for the dentist to open. I was the first call of the day and they got me right in.

The dentist came in and put his arm on my shoulder. "Hey! Don't worry, Sabra. We're going to fix you up," he said.

He took an X-ray to be sure and said, "Easy fix!"

In ten minutes, it was all better.

"You're a true hero," I said. "Seriously, if you ever wonder if your work matters, I'm here to say, you saved the day. You fixed a problem that kept me up all night."

He smiled and went to see the next patient, and I skipped out of there, relieved and feeling blessed.

Lord, thank You for the unsung heroes who make emergency appointments and fix broken teeth and calmly soothe our fears. —Sabra Ciancanelli

Digging Deeper: Psalm 34:4–5; Romans 8:28

Friday, August 9

For we are God's handiwork, created in Christ Jesus to do good works....—Ephesians 2:10 (NIV)

My husband, Wayne, and I have always enjoyed road trips. On a recent one, we'd stopped for gas in one of those stations that has a small grocery attached, along with a fast-food franchise. We took the opportunity to eat lunch. While we were enjoying our meal, I noticed a young man gazing at the overhead menu. I heard him sigh and turn away.

I wondered if he was hungry and couldn't afford the meal. After we finished eating, I stepped into the grocery area to pick up a couple of bottles of water for our trip. I saw the same young man again. He was wandering down the aisle, looking at the food items, checking the prices, and then returning them as if they were more than he could afford.

I finished our purchase and returned to the car, while Wayne finished up in the restroom. As I sat in the vehicle, I felt the Lord speak in my heart, telling me to give the young man some money. I didn't feel I could go up to a stranger and hand him money. It would be insulting. Then I felt a nudge to tell the young man I found this twenty-dollar bill on the ground and that it must be his. I wrestled with this, and before I knew it, Wayne returned and started the car. Ever since that day, I've regretted leaving without following God's lead. I missed a blessing, and I have a new determination to listen when the Lord speaks and act promptly.

Lord, please help me to not only listen to Your still, small voice but also to respond immediately. And please take care of the young man from the market.
—Debbie Macomber

Digging Deeper: Deuteronomy 28:1–2; Proverbs 2:1–5; James 1:22

Saturday, August 10

Therefore, my friends, I want you to know that through Jesus the forgiveness of sins is proclaimed to you. —Acts 13:38 (NIV)

Sometimes I can be selfish. While visiting family recently, my sister asked me to go with her to the funeral of our friend, Virginia. As I pondered her request, the decision I *thought* I had before me was to either honor my need for rest or to honor the life of Virginia, a person who had greatly helped me when I was ill with a brain tumor.

Sadly, I chose myself over Virginia. There were a lot of good reasons why I didn't attend the funeral. But the truth is I chose myself over her. Driving back home to Kentucky, this selfish decision weighed heavily on me. There was no way I could get a do-over, I thought.

But then I had a dream. In it, I was sitting on a stone bench at the church that we all attended. Suddenly, Virginia was walking past me guiding a horse. I knew instantly what it meant.

To change, we have to be ready to be thrown off our horse, like it is said to have happened to Paul on the road to Damascus. The dream was telling me that in God's Kingdom, do-overs are always possible. When we are ready to change, God will always provide a way where no way previously existed. I was freed of my guilt and filled with gratitude.

O God, how good and kind You are to us. Even in our selfishness, You show us mercy. Our cup overflows with gratitude. Amen. —Adam Ruiz

---

Sunday, August 11

**The God-setting-things-right that we read about
has become Jesus-setting-things-right for us.
—Romans 3:22 (MSG)**

Every Sunday night, my friend Anita and I enjoy a
soup-and-salad supper together. Then, we embark
on a trip to the United Kingdom, preferably to a
destination where there's been a recent spate of murder
and mayhem. We travel via the magic of television,
which means we get to enjoy a bowl of ice cream along
the way. Anita and I prefer British whodunits over
their American counterparts because there's less gore
and more gorgeous...scenery, that is. And who doesn't
love the musicality of a British accent?

As weird as it sounds, our Sunday night tradition
offers us a welcome respite. Some people relax by
watching the Hallmark Channel. We prefer losing
ourselves in stories that reflect the mystery and
unpredictability—and even the evil and inequity—
that's part of living in this fallen world. As mysteries
are solved, motives are unearthed, and justice is
meted out, our hearts and minds are calmed. As
the credits roll, it feels as though all's right with the
world, once more.

I've come to realize my apparent addiction to
British crime dramas is born out of a deep-seated

longing for good guys to win and bad guys to get what's coming to them. In other words, my heart craves Old Testament law more than New Testament grace—at least in regard to other people. I want justice for those who've hurt me but mercy for my own misdeeds. How grateful I am that God is God, and I am not.

Almighty God, this world can be a confusing, unjust, and evil place at times. But You are a God of love, order, and grace. Help transform my heart to become more like Yours. —Vicki Kuyper

Digging Deeper: Micah 6:8; Zechariah 7:9; Matthew 5:38–39

Monday, August 12

SEEKING CONNECTION IN THE BIBLE'S STORIES: Peter's Second Chance
I do believe; help my unbelief! —Mark 9:24 (NASB)

Peter has just spent the worst night of his life after Jesus's arrest in the Garden of Gethsemane. He has emphatically denied any association with Him. The same Jesus he has loved and followed for three years as one of the inner circle of twelve disciples. He had once boldly declared, "Lord...I will lay down my life for You" (John 13:37, NASB).

Peter's faith fled. Or did it? The continuing story shows Jesus, after His resurrection, offering Peter a second opportunity to declare his love and belief. Peter becomes a bold, unstoppable voice for Christ.

I went through a faith crisis recently with my husband, Terry's, cancer surgery on his remaining kidney. I was sleepless with worry the night before. Then upon arrival, the surgery was suddenly canceled; the doctor was ill.

Eight days later, when we tried again, I felt complete peace. My second chance at faith came when I'd read two Bible stories during the week. In one, Jesus in His hometown "could do no miracle there" (Mark 6:5, NASB1995) because of unbelief; in the other, belief brought the miracle and the Roman centurion's servant was healed (Luke 7:2–10). Unbelief blocks—and belief unlocks—what God is able to do.

I asked God to help me believe—even as I acknowledged His sovereignty in all things. Like Peter, absolute trust is what I most wanted. I waited through the surgery sheltered. It turned out to be a very tricky procedure, but the surgeon accomplished what he wanted and left Terry's kidney intact. He called it a miracle.

Jesus, have compassion on my weakness. You know in my heart of hearts I believe. —Carol Knapp

Digging Deeper: Luke 22:54–62; John 21:15–17

Tuesday, August 13

Old things have passed away; behold, all things have become new. —2 Corinthians 5:17 (NKJV)

Randolph County is repaving our road because it can no longer be fixed with patches. I stand at the edge of the road, admiring these artists in asphalt. I can feel the heat of the new paving from twenty feet away, and the vapors smell like a burnt ham.

A big truck filled with black, granulated asphalt dumps its load into what looks like a yellow army tank. Workers in lime-green vests and silver hard hats climb all over the machine, adjusting levers and wheels, and a thick mat of new pavement slides out from under the machine and lies like a heavy carpet over the old, tattered tar. Finally, compacting machines roll back and forth, smoothing out seams in the new roadway. A loud symphony of noise rises from all this activity, as stirring as Richard Rodgers' "Victory at Sea." I wave at the workers and give them a thumbs-up. They smile and tip their hats.

As I watch this blacktop beautification, I am thinking that some things in life can reach a point where they can no longer be fixed with patches. Like a friendship I have neglected too long. I may need to start all over, laying down fresh kindness, smoothing out misunderstandings, giving quality time and attention to my old friend.

Above all, I know that I need to bring the Lord into this relationship. He is our Common Friend, who alone can orchestrate our renewal.

I thank You, Lord, for opportunities to quietly start all over again with those I love.
—Daniel Schantz

Digging Deeper: Job 42:10;
Proverbs 17:17

In his hand is the life of every living thing and the breath of all mankind. —Job 12:10 (ESV)

Do you smell the lake, boy?" my friend Kendall asked the dog. "We're almost there."

Sport wagged his tail. Though Sport belonged to me, he had become fast friends with Kendall over this camping trip. We crested a hill, and the lake crept into view. The August sun glanced off the water's surface. I shaded my eyes as we descended. We stopped at the edge of the lake. Sport watched the water lap at the sand.

"Do you like to swim, boy?" Kendall asked Sport. Sport tilted his head.

"He's never been before," I said.

Kendall began to roll up his pants.

"Well, then, unclip him," Kendall said. He waded into the water.

"But Sport doesn't know how to swim," I said.

The water was above Kendall's knees now.

"He's a Labrador, right?" Kendall asked. "He knows how to swim."

Sport whined, pulling his leash toward Kendall. I held firm. I loved this dog. I'd raised him from a puppy, and I felt responsible for him. Could I trust Sport's instincts? Could I trust that God built him to swim? I bent down, holding Sport's face and looking into his eyes. Then I unhooked his leash. Sport stood still, unsure of his freedom. Then he bounded into the water, out of my reach.

As Sport pushed into the lake, he slowed. He flailed his paws, struggling against the water. His head dipped below the surface. My chest tightened. Then, Sport's head bobbed up. His tread synchronized, and his movements steadied. He began to swim. I watched my dog paddle out to my friend. Free-spirited, but held in the hands of his Creator.

Father, help me to trust in You, the Creator of all.
—Logan Eliasen

Digging Deeper: Psalm 147:9;
Matthew 6:26

Thursday, August 15

Is not my word like fire? saith Jehovah....
—Jeremiah 23:29 (ASV)

I answered an email, pushed back my chair, and scowled. I'd been dealing with a couple neighbors complaining about my cat, Stealth, saying he was killing their chickens and attacking their cats in the middle of the night. But each night shortly after dark, I had been locking him in the barn. Suddenly, I heard a dull thud from the living room below. Then a scratching from inside the woodstove.

I skipped down the stairs and heard the fluttering of a bird. Thank goodness it was August and the stove was cold. After draping a sheet over me and the stove so there wasn't any light to draw the bird,

I tossed an old pillowcase over the bird and pulled it out. Carefully, I cradled it, walked outside, and unwrapped the cloth. A baby flicker blinked at me, still trying to gather its wits after the fall down the chimney. In a few minutes, the bird flew free but I didn't; I kept rehearsing the false accusations.

Days later, I heard another thud. And the next day too. When the bird fell down the chimney for the sixth time, negativity ruled my thoughts. I lectured the baby before it flew away, "Why don't you learn?" My heart echoed the question, *Why hadn't I learned not to let myself get mired in anger and negativity? I should be focused on what the Lord says, not on what my neighbors are saying.*

After calling the chimney sweep, he shared that bugs move into chimneys by late summer, enticing the bug-eating birds. The answer was simple—for both my negative thoughts and the bugs, build a fire to burn them out.

Lord, I need the fire of Your Word to burn away the false accusations from my mind and help me replace them with thoughts of Your Word. Amen.
—Rebecca Ondov

Digging Deeper: Proverbs 4:23;
2 Corinthians 10:5

Friday, August 16

But let all who take refuge in you be glad.... Spread your protection over them....—Psalm 5:11 (NIV)

"What's Gracie barking at?" Julee said.

I jogged down to the apple tree. Our golden had treed a small, dark creature now curled at the top branch. *Probably a black squirrel,* I thought.

"C'mon, Cujo, you made your point."

Gracie pranced up the hill behind me, casting an occasional woof over her shoulder. Dogs. Always have to have the last word.

When it was time for bed, Gracie came over to me, limping slightly. She sat and showed me her paw. There were thin, silvery quills mixed in with her golden fur. That was a porcupine she'd treed, probably a youngster.

I dug out some pain pills she'd had for a strained back. I wanted her to sleep deeply enough so she wouldn't chew the quills and have one end up in her throat. I'd take her to the vet first thing tomorrow.

In the morning, Gracie's veterinarian, Dr. Phillips, said she would try to remove the quills without sedation. My whole body tensed as they led Gracie to the treatment room. I stood there holding her leash and begging God to please, please, please not let it hurt. It seemed like hours before they brought her back.

"How is she?"

"Amazing. She didn't flinch; she didn't even yelp. We must have pulled out thirty quills." She showed me the quills floating in a surgical dish. My knees went weak.

They sent Gracie home with antibiotics and a new toy.

Did God keep her in His arms while they took out the quills? I like to keep that image in my imagination and in my heart. I have a brave dog and a loving God.

God of love, You love all creatures. Thank You for loving Gracie. And even that porcupine, I guess.
—Edward Grinnan

Digging Deeper: Psalms 42:3–3, 91:9–11

Saturday, August 17

LORD Almighty, blessed is the one who trusts in you. —Psalm 84:12 (NIV)

My dad walked across his backyard, tall milkshake glasses clanking on a tray. "Mama made these," he said as he reached over the wall of the pool to hand them to twelve-year-old Isaiah and me.

Swimming at Mom and Dad's was different for us. My husband and I knew, when we moved from the home we'd raised our boys in, that we'd miss the pool in our own backyard. It had been our gathering place. Where we'd toss a football or dive for marbles with our boys. Where we'd split a watermelon right on warm deck boards or admire the stars while floating on tire tubes at night. Without this place of connection, would our relationships take a hit? It broke my heart to think of it.

After all, I'd grown up with a pool in the yard.

"I know how you'll miss your pool," my dad said when summer came close. "I can open my pool one last year." My parents' pool was weathered and weary, but it was filled with memories miles deep.

And dad opened the pool one last time.

Now I sipped a shake that tasted like my childhood as Dad disappeared to grab chairs for the deck. Soon he and Mom joined us while evening softened the sun.

"Want to play catch with us, Papa?" Isaiah asked when we'd finished our treat.

"Toss 'er here," Dad called from his chair.

Isaiah grinned and threw the football.

So often I want to close my fist around the things I cherish. But blessing, in the Lord's hands, flows deeper. Bringing more than I'd hoped there could be.

The breadth of Your blessing is more than I can fathom, Lord. I do trust in You. Amen.
—Shawnelle Eliasen
Digging Deeper: Isaiah 26:3–4

Sunday, August 18

Only fear the LORD and serve him faithfully with all your heart. For consider what great things he has done for you. —1 Samuel 12:24 (ESV)

Summer Sundays at the barn are typically peaceful but not this Sunday. Our horse, Snow, was struggling to breathe and had foam discharging from her nostrils. Our trainer advised us it was choke, an obstruction in the esophagus that is usually nonfatal, and to call the veterinarian. Although the trainer assured me Snow would be alright, I kept imagining the worst.

By the time our veterinarian, Dr. Woodall, arrived, I was mentally exhausted. His arrival brought calm and competence to our emergency. As I handed off Snow to Dr. Woodall, it dawned on me I had never once asked for the Lord's intercession. I silently prayed the Lord's Prayer because my cloudy mind struggled to formulate spontaneous prayer. I felt I could breathe again as the words "Thy will be done" floated from my inner voice. I was able to take direction from Dr. Woodall, and I held the tube as he unclogged Snow's esophagus. Dr. Woodall was the daily bread I prayed for. His skill was evident in not only helping my suffering 1,200-pound horse but also managing the scared, upset human who loves Snow.

As I walked into the back door of our home late that night, I began to inwardly reflect on the events of the day. Letting go of panic and truly relying on the Lord's will is sometimes hard for me. Despite this, I shall try to persist to rely on the Lord for my daily bread. Some days my daily bread is peace in the midst of turmoil.

Father, make me a blessing to those around me in deed and word, in both peaceful and challenging times. —Jolynda Strandberg

Digging Deeper: Acts 20:35; Hebrews 6:9–12; 1 Peter 1:10–12

Monday, August 19

SEEKING CONNECTION IN THE BIBLE'S STORIES: Job's Grief

And He said to them, "My soul is deeply grieved, to the point of death...." —Mark 14:34 (NASB)

Sitting shiva is a Jewish tradition following the funeral of a loved one. Shiva means seven. For seven days, friends come to share the sorrow of the bereaved family. In the Bible's book of Job, his three friends sat with him "seven days and seven nights, with no one speaking a word to him, for they saw that his pain was very great" (2:13, NASB).

Job has lost nearly everything. In his suffering, he wishes he'd never been born. As he expresses his deep pain following shiva, his friends have had enough and they jump in with advice and rebuke.

They say he must have done something wrong to have all this trouble, that he needs to seek God more, that he's impatient in his distress, and that they would be handling grief differently. Job ends up telling them, "Miserable comforters are you all!" (16:2, NASB).

My recently widowed sister-in-law and I have been having grief talks. She's read a book about how uncomfortable people can be with pain and suffering—wanting to hurry the grieving person through it. They give unsolicited advice and recite from their own experiences.

I'm embarrassed to find myself among Job's shiva friends—saying the wrong things in an attempt to comfort or cheer, giving ignorant input in the face of profound loss, making judgments. Job's friends were right to sit silently with him in the beginning. But they couldn't handle it once he got honest about his searing pain.

Jesus faced people's pain with them. He didn't minimize His own suffering. He is the One who can guide me in "sitting shiva" with those who grieve.

Lord, in the presence of others' sorrow, let me cry Your tears. —Carol Knapp

Digging Deeper: Psalm 77:1–15; John 11:35; Romans 8:31–39

Tuesday, August 20

He gave his life to purchase freedom for everyone. This is the message God gave to the world at just the right time. **—1 Timothy 2:6** (NLT)

I filled my online cart with all sorts of goodies that I had perfectly selected. Shopping has always been exhilarating to me. Since I was a little girl, I loved new school supplies or a heaping pile of new outfits and shoes. As an adult, I hit the purchase button on my favorite websites frequently.

It's easy to cover things up with clothes and makeup to hide some of the other things I'm grappling with. Maybe, this morning, I've taken offense to something someone said and let bitterness seep in. Yesterday, I had a harsh tongue with my family. For a lifetime, I have battled with pride and unforgiveness. And my fear of rejection may have cost me my last chance.

As I excitedly anticipated my package delivery, I began to think about how, in a similar way, God excitedly anticipates the delivery of me into His arms. Psalm 18:19 tells me that God does not just settle for or simply tolerate me but that he delights in me. He loves me, as I am, without ever bargaining the cost down. He paid full price at my worst. Maybe I am harder on myself than He would like sometimes. Knowing He purchased both me and my freedom is worth more than anything I can ever shop for here on Earth.

God, thank You for giving me love and grace that is bigger than all my flaws. Thank You for providing for all my deepest needs, freely and eternally.
—Nicole Garcia

Digging Deeper: 1 Corinthians 6:19–20; 1 Peter 1:18–19

Wednesday, August 21

Starting a quarrel is like breaching a dam; so drop the matter before a dispute breaks out.
—Proverbs 17:14 (NIV)

I tried to offer a listening ear as my sister told me details of her friend hurting her feelings. Finally, I interrupted. "Is this doing you or anyone else any good?"

"No," she answered, then started in again. "I don't think I did anything wrong; I don't know why she thinks I did."

"What does God think?" I asked.

"I think He's very happy with what I did."

"Good, then leave it at that."

"You're right. I should," she said, then picked right up where she'd left off.

"Let it drop. You're only hurting yourself." I knew my advice was easier said than done.

This exchange caused me to think about my daughter Rachel and her young dog, Piper. When Piper picks something up that's not good for her, Rachel says, "Leave it." Piper drops the item momentarily, then picks it up again and gnaws on it some more. Another "leave it" and Piper drops it, then quickly retrieves it, shaking it between her teeth. After several rounds of this, Piper finally lets it go. Piper's reluctance to drop something that isn't good for her is like what I and my sister have been guilty of.

Not long after my conversation with my sister, frustration swirled in my mind as I rehashed something someone close to me had done weeks before. *Why can't they understand how much that hurt me? Should I tell them?* Suddenly, I heard my sister's voice and saw Piper's image.

Leave it. Let it go, I heard God say to my heart. This time I obeyed.

Lord, when I hear You in my heart, telling me to "drop the matter,"

help me to obey. It feels so much better when I do.
—Kim Taylor Henry

Digging Deeper: Psalm 37:8; Proverbs 20:22, 24:29

Thursday, August 22

Call to me and I will answer you, and will tell you great and hidden things that you have not known.
—Jeremiah 33:3 (ESV)

We are so lucky to live in a tiny community that has everything we need, including the hospital my kids were born in, which we can almost see from our house thanks to our hilly neighborhood.

The kids love hearing the stories of being born as we pass the hospital, which we often do on the way to the store or school. I tell them about which window was theirs, how mad they were when they first arrived, and even how one of them, who shall remain nameless, soaked everyone just after arriving.

After a few dozen rounds of their own stories, they started to ask who was in that hospital now. We talked about new mamas who might be waiting for their babies to arrive, the dads who were probably a little nervous, and the doctors who were bustling about.

Now, when we pass the hospital, instead of asking about their own stories, they say a quick prayer for the people inside. *Help the babies like their new blankets. Keep the mamas safe. Help the babies not to be scared.*

What a perfect way to learn to fold prayer into your daily life, pausing to ponder landmarks as you pass them. Even when the kids aren't in the car, I find myself sending up a quick prayer for everyone inside that building and welcoming those new babies as they start their long, fun journey.

Lord, let my prayers flow freely as I go about my day. Let me take every chance I have to worship You and declare Your glory. —Ashley Kappel

Digging Deeper: Matthew 6:9–13; Ephesians 6:18; 1 Thessalonians 5:17

Friday, August 23

Be still, and know that I am God; I will be exalted among the nations, I will be exalted in the earth. —Psalm 46:10 (NIV)

I was up early in the morning but decided to stay in bed to pray and meditate. I had a lot on my mind. My transitional pastor position at the church where I had been working was ending by year end. "Lord, where do we go next?" I prayed. "God, show us the way we need to go." While praying, I dozed off. Then I heard myself saying loudly over and over, "Be still, and know that I am God."

The sound of my own voice reciting these words woke me up. I reached for my Bible and read Psalm 46. I wasn't sure what to make of the moment or the message. What was God trying to say to me? Was this some kind of answer to my prayers? I shared my experience with my wife and a close friend and no one else.

As I searched for a new position, the words, "Be still, and know that I am God" gave me peace and the assurance that all was going to be well.

Five weeks before my assignment ended, I received a call out of the blue. It was a church in Naples, Florida, seeking an interim pastor. Someone had referred me to the search committee. It was the right church at the right time. I just needed to be still and trust God.

Lord, teach us to be still and lean on Your presence and promises for us. —Pablo Diaz

Digging Deeper: Psalm 131:12; Isaiah 32:17

Saturday, August 24

When we put bits into the mouths of horses to make them obey us, we can turn the whole animal. —James 3:3 (NIV)

My five siblings and I couldn't be more diverse. Politically, we are Democrats, Republicans, and anarchists. Spiritually, we are Christians, atheists, and New Age agnostics. We live in California, Colorado, and Oklahoma. No two of us agree on most subjects, and, in the way of siblings—especially siblings raised in volatile households like ours was— we either fight it out or break it off. At any given time, at least one sibling isn't talking to another.

Phone calls are tricky to navigate without angry disagreement, hostility-fraught silences (my usual cowardly tactic), or the resentment-charged account of a fight that just happened between the sibling I'm talking to and another. So, two of my sisters recently took to texting only to avoid phone conversations erupting into rage. One of them reported enthusiastically that texting has not only eradicated the fights but significantly improved their relationship.

"I get to read it before I hit Send and delete whatever might make her mad, so that's good. But the best part is that I just like her more via text. And it seems like she likes me."

My sister's report reminded me of an analogy Jesus's brother James uses in discussing how hurtful our words can be, so we talked about that: how texting can apparently bridle their mean tongues and, like a bridle on a horse, direct us to better places in our relationships. It was exciting to witness God working, between us all, to achieve his goal for his children: love.

Father, I love how You use everything—technological developments, phone conversations, Scripture—to reach us. Help me use every opportunity You devise to do Your work. —Patty Kirk

Digging Deeper: Deuteronomy 6:4–9; Psalm 39

Sunday, August 25

Before I formed you in the womb I knew you, before you were born I set you apart.... —Jeremiah 1:5 (NIV)

"I can finally announce," I declared on social media, "I'm going to be on Food Network for a baking challenge!"

The show had taped months before, and although I didn't win, I was still excited for the upcoming episode. The response to my post was overwhelming, and everyone assumed I won.

"You'll have to watch and see," I'd answer.

I hated to disappoint their belief in me but was still happy about what they'd see. While I thought my cookies were a mess after the ninety-minute challenge, the judges' comments recognized my ambitious vision and my artistic ability, and they enjoyed the taste.

The day the show aired, my excitement quickly soured. My cookies looked worse than I remembered, I was shown running around like a lunatic, and they edited out all of the positive comments from the judges. I was mortified. I wanted to disappear as I heard my phone buzzing with calls and messages. This was not the image I wanted to put out there of myself.

When I finally read my messages, my friends and family made it clear. They already have a true image of who I am, and nothing would change that. They were proud, not because of a win or beautiful cookies; they were simply proud of me for being just that: me. They reminded me to see myself through God's eyes, not the camera lens of self-doubt.

Lord, help me to love and know what You've created me to be. Instead of focusing on an image for others to see, help me to live authentically and focus on who I am in You. —Karen Valentin

Digging Deeper: 1 Samuel 16:7; Ephesians 2:10

SEEKING CONNECTION IN THE BIBLE'S STORIES: Lydia's Hospitality
...I was a stranger, and you invited Me in....
—Matthew 25:35 (NASB)

Lydia is someone I'd like to know. Not that I'm even close to being a businesswoman. She was a successful "seller of purple fabrics" (Acts 16:14, NASB) and an early convert to Christianity. Only the wealthy wore garments of purple—and Lydia herself seems to have been well off.

She came from a Greek city, Thyatira, which is now part of Turkey. Somewhere along the way, she moved to Philippi, a Roman colony in Greece. When the Apostle Paul arrived in town and went to the river on the Sabbath for an open-air meeting, Lydia was among the women gathered there.

Though a non-Jew, she is called a "worshiper of God" (16:14). As Paul spoke of Jesus who came as Savior for the world, "the Lord opened her heart to respond" (16:14). She and all her household were baptized. Her next act was to persuade Paul and his companions to come be guests in her home.

Thus began the first house church in Europe—which grew and grew and generously supported Paul's ministry. What I love about Lydia is she practiced "open heart, open home."

Our son's high-school friend lived with us through an unstable home situation. Now with a family of his own, he's told me how it helped him then and helps him still. This continues to a second generation with our granddaughter's teen friend—fending for herself far too young—in need of welcome. She's always included in our family gatherings—even seeking to drive the distance and spend her own time with us or to call and ask for prayer.

Lydia and I share a love for homegrown hospitality that affects lives beyond our own doorstep.

Jesus, opening my heart and home in Your name is an act of worship. —Carol Knapp

Digging Deeper: Luke 10:1–7; Romans 12:9–13; Colossians 3:9–11

Tuesday, August 27

Hast thou not known? . . . the everlasting God, the LORD, the Creator of the ends of the earth, fainteth not, neither is weary? there is no searching of his understanding. —Isaiah 40:28 (KJV)

Our annual Zimbabwe trip was just days away, and I had a new camera, which was a top priority in recording our work. It was fancier than my worn-out camera, and I knew I had a lot to learn. My plan was to load instructions from the Internet and use the twenty-four-hour plane trip to study my new toy.

I was in a huge rush when I printed the forty-page manual, and I didn't give it a glance until we were in the air.

"Ohhhh, I am truly the dumbest person in the universe," I wailed softly to David, as I pulled the stack of papers out of my bag and saw they were for another camera.

Once in Zimbabwe, I found my new camera similar enough to my old one, and I was managing well.

At breakfast, a clearly distressed lady approached our table. She introduced herself as a writer on assignment with an international children's organization. There to report the plight of Africa's AIDS orphans, she had been given a complicated camera with no manual. With tears in her eyes, she said, "I hoped your camera was the same and you could help, but I see it's not."

I was stunned. "Can you give me the make of your camera?"

Within minutes, I was back from our room, papers in hand. They were, of course, the exact instructions she needed to operate her camera...saving lives in the process.

I wasn't really surprised. That's simply the way the God I've come to know works.

Father God, You surely delight in surprises. I am humbled when You choose me to be a part of Your magic. Thank You. —Pam Kidd

Digging Deeper: Ecclesiastes 11:5; Nahum 1:7

Wednesday, August 28

Finally, brethren, whatsoever things are true, whatsoever things are honest, whatsoever things are just, whatsoever things are pure, whatsoever things are lovely, whatsoever things are of good report; if there be any virtue, and if there be any praise, think on these things. —Philippians 4:8 (KJV)

My friend Honey was like an extra grandmother to me. She died several years ago, but I loved her dearly and still think of her nearly every day. She was the most positive person I've ever known.

One thing Honey loved was an uplifting scripture or inspirational quotation. She kept them everywhere: on her fridge, on her mirrors, on little sticky notes or index cards all over her house. She had notebooks filled with verses or wise words she'd copied down by hand.

I'd always assumed that Honey surrounded herself with these encouraging thoughts because she was such a positive person. But after she died, her granddaughter Casie told me something that surprised me: "Grandmom didn't write these things down everywhere because she was so positive; she was so positive because she wrote those things down everywhere."

Casie had become Honey's caregiver before she died, and she'd seen Honey suffer in the final months of her life. She witnessed Honey's struggle to stay positive and how she relied on the Bible to stay focused on Jesus. Honey aimed her attention on "whatsoever things were lovely." She didn't just instinctively see the sunny side, but "[took] captive every thought to make it obedient to Christ" (2 Corinthians 10:5, NIV).

Nowadays, I often have a verse or two taped to my computer screen or my mirror because Honey taught me that as someone "thinks within himself, so he is" (Proverbs 23:7, NASB).

Lord, train me to set my mind on what is good.
—Ginger Rue

Digging Deeper: Romans 12:2; 2 Timothy 1:7

Thursday, August 29

But in the church I would rather speak five intelligible words to instruct others than ten thousand words in a tongue. —1 Corinthians 14:19 (NIV)

I like acronyms. When I lived in Wisconsin in the 1980s and '90s, I formed a women's group called SWILL. It stood for *Southeastern Wisconsin Interesting Ladies League.* A woman in that group formed her own group called FOSSILS, which stood for *Friends Over Seventy Seasoned in Life Society.* One of my pilot friends told me about GUMPS, something every pilot with a commercial license knows to check before landing. GUMPS stands for G = gasoline; U = undercarriage or landing gear; M = mixture of gas and air; P = propeller RPMs (make sure the prop is at maximum pitch); S = seat belts on.

Acronyms help me remember things. One day, I decided I needed an acronym for readjusting my sometimes do-I-have-to-go attitude before I leave for church on Sunday mornings. It's usually a warm, wonderful sunny day and the thought of sitting inside has me dragging my feet. So I came up with the acronym PAGES, which stands for P = prayerful thoughts; A = attitude; G = giving spirit; E = envelope contribution; S = servitude. As I walk out the door determined to pray with a good attitude and a giving spirit, ready to serve where needed, I know that all my PAGES are in order and somehow church becomes a sacred experience. Hey, maybe SACRED stands for *Sincere and Creatively Respectful Each Day.*

Lord, thank You for ways to keep my mind and body in tune with my heart and soul when it comes to worshipping You. —Patricia Lorenz

Digging Deeper: Proverbs 16:1; 2 Thessalonians 2:16–17

Friday, August 30

Each of you should use whatever gift you have received to serve others, as faithful stewards of God's grace in its various forms. —1 Peter 4:10 (NIV)

After monsoon rains fell in late August, bringing necessary moisture to the Sonoran Desert, my granddaughter, Juniper, and I decided to walk to a nearby park. I paid little attention to the moisture-drenched air or to her toddler chatter. I was pondering an upcoming work deadline that had me paralyzed with doubts because I felt unqualified for the project. Surely someone with more skills was needed. Or more creativity.

Unconcerned with my inner turmoil, Juniper pointed to a six-inch nest that had been tossed on the sidewalk. Besides three types of grasses, the unknown bird had woven a length of string, a paper straw wrapper, and a ripped T-shirt seam into the nest. The intricate design was strengthened with a layer of mud on the bottom.

At the playground, Juniper gathered stones, piling them in precise fashion. Casting aside brown rocks, she chose white ones, the cleaner, the better. Juniper balanced a second layer, patiently replacing stones when they tumbled down. "Making a castle," she declared when I questioned her. With careful thought and deliberation, Juniper created her little house using what she had available.

Grasses. A paper straw wrapper. Stones. Watching my granddaughter, I realized the answer to my work situation was not going to be found in some unknown source but by using the gifts God had placed inside me. With a little creativity, I knew I could finish the job.

Master Designer, as I create at work and at home, help me focus on what I have, rather than what I lack.
—Lynne Hartke

Digging Deeper: Matthew 5:16; 1 Corinthians 3:9–11; Ephesians 2:10

Saturday, August 31

REMEMBERING GRATITUDE:
An Encourager's Influence

Therefore encourage one another and build each other up....—1 Thessalonians 5:11 (NIV)

When I applied for a coveted position in healthcare, a friend referred me to a man named Henry. He held a degree in teaching but currently worked at home doing word processing. Henry was known for making people look pretty on paper in the form of professional resumes. He transformed my cut-and-taped notes into a work of art, both in the layout and the words he upgraded.

I'd done a bunch of things in my career, but I never dreamed of calling any of it coordinating, motivating, and orchestrating. Henry shrugged off my amazement, instead affirming my accomplishments. "I just put a few flowers in a vase," he said. "You've got that other stuff."

When I began to write articles for medical and nursing journals, a tumor affecting my vision meant scribbling content on a legal pad. Henry elevated that as well. The day came when my vision was restored, but my revered spiffer-upper was moving away to accept a college teaching job.

There could be no more articles without Henry's touch. My typing skills were marginal, and I knew nothing about working a word processor. Besides, my brain worked pen to paper, not fingers to machine. Henry offered to teach me the technical. "You'll access a different part of your brain," he insisted. "Your writing will improve tenfold."

Today, when I mentor someone, I try to encourage them as Henry did me—and as Paul did the Thessalonians in their own uncertain days. In my mind, I'm smiling when the long-ago words of Henry pass my lips. "That's just a little trick of the trade," I tell them. "You've got that other stuff."

Encouragers are the lifeblood of our lives, dear Lord. Thank You. —Roberta Messner

YOU WERE CALLED TO PEACE

1 _____

2 _____

3 _____

4 _____

5 _____

6 _____

7 _____

8 _____

9 _____

10 _____

11 _____

12 _____

13 _____

14 _____

15 _____

16 _____

17 _____

18 _____

19 _____

20 _____

21 _____

22 _____

23 _____

24 _____

25 _____

26 _____

27 _____

28 _____

29 _____

30 _____

31 _____

September

In his days may the righteous flourish, and peace abound, till the moon be no more!

—Psalm 72:7 (ESV)

Sunday, September 1

To every thing there is a season, and a time to every purpose under the heaven. —Ecclesiastes 3:1 (KJV)

Recently, I've been reflecting on God's perfect timing in the journey of my career.

After graduating from seminary in 1977, I served as a pastor of five wonderful churches for a total of thirty-three years. Then, at age fifty-nine, I founded and directed The Institute of Life Purpose at my alma mater, Mercer University, for another ten years. As I approached my seventieth birthday, I began to feel it was time to retire. Two years ago, my wife, Beth, and I entered into this new season of life together. It has been a wonderful new chapter!

I continue to teach one course at Mercer. And I am enjoying my favorite avocation as a writer. Most important, I continue to have frequent conversations with Mercer students at the coffee shop. I also spend more time visiting with my grandchildren, participating in my many hobbies, and sleeping a little longer in the mornings.

However, I must admit that this new transition has also been tinged with fear and anxiety. How will I adjust to this new season of retirement? How will I handle the loss of identity, the fear of growing older, and the apprehension of exploring new territory? I have realized once again that no new chapter of life can be entered without the flutters of fear. We are all complex creatures of conflicting emotions. We must trust that God made us this way for good reasons.

When we walk faithfully with God, He will turn every chapter into a worthy venture. And the Good Shepherd will always lead us to green pastures and still waters (Psalm 23:2).

Father, in the midst of transition and change, may I feel Your hand upon my shoulder and hear Your calm voice of reassurance. May I know that You are with me. Amen. —Scott Walker

Digging Deeper: Psalms 27:1, 91:1–2; 2 Timothy 1:7

Labor Day, Monday, September 2

...for there is a reward for your labor.
—Jeremiah 31:16 (JPS)

My colleague Joan worked as a personal assistant for one of the worst bosses I'd ever seen. I was aware of their ongoing interactions because it was a very small office, but I tried not to pay attention. I did not want to embarrass Joan, who was often given directions rudely, sometimes berated for a minor mistake or a misunderstanding that could have been the boss's doing, and often treated as if she was incompetent or stupid.

Joan was a calm, good-natured woman who astonished me with her capacity to let abuse wash past her without it seeming to disturb her serenity in any way. I wanted to ask how she did it, but that would have meant letting her know I witnessed the humiliation I was sure she was enduring on a daily basis. Instead, I simply watched out of the corner of my eye and winced for her.

I had almost reached the point when I would have had to say something, but then I got my answer by accident. Joan was typing the boss's correspondence one afternoon when the boss interrupted her, tossing a heavy folder onto Joan's desktop with a loud bang. When Joan looked up, the boss said, "That's what you have to do next."

Joan smiled, and corrected gently, "No, that's what I *get* to do next."

In that moment, I realized that Joan had chosen to see her unpleasant working situation as an opportunity.

It made me wonder if I'd been missing an opportunity in my own life to respond to hostility with gentleness and to start thinking of the things I *have* to do as the things I *want* to do.

If I can tell myself that even the most unpleasant situation is a gift from You, Source of All That Is Good, I can do it with a light heart.
—Rhoda Blecker

Digging Deeper: Deuteronomy 30:9; 2 Chronicles 34:12

Tuesday, September 3

Amen, I say to you, whoever does not accept the kingdom of God like a child will not enter it.
—Luke 18:17 (NABRE)

This morning when driving to work, I listened to a sports talk show.

Today, the hosts were arguing about a recent school board decision that impacted their school-aged children. As I listened to their heated debate, I began to notice that, along with the radio hosts, other people around me seemed upset too. I was surrounded by people who were full of anger, each for their own reason. Only they were in their cars, weaving in and out of traffic and driving carelessly.

Then something surprising happened. Driving along a boulevard, I noticed that all the cars in front of me had suddenly stopped. I wondered why. Peering over my steering wheel, I saw a large number of geese casually walking from the grassy area where they had been to the other side where a pond awaited them. As they serenely walked in front of us, I realized how trusting the geese were and how respectful all the drivers had become.

And then something lovely happened inside me. As I watched the geese, I gave thanks for their appearance: "Slow down," they seemed to say. "Enjoy the sunrise," they encouraged.

As I continued my morning commute, I felt an urge to be more like the geese. They were "in the moment," whereas I had been driving but stressing about unfinished work, lamenting an unfortunate phone call, and distracted by angry voices and drivers until I became one of them. But the geese had changed me. I now knew that this moment was as perfect as it needed to be. This realization allowed me to accept the day as it unfolded, knowing that infinite possibilities to love awaited me. It was going to be a glorious day.

> **May our life be pleasing to You and give You glory. Amen.** —Adam Ruiz

Digging Deeper: Luke 2:13-14; John 16:33; Galatians 5:22–25

Wednesday, September 4

He giveth power to the faint; and to them who have no might he increaseth strength. —Isaiah 40:29 (KJV)

The TV was blaring where I waited for my car. Earlier, the car's emergency light had caused me to forgo lunch for an oil change. Piles of to-dos waited in my office. Worse, I was dreading an afternoon appointment with a high-maintenance person with whom I cochaired a committee.

God, I'm weary. Give me the strength to weather this day, I was half-praying when the smell came. It was a mixture of old grease, tire rubber, with a bit of car exhaust thrown in.

And suddenly I was back in the old gas station of my childhood. Mr. Tillery, whose name hung over the door, was there, a plug of tobacco tucked back in his jaw. He grinned, as I slid back the lid of his old chest cooler. I stuck my head inside, trying to decide between a grape Nehi or an RC Cola. My grandfather's deep laugh filled the station as he suddenly swooped me up in the air. "Time to test your strength, lad," he said, plopping me on the grimy counter in front of Tillery's strength machine. There, for only a penny, you could grip the handle and measure your strength. Squeezing with all my might, the needle barely hit ten. Now Pa took hold, and the needle shot all the way up to 250. Everyone was cheering, but Pa looked at me with a serious eye. "Don't be discouraged, son; strength takes practice."

"Mr. Kidd," the attendant was calling, "car's ready." And I was back in the present, driving toward my office. "Test Your Strength Daily" had been written across that old machine. Right now, it might as well have been a Post-it note from God because I was feeling stronger by the minute.

Father, Your encouragement is my strength.
—Brock Kidd

Digging Deeper: 1 Chronicles 29:12; Isaiah 40:21

Thursday, September 5

Your Father knows what you need before you ask him. This, then, is how you should pray: "Our Father in heaven..." —Matthew 6:8–9 (NIV)

Fingering rosaries. Lighting candles. Repeating phrases. Around the world, there are so many ways to pray. Does God hear my informal intercessions alongside others'?

Recently, I've been praying especially for my friend Tatiana. Her Christian traditions and life experiences as an adult immigrant are different from mine, yet we have a heart connection. Her home country is currently war torn. Her elderly mother, called Zina, lives in a particularly vulnerable city. I've met Zina several times on her visits here to the States. I fondly remember her smile.

Tatiana is worried about Zina, virtually homebound after a stroke. Is she safe? Can she be relocated? If plans could be put in place, would Zina move willingly or insist she intends to hunker down?

One evening, I emailed a message of support, as I had been since the situation worsened. "Praying you will not be living in fear, as hard as that is," I wrote.

She quickly responded, "Thank you so much. And please pray for my mother, Zinaida." I'd never heard anyone use the longer name. I didn't see it as important until an hour later, when Tatiana sent another short message, providing Zina's last name also.

Why do I need this extra information? I wondered. I was confident that God knew which Zina—Zinaida—I was praying for. He knows every detail of our hearts. Even so, I presented her many-syllabled name to our Father in heaven. Even now, I light a candle and plead for her in her precarious situation.

God of mercy, I trust in You to know our hearts and hear our prayers, whether they are formal or informal, precise or imprecise, perfect or muddled.
—Evelyn Bence

Digging Deeper: Ephesians 1:16–19, 6:18

Carry each other's burdens, and in this way you will fulfill the law of Christ. —Galatians 6:2 (NIV)

As a social worker serving youth in foster care, I often discuss secondary trauma with my team. A year into my current position, I had witnessed the trauma of children and families on my caseload—domestic abuse, neglect, drug exposure. Yet I wasn't aware of a time that I had personally experienced secondary trauma.

One day recently, I sat with my husband, Anthony, watching a documentary featuring a favorite pop star. In addition to a huge music career, this artist had found success acting in film and television. As a child, she was cast in a popular sitcom as an abused child. The documentary featured a montage of scenes from this role, and in one, the evidence of her mother's abuse was revealed—a burn on the girl's back in the shape of an iron.

I felt my shoulders tighten and my eyebrows furrow. I couldn't understand why this scene affected me so deeply at this point in my life. Later, after I had processed my emotions, I realized I had experienced secondary trauma. Though a fictional account, I had just seen the evidence of the abuse and trauma my foster kids knew all too well. My body and brain had made a clear connection.

The next day in a meeting with coworkers, we began with a check-in, and I felt safe to share my experience. After I shared, my coworkers shared their own stories of secondary trauma while watching television, listening to music, reading magazines—at times they least expected. We discussed our ongoing need for self-care and each other's support.

I felt understood and cared for among these people who were so willing to help carry my burdens.

Lord, thank You for my circle of community, full of understanding, care, and support.
—Carla Hendricks

Digging Deeper: Hebrews 6:10–11, 10:23–25

Saturday, September 7

Look...one who brings good news...
—Nahum 1:15 (NIV)

I was afraid to open my Bible. My husband and I were in a dispute over a driveway easement with a neighbor, and our quarrel was coming to a head. Throughout the ordeal, we'd prayed for reason and justice to prevail, and we also prayed for our neighbor. We prayed that we would always show grace, even when we didn't feel it. We vowed to act in a godly fashion and not let our anger run unchecked. Think. Pray. Then speak. But nothing in our situation was changing. I knew I should continue to consult God first in all things, but, honestly, I didn't want to read about turning the other cheek. We'd been turning it for two years!

To get my mind off of the situation, I grabbed the paper and opened to the crossword. Goosebumps rose when I read 30-down: "Located between Micah and Habakkuk."

Precious Father, I get Your clue!

I dropped the paper and grabbed my Bible. I opened to Nahum and read of his vision God sent as a message to comfort Judah, God's people, from their ongoing battle with Nineveh. "The LORD is good, a refuge in times of trouble. He cares for those who trust in him" (Nahum 1:7, NIV). My heart lifted, and my soul rejoiced. The passage spoke of peace, strength, reassurance, victory!

Eventually, our disagreement was resolved amicably. But not before I knew who was behind this victory.

Lord, You are slow to anger and great in power (Nahum 1:3). Regardless of the human battles we face, in You the victory is already won. Lord, I trust YOU! —Erika Bentsen

Digging Deeper: 2 Samuel 22:3; Psalms 73:28, 91:2

Sunday, September 8

The eternal God is your dwelling place, and underneath are the everlasting arms. —Deuteronomy 33:27 (ESV)

The women, who sat around the table, gasped when Shelli opened the box of necklaces the church had purchased for the children. Instead of being neatly piled, all the string necklaces with the plastic crosses had become one big, tangled ball. I laughed, saying, "I can get them untangled in no time. When I worked in the mountains on horse pack trips, I was constantly unknotting ropes."

Carefully, I lifted the mess out of the box and entwined my fingers in the center. The tangled mess reminded me of what my life looked like nearly two decades ago, after the devastation of a divorce when I had no skill with which to make a living.

Gently I added tension by separating my hands as I shook the ball. A couple strands fell. I untangled the outside strands as far as I could. The tension was much like when I moved to a new town, where I hardly knew a soul, had almost no money, and took an unfamiliar, high-stress job. Through days of persistent struggle and prayer followed by nights of crying myself to sleep, God had guided me on how to straighten out the mess I was in—one strand at a time.

The gals watched in awe as with a simple twist here and a shake there, the knotty ball started to look like necklaces. Untangling the mess appeared easy, but developing this skill had taken years of patience and practice—not unlike what it had been to create my new life.

Lord, thank You for carrying me and guiding me to help turn my life right-side up. Amen.
—Rebecca Ondov

Digging Deeper: Romans 6:18; Hebrews 2:14–18

Put on the whole armor of God, that you may be able to stand against the schemes of the devil.
—Ephesians 6:11 (ESV)

I was on a virtual work meeting when I spotted the stink bug crawling back and forth on the cord of my monitor. He balanced himself beautifully, entertaining me, as I listened along to a presentation.

I love stink bugs; their cute little bodies, shaped like a shield, always make me think of armor, and today as I listened to my colleagues talk about key performance indicators, I kept an eye on the little stink bug exploring my desk.

A coworker said a rude remark, another raised her voice, and I felt myself tense up. The meeting went downhill quickly. Working from home can be challenging, and sometimes it seems the screens between us make for more contentious meetings.

I looked around the squares of my fellow workers' faces—all showing discomfort as another coworker took control and gently and calmly brought us back to peaceful dialogue. The stink bug climbed the edge of my monitor and put his little face right into the camera, looking into the lens as if he were investigating my world.

I leaned in to see if I could see his little face, and the stink bug stayed for a moment or two before he went back to balancing on the cord again, taking with him the drama of the meeting and leaving me with a better perspective.

Lord, Your Word is my shield. Thank You for reminding me that sometimes all I need is to refocus away from life's uncomfortable moments to see the larger purpose of what really matters. —Sabra Ciancanelli

Digging Deeper: 2 Corinthians 4:18; James 1:12

Tuesday, September 10

Many are the plans in a person's heart, but it is the LORD's purpose that prevails. —Proverbs 19:21 (NIV)

Several unexpected appointments had derailed my to-do list, and I was trying not to be crabby as I waited at the stoplight. That's when I heard the unmistakable sound of skidding tires and crushed steel. I looked up at the intersection a split second after the accident happened and saw an elderly woman step out of her car, clutching her chest.

I immediately jumped out of my vehicle to see if she needed help. She told me her chest hurt, so I grabbed my cell phone and dialed 911. I kept asking her if she was OK, and she looked up at me with wide eyes and said, "Can I just hug you?"

Without an ounce of hesitation, I wrapped my arms around her and held her tight. She clung to me in that busy intersection, as people drove around us, and I could feel her start to calm. Eventually, her chest pain went away, and we were able to talk to the other driver, who was unharmed. I waited with her for the police to arrive and helped her untangle her thoughts as she told her side of the story. Eventually, I wasn't needed, and I drove off toward home.

As the situation began to settle in my heart, I became aware of the series of events that led me to that moment. Nothing had gone as I had hoped that day. If my plans had succeeded, I would have missed a Divine Appointment, one that turned out to be more important than anything else I had planned.

Lord, sometimes I feel frustrated when things don't go as I hope. Help me to remember that Your plans are better than mine and nothing is accidental in Your kingdom. —Gabrielle Meyer

Digging Deeper: Proverbs 16:9; Ephesians 3:1

Wednesday, September 11

Surely there is a future, and your hope will not be cut off. —Proverbs 23:18 (NRSV)

The streets in New York were painfully empty those first few days after the World Trade Center was destroyed. The downtown skyline was missing its usual punctuation points. Police cars and emergency vehicles passed, sirens blaring. And signs went up all over town with faces of the victims: "Missing..." "Last seen on the 97th floor..."

Everyone traded stories, seeking some signs of reassurance, some sense that God could be present here, when things didn't make any sense anymore. One friend told us, with incredulity, how that morning her husband would have been at his office on the upper floors of the World Trade Center, but she had a meeting to attend and because of it he had to take their son to nursery school. An errand that miraculously saved his life. They were both grateful, even as he mourned the deaths of his colleagues.

The story that resonated most with me came from a dad whose son had started his first day of high school only blocks from the towers. Disaster struck in that first hour of classes and the kids had to be sent home. The only way was to walk. No subways or buses were running.

A streetwise fourteen-year-old, he knew his way home, but the horror was haunting. He started walking. He'd gone for a mile or two when he saw his father coming toward him the other way. They embraced, and the son said, "I knew you'd come."

I knew you'd come. Isn't that the sort of phrase that lodges in all our minds when tragedy strikes? We know, despite the sorrow, despite the pain, that our Father will come.

May You come to me, Father, when I need You most.
—Rick Hamlin

Digging Deeper: Psalm 23:1; Isaiah 40:31; Romans 12:12

Thursday, September 12

Being confident of this, that he who began a good work in you will carry it on to completion until the day of Christ Jesus. —Philippians 1:6 (NIV)

When I read my son's official ADHD diagnosis, it felt as if I'd passed down a curse. His struggles in school were the same I'd faced when I was his age.

"He's too far behind," his teacher had said in a meeting that left me in hysterics. "He'll have to repeat third grade and go on medication if he returns."

There was little known about ADHD when I was a child, and I assumed the grown-ups who called me "stupid" in frustration were correct. But here I was over thirty years later, and still no one could help or truly see my son.

I spent the summer focusing on the blessing instead of the curse. I reminded him of my own accomplishments, knowing that despite the challenges, my ADHD helped me to succeed as well. I prayed his new school would focus on the amazing things his uniquely wired brain could do, instead of what it could not.

Days after school began, I tensed up as his teacher approached me.

"Your son has such a beautiful soul," she said, as my body relaxed, knowing she was an answer to my prayer, "and the way he approaches a problem is an amazing thing to watch."

Lord, help me to navigate this life, fully confident in the knowledge that You are my creator. Help me be true to the vision You had when You gave me life, even if some fail to see it. —Karen Valentin

Digging Deeper: Psalm 139:14; Isaiah 40:31

Friday, September 13

But one thing I do: forgetting what lies behind and straining forward to what lies ahead, I press on toward the goal for the prize of the upward call of God in Christ Jesus. —Philippians 3:13–14 (ESV)

"How are classes going?" I asked.

My brother Sam and I were walking across the University of Iowa's campus. The terrain was familiar to me, as I had graduated from the law school here several years before.

"Finals start on Monday," Sam said. "I'm exhausted from studying. But I only have one more week to get through."

I was jealous. I, too, was exhausted. But my work had no clear end. There were always new cases and responsibilities.

"Wasn't your old apartment in that direction?" Sam asked, pointing.

"It was," I said. "Let's walk by it."

We stopped on the sidewalk in front. I counted units until I saw the one that had been mine. Light glowed from the window. It seemed welcoming. I felt as if I could walk into that apartment and back in time. Back to when I had fewer obligations.

"Remember how small that apartment was?" Sam said.

The space inside my apartment had been tiny. In the four years since I graduated, my life had changed. I'd adopted a puppy. I was hosting a weekly Bible study. I'd begun refinishing antique furniture in my garage. My life no longer fit within this small apartment.

"Ready to go?" Sam asked.

I nodded. Grateful for the blessings behind me. And excited for those ahead.

Father, help me to move forward with confidence in You. —Logan Eliasen

Digging Deeper: Proverbs 1:5; Luke 2:52

Saturday, September 14

First we were loved, now we love. —1 John 4:19 (MSG)

Although I snuggled in my prayer chair with my Bible, my heart was distant. After reading my daily goal, I snapped my Bible closed and was thinking about my exciting day. At noon, I would take Willow, my German shepherd puppy, to the trainer for another lesson in nose work. I'd always wanted a dog that would be able to track and find things.

As I drove down the driveway at the trainer's, Willow enthusiastically barked. She barely stayed in a heel while we walked into the indoor horse arena for our lesson. But after Tonya hid Willow's toy and I asked the pup to find it, she poked around hither and yon. Then she found it. After the third try of the pokey puppy dawdling around the barn, I looked at Tonya and said, "I don't understand. At home she finds it."

Tonya nodded wisely. "If you watch Willow, she's really not interested. She's only going through the motions to please you. Her heart's not in it."

I was crushed. My dream wouldn't happen with this pup.

Then I gulped when I thought of my morning. I'd done the same thing during my Bible study. I had merely gone through the motions, checking it off my list. Willow was a dog and there wasn't much I could do if she wasn't interested. But I could choose to engage my heart with God during my quiet time.

Lord, help me to see how much You desire to fellowship with me. Help me to cultivate that same longing inside my heart every day. Amen.
—Rebecca Ondov

Digging Deeper: Psalms 42:1–2, 63:1–8; Isaiah 26:9

Sunday, September 15

Purify me from my sins, and I will be clean; wash me, and I will be whiter than snow. —Psalm 51:7 (NLT)

I was a self-professed germophobe long before the onset of the global pandemic. I dutifully sanitized my children's hands after trips into shopping malls and grocery stores. I sent them to school with travel-sized sanitizer strapped to their backpacks. So when it seemed everyone in the world suddenly became aware of the importance of hand hygiene, my family was already accustomed to it.

One Sunday afternoon, I set out to take my son to his first Spartan race, an extreme obstacle course that involves navigating rugged trails, climbing hills, dragging sandbags, crawling ropes, jumping through muddy pits, and the like. By the end of the exhilarating run, he was exhausted, dipped in mud, and hungry.

Before we headed for the concession stand, I doused his grimy hands in sanitizer. It helped a bit, but muddy residue still remained. Anxious to get food in his belly, he grabbed a bottle of water from the side pocket of my backpack.

"Nothing washes dirt away better than water," he said, dumping it into his palms.

God speaks to us anywhere He sees fit, even surrounded by throngs of muddy, sweaty runners in the middle of an overgrown field. At that moment, He reminded me that the living water of His Word was available to cleanse me—wholly and completely. It washes away my sins, cleanses me of unrighteousness, purifies my thoughts, sanctifies my spirit, and refreshes my soul. No amount of sanitizer could ever do that.

Lord, wash away my impure thoughts and motives. Create in me a clean heart. —Tia McCollors

Digging Deeper: Psalms 51:10, 119:9; John 15:3; Ephesians 5:26

Monday, September 16

I have strayed like a lost sheep. Seek your servant, for I have not forgotten your commands.
—Psalm 119:176 (NIV)

Hello, this is Gracie speaking, Edward's golden retriever, back by popular demand. I love the fall, don't you? I adore the smells. But they can make me crazy! Which is what happened recently. I got lost. Yes, I, Gracie, got lost.

We were at Monument Mountain reserve in the Berkshires. Suddenly, a smell took control of my nose! I went shooting off into the woods. Edward has this whistle he blows. I could hear it, faintly.

Have you ever been lost? Even now, when I think about it, it scares me. To imagine that you'll never find the people you love. I knew Edward was doing something he always does when he's scared, that thing they call praying.

I ran all the way to the top of the mountain. There I saw an angel! Well, OK, it was just a guy with a backpack. I let him look at my collar. He took out that thing that people talk into. Nodded his head. Then he got some string from his pack and tied it to my collar. I thought I could trust him. He smelled honest.

We went all the way down and there was Edward! The look on his face! I almost ran away again. Then he was hugging me and rubbing my ears.

I still love fall, with its smells and its colors, most of which I can't see. Just remember when you are lost that you never really are. There will always be someone looking for you, someone praying for you, someone who loves you. Someone who will find you.

Lord, Gracie reminds me that at times we all feel lost. It is then that we wait on You to find us.
—Edward Grinnan

Tuesday, September 17

Let the field be joyful, and all that is therein.
—Psalm 96:12 (KJV)

My husband, Don, and I intended to get another
dog soon after our golden chow died, but Don's
failing health and death intervened. Months later,
I tried a shelter dog. She attacked and killed my
daughter's beloved Maltipoo, Drake, leaving us
brokenhearted. So I decided to remain dogless; I
wouldn't risk another tragedy.

Then a veterinarian friend called. "I have the
perfect dog for you," she said. "Pepper is a short-
haired mixed breed with stand-up ears. She's gentle,
spayed, housebroken, and leash trained. Her owner
can't continue caring for her."

So I brought Pepper home...and quickly
discovered she wasn't quite perfect. She was
extremely destructive when left alone; separation
anxiety, I was told. She destroyed three door
moldings, two ballpoint pens, my reading glasses,
several books, a sofa pillow, and a wicker basket of
dried flowers, plus damaging other items. When
I crated her, she bent the wires and escaped. The
evening I left her in the garage, she ate the air-
compressor hose. It took her ten minutes to dig out
of the fenced dog run in my yard and two hours to
destroy the flower-bed irrigation system.

But Pepper has one huge redeeming quality: she is joyful. She runs happy circles around the yard; adores going for walks; and wiggles with excitement when we go for pickup rides or company comes. So I'm helping her learn boundaries and good behavior. And she's teaching me to take risks, step out in faith, and rediscover joy!

Thank You, Lord, for my joyful, not-quite-perfect dog. —Penney Schwab

Digging Deeper: Proverbs 12:10; Isaiah 49:13; Philippians 4:4

Wednesday, September 18

My future is in your hands. —Psalm 31:15 (GW)

I decided to splurge. Instead of throwing together my usual peanut butter and jelly sandwich, I picked up lunch at my favorite Asian restaurant. The stir-fried entrée was a welcome treat, especially when enjoyed via the challenge of chopsticks. But one of my favorite parts was yet to come—the fortune cookie.

I've collected every paper fortune I've received for over a decade. These playful glimpses into my future may not be accurate, but they sure are fun to read. The last fortune I received had promised I'd travel to Asia but unfortunately didn't include the date or a roundtrip ticket. My all-time favorite simply said, "Laugh and grow fat." That was one prediction sure to come true.

But when I cracked open my cookie this time, there was nothing inside…except cookie. I turned it over in my hands, hoping the fortune was somewhere hidden in the cookie's folds. Nothing. Disappointed, I munched the crunchy wafer, but it didn't seem quite as enjoyable without that little random wish.

I felt a bit cheated, as though that piece of paper could actually hold any true knowledge of what lay ahead. *I guess no one, but God, really knows the future,* I thought. Then I realized He'd already shared some of that knowledge with me. I knew God worked all things together for good, that nothing could separate me from His love, and that one day I'd spend eternity with Him. What more did I really need to know?

Father, let me rest in what I know of tomorrow and trust You for what remains a mystery. —Vicki Kuyper

Digging Deeper: Proverbs 31:25; Jeremiah 29:11; Ephesians 1:11; Philippians 1:6

Thursday, September 19

Be kind to one another, tenderhearted, forgiving one another, as God in Christ has forgiven you. —Ephesians 4:32 (NRSVUE)

We got the kids off to school and sat down in the living room. "I need to talk with you," my wife said. I had no idea what was coming next.

"We have serious problems," she said. "I can't go on like this."

"What is it?" I asked, innocently and stupidly.

"You know," she said.

Yes, I did. We hadn't exchanged more than a few sentences with each other for days. Not exactly the tenderhearted kindness that Ephesians urges. Busy days ushering kids to and from school and appointments had followed a weekend filled with religious services and gatherings with friends, which had come after a singular fight. What was the fight about? Over which kitchen drawer should hold small pieces of Tupperware. Seriously. That's where it all began. We hadn't spoken for a week.

All of this flushed into my mind as my wife's anger began to rise again. I didn't know what to say. I often don't know how to talk about what has gone wrong. I often don't know where to begin or what to say.

But suddenly I realized that she was right, we were going the wrong direction, and we had to start over. I got down on one knee. "I'm so sorry," I said.

Give me the grace to see where I've gone wrong, Lord, and the way back to You. —Jon M. Sweeney

Digging Deeper: Psalm 30:5

Friday, September 20

**As far as the east is from the west, so far has he removed our transgressions from us.
—Psalm 103:12 (NIV)**

The night before Wayne and I were due to fly across the country, we went out to dinner with friends.

However, when the bill arrived, my husband couldn't find his wallet. Thinking it must have fallen out of his pocket while he was in the car, I took care of the bill. However, his billfold wasn't in the car. Nor had the valet found it. Convinced he must have left it at home, we looked there with no luck. His wallet had gone missing, along with his identification, his credit cards, and cash.

After a thorough search, Wayne decided the only thing he could do was contact the credit card companies and cancel all our credit cards. He had his passport, so we could at least get on the plane.

The following morning, as we readied for the trip to the airport, a sheepish Wayne came to me and announced he found his wallet in his pants pocket. He'd placed it on the opposite side of where he normally kept it.

I shook my head and said, "This goes on your permanent record."

The family picked up on the saying, so any time one of us does something that makes our eyes roll, we say, "It's on your permanent record."

Thankfully, God doesn't keep track of our sins as humans do. When we invite Christ into our lives, He takes away our sins and washes us clean. There's no permanent record with the Lord.

Lord, thank You for always forgiving me. I only need to confess to You, and You graciously forget my sin. Please help me to be more forgiving, like You.
—Debbie Macomber

Saturday, September 21

I will establish my covenant as an everlasting covenant... to be your God and the God of your descendants after you. —Genesis 17:7 (NIV)

I drove home from our county's tree sale, smiling as waxy red leaves tickled my right ear and shoulder. I couldn't wait to plant my four-foot-tall scarlet oak.

Growing up in upstate New York, I could see the Vermont hills from my bedroom window. I loved the way the bright autumn reds, oranges, and yellows sparkled against the deep evergreens. After thirty years in central Indiana, I still miss those saturated colors.

I studied my county's list of native trees for sale; many offerings read "dull yellowish green fall color." Ugh. Then I found the scarlet oak! Our wide front yard would be perfect for its shade in hot summers and its brilliant leaves in the fall.

Several friends asked me why I would plant a tree that would take decades to reach its full size. I replied with my favorite Greek proverb, "A society grows great when old men plant trees whose shade they know they shall never sit in."

When I told my friend Kathy of my plans, she replied with a story of her own. "Remember when I went to the Holy Land with that group from our church? Our tour guide in the Mount of Olives said their olive groves are planted so that their children and grandchildren can harvest the fruit." Like faith itself, the trees are a gift to future generations, one that will help nourish them through times we can't imagine.

My husband dug the hole for what he called my "twig." I staked its narrow trunk. I lovingly tucked mulch around it. I water it faithfully.

I named our tree Mighty Oak.

> **Heavenly Father, You call me by name
> and know my potential.
> I trust You to hold my future in Your loving hands.**
> —Leanne Jackson

Digging Deeper: Genesis 1:11; 1 Peter 3:3–4

Sunday, September 22

To him who is able to keep you from falling and to bring you faultless and joyful before his glorious presence. —Jude 24 (GNT)

When you are parents to the offspring of a Great Dane and Labrador retriever, you live life in a big way. Buy a big dog bed, transport him in a big pet porter, and store big bags of dog food. As a youngster, Casey grew tall enough to place his front paws on my shoulders and still be a head higher. Always glad to see us when we returned home from work, he occasionally greeted me with too much enthusiasm. Picture a woman in business clothes sandwiched between a concrete sidewalk and a dog the size of a miniature pony.

To exercise our playful pup, we took him to a nearby field adjacent to a new subdivision. One day while sniffing construction debris, Casey wedged his large head into a box. Frightened and unable to see, he ran in circles as we tried to catch him. The chase ended when he plowed into my husband, they tumbled to the ground, and I removed the box.

We walked home with Casey on his leash and laughed about life's ups and downs with a big dog—some of them exciting, others silly, and a few painful. Weeks later, when our pastor based his Sunday sermon on Jude 24, once again we chuckled on the way home—having firsthand knowledge of falling flat on our faces and other places, but grateful our Heavenly Father is able to keep us standing in His presence with nary a cut or bruise.

God, thank You for holding me upright when I stumble in life. —Jenny Lynn Keller

Digging Deeper: Psalms 37:23–24, 55:22; Matthew 7:24–25

Monday, September 23

God wanted them to look for him and perhaps search all around for him and find him. But he is not far from any of us. —Acts 17:27 (ICB)

A student was out sick for three weeks in Advanced English Grammar, a course my students say is the hardest they've ever taken. Throughout my student's illness, she emailed me repeatedly, sometimes wielding ALL CAPS. Her apparent anger irked me, but I made myself respond encouragingly each time, offering class updates and prayers for her recovery. I prayed then and there, knowing that the second my fingers hit "Send" her plight would whoosh off into the louder needs of my other students: appointments coming up, an announcement about syllabus changes I needed to send, piles of tests and papers yelping "Grade me!"

Upon my student's return, I advised her to drop my course.

"Grammar builds one week to the next," I said.

To my amazement, my student was relieved. She wanted to drop but didn't want to disappoint me.

"I'm not disappointed!" I reassured her. "You can't succeed this semester, but you will next year."

Later I got another email from her, more ALL CAPS than ever, thanking me for my emailed prayers and reporting that *she'd* been praying for *me* ever since our first course together years earlier.

"YOU are not forgotten, even when you think you are," she concluded. Wow. I felt so unworthy, so loved.

How cleverly God circulates among us, hovering always nearby, like a teacher among blindfolded children, guiding them closer to the goal, keeping them from hurting one another.

Father God, thanks for my students and all
my other siblings. What would I do without them?
—Patty Kirk

Digging Deeper: Jeremiah 23:23–24; Acts 17:22–34

Tuesday, September 24

**Therefore do not worry about tomorrow,
for tomorrow will worry about itself.
—Matthew 6:34** (NIV)

Those of us who have lived in the southern United
States for a while are familiar with hurricanes. In
fact, we mark time by the storms, calling them by
their names. Names like Charlie, Andrew, Betsy,
Katrina, and others are hurricanes we remember.
I moved here right before Hurricane Ivan did.

I had barely settled into my new place and had started
a new job that required some traveling when Hurricane
Ivan showed up in the Gulf of Mexico. Hurricanes
are fickle, and one never knows exactly where they'll
make landfall or how big they'll be when they do.
I only hoped it wouldn't hit us directly. So when
the hurricane took aim at our area and increased in
strength, I worried about what to do. I was supposed
to go out of town for a meeting the same day it
was expected to hit. Many people in my area were
evacuating. I lived alone with a dog and a cat. What
would happen to them with everyone leaving?

Having always been pretty independent, I was in
charge of most of the things in my life. However, no

one is in charge of a hurricane except God. Knowing what kind of devastation such a storm can do made me worry about what would happen to my home, my pets, and my future. I prayed for wisdom and protection, looked at my new condo for what could be the last time, packed my car and my pets, then headed north toward my meeting. I had to trust God for the outcome, and thankfully I was able to return to an undamaged home.

Lord, thank You for taking care of my tomorrows so I do not need to worry. —Marilyn Turk

Digging Deeper: Psalms 85:2, 143:8; Luke 12:25

Wednesday, September 25

But the fruit of the Spirit is love, joy, peace, patience, kindness, goodness, faithfulness. —Galatians 5:22 (ESV)

A little bundle of life named CoCo, our Yorkshire terrier, is the epitome of joy in our home. He has personality in droves and often plays until exhaustion. One afternoon, while putting away all of his toys into his toy basket, I noticed each and every one of his stuffed toys was ripped and bleeding fluff. Not one toy was spared.

CoCo watched me tidy the toys with his head tilted, ready to pounce on any toy I decided to throw down the hall. I couldn't help but throw his favorite, and so began our spontaneous play session. CoCo, like most dogs, plays without hesitation and with his whole presence. His basket full of destroyed toys was evidence of a fully enjoyed life. Maybe a little less seriousness and more playtime is just what I needed too.

I am a serious person, a proper adult. But God also wants me to be joyful and rejoice in Him. In an effort to embrace the joy CoCo modeled that afternoon, I pranced up to my seven-year-old and made a silly face.

He laughed and questioned, "What's wrong? You're being silly."

Right then I knew I needed more playtime with him. I replied, "I just love you and want to play with you."

He hugged me and gave me a raspberry.

We proceeded to play and spent time talking and being silly. My heart was filled with a life fully enjoyed.

Heavenly Father, thank You for CoCo's lesson; help me increase my joyfulness so I may bring peace and love to others. —Jolynda Strandberg

Digging Deeper: Deuteronomy 16:14–15; 1 Kings 1:39–40; Luke 2:9–11

Thursday, September 26

REMEMBERING GRATITUDE:
The Karate Kid
Pride goes before destruction, a haughty spirit before a fall. —Proverbs 16:18 (NIV)

I was waiting to have my car serviced between three hairy medical appointments when a lady fell into an empty chair. "An oil change is the laaaast thing I need," she wailed. *Try* my *life, baby,* I inwardly grumbled. *A fifteen-minute oil change is the highlight of* my *day!*

A scrap of conversation caught my attention. Another customer had learned that the kid in our midst was into karate. "How does a person earn one of those black belts?" he was asking.

"Oh, the masters tell you that takes a lifetime," he said. "Maybe not even then." I puffed right up at his words. I'd earned a black belt in suffering in grade school. "You can buy a black belt to wear around your waist at a store," he continued. "But earning one takes time." I was stunned to hear it involved humility.

You might think I forgot the kid. The one who sheltered an entire waiting room with the kind, knowing eyes that looked into my heart. But in the two decades since, he still points the way. Before he entered my life, I thought pride was having the best house on the block, a fancy-dancy car, a child you could brag on. But pride had found me when I'd forgotten to be humble, so caught up in my own problems, sure that mine were worse than anyone else's, that I'd failed to see the often-hidden suffering of others.

When times get rough, I sometimes slip into errant thinking. But the karate kid stops me in my tracks. For when his eyes found mine, I saw God's, and He wasn't talking karate.

___

Friday, September 27

CELEBRATE!! A Joyful Funeral
...for I will turn their mourning into joy, and
I will comfort them and make them rejoice.
—Jeremiah 31:13 (TLB)

I walked toward the church that sunny September
morning, filled with sorrow. Today was Nyah's
funeral. We had been praying for the beautiful
sixteen-year-old girl since she was diagnosed with a
malignant brain tumor four years ago. It was serious,
but we thought she'd be cured. A couple months
ago, a test revealed new inoperable tumors. Hospice
came in. Nyah shifted into this new direction
with greater acceptance than most of us. She had
something new to anticipate.

I stepped into the church, filled with her favorite
music playing loudly and bunches of balloons in her
favorite colors of teal, mint, and white. I smiled. The
service began, and the Nyah stories overflowed with
descriptions of her contagious hope and humor. We
learned that she'd planned her whole service. She
wanted a joyful birthday party.

As the service ended, we turned to exit and
noticed that curtains had closed off the back of the

room. They were opened as we began filing out, revealing festive tables with teal, mint, and white cloths, laden with chocolate cupcakes that were frosted in the theme colors, turkey sandwiches, and lots of ice cream. The room buzzed with happy sounds as everyone got a helium balloon.

"As you know," a friend announced, "Nyah wanted this to be a birthday party celebrating her birth into a life of glory with Jesus, so let's release our balloons, and when she looks down, she'll know we are celebrating." With that, we released balloons that soon covered the high ceiling.

Thank You, Lord, for giving us the capacity to experience sorrow and joyful celebration at the same time. —Carol Kuykendall

Digging Deeper: Nehemiah 9–12; Psalm 84

Saturday, September 28

I will give you a new heart and put a new spirit in you; I will remove from you your heart of stone and give you a heart of flesh. —Ezekiel 36:26 (NIV)

My husband and I became empty nesters a few weeks ago when our daughter, Micah, started college. The change from having an active teen bouncing around to open schedules had me wandering aimlessly around the house. Micah had been the focus of my attention for the last eighteen years. Now she was gone. I didn't know how to navigate this new season of life.

Saturday morning, I heard my husband, Michael, rummaging in the attic. I walked into the garage. Decorative scarecrows leaned again the wall. We'd not set up harvest displays since Micah was in elementary school. I figured the decade-old quintet was bound for the trash can.

"Let's go to the garden store for some decorations," suggested Michael.

I thought he'd lost his mind, but we had a blast picking out pumpkins in all shapes, colors, and sizes. We also loaded gourds, cornstalks, yellow mums, and hay bales into the back of his SUV.

At home, we arranged pumpkins with scarecrows on the porch, put three scarecrows behind a hay bale under the canopy of our oak, and planted mums with mini pumpkins beside the mailbox. We ran to the curb to survey our displays countless times over the next few days. *Maybe we'd both lost our minds.*

Then it hit me. Michael knew I needed something to fuss over. Now I knew how we'd get through this next season of life—together.

Help me lean in to You, dear Lord, and those I love, knowing life, like seasons, always changes.
—Stephanie Thompson

Digging Deeper: Ecclesiastes 7:10; Isaiah 43:19; 1 Corinthians 2:9

For where two or three are gathered together in my name, there am I in the midst of them.
—Matthew 18:20 (KJV)

David was a brilliant atheist, just finishing his PhD in anthropology at Brown when the Light of God came calling. Suddenly a believer and longing to learn more about "this Jesus," he came to Vanderbilt Divinity in Nashville. We met, fell in love, and only then discovered that God was calling him to be a minister. We were hesitant. But both people of faith and those seeped in doubt were drawn to David. It seemed right.

David's goal was to create a church that reflected God's kingdom on earth. Overlay this with Jesus's teachings, and you will get his concept: love God, love all His children, serve.

Church became our sacred space, our family, our friends.

We were warned: "Don't make church your life." We thought we knew better. Then retirement came.

The National Presbyterian Church has guidelines that encourage retirees to disengage from leadership to give full rein to successors. Unfortunately, these rules opened a window to an envious staff person who viewed David's relationship with the church as a threat to their position. Working to undermine his memory, they even reported us to presbytery for "interfering" by visiting a dying friend. It was brutal. The day a misled presbytery rep told David our church would be better off if it considered him dead, I became "unchurched"—still worshipping in my heart but unable to return to that particular building.

Still, we had each other, and together, we moved on. Then a knock at our door. A neighbor, Phyllis, also hurting from being "unchurched," had a request. Would David lead a simple neighborhood church?

We meet on our front porch or in some neighbor's living room. David leads. We laugh. We learn. We hold each other up. We *are* church.

Father, with You by our side, we journey on.
—Pam Kidd

Digging Deeper: Isaiah 56:7; Galatians 3:28

Monday, September 30

The heavens are telling the glory of God; they are a marvelous display of his craftsmanship.
—Psalm 19:1 (TLB)

In 1995, when I turned fifty, I was blessed to go to the big island of Hawaii as well as two other islands in the archipelago, Oahu and Kawaii, with my daughter Jeanne; her boyfriend (now husband), Canyon; and my son Andrew. Then twenty-five years later, when I was seventy-five, I got to go again to visit Jeanne, Canyon, and their daughter, Adeline, while they were living in Maui for a year.

Determined to write a daily journal during my sixteen-day Hawaii visit, I fell short by fourteen days. There was just too much swimming, snorkeling, hiking, exploring, and sightseeing to do. On page two of the world's shortest journal, it lists my favorite Maui things: 1. Snorkeling everywhere! 2. Ah, family! Long talks with Jeanne, Canyon, Adeline & Ethan (my California grandson who joined me in Maui). 3. Swimming in the ocean. 4. Catamaran ride to the volcano for snorkeling. 5. Sunset at Kaanapali Beach. 6. Sea turtles, coral, and fish everywhere we snorkeled. 7. Black sand beach. 8. Treacherous Koki Beach on the road to Hana.

My eight favorite things had everything to do with the beauty of God's world and the people I shared it with. Nature and people. I'm starting to wonder if that's all we really need to relax and unwind.

Ever since that trip, those sea turtles, sunsets, and snorkeling days still fill my heart with joy because God also gave us the gift of memory. Maybe the journal wasn't as important as being present and focused every day as the adventures of experiencing God's glorious world unfolded before my eyes.

Heavenly Father, thank You for keeping the memories of so many people, places, and events alive in my mind and heart, for they bring me closer to You who created it all. —Patricia Lorenz

Digging Deeper: Isaiah 35:1–2; Hosea 14:5–7

YOU WERE CALLED TO PEACE

1 _____

2 _____

3 _____

4 _____

5 _____

6 _____

7 _____

8 _____

9 _____

10 _____

11 _____

12 _____

13 _____

14 _____

15 _____

16 _____

17 _____

18 _____

19 _____

20 _____

21 _____

22 _____

23 _____

24 _____

25 _____

26 _____

27 _____

28 _____

29 _____

30 _____

OCTOBER

Do not be anxious about anything,

but in every situation, by prayer

and petition, with thanksgiving,

present your requests to God.

—Philippians 4:6 (NIV)

For every house is built by someone, but He who built all things is God. —Hebrews 3:4 (NKJV)

One day the building was there. The next it wasn't. My favorite community restaurant had closed months earlier, and the building had been up for sale ever since. To my surprise, one afternoon when I drove by, I noticed the building in rubbles. Construction fences and equipment blocked most of my view and cautioned pedestrians to stay clear while work was in progress.

I watched over the next few months what seemed to be a painstakingly slow and tedious process of rebuilding the area.

At times, I've felt my life was a mess—surrounded by dusty rubble and fallen debris—and knew that only God could reconstruct it. My prayers for God to change my life have led to frustration when the results don't happen as quickly as I'd like. Doesn't God want me to be more patient? Shouldn't it be easier to mend strained relationships? God, what's taking so long?

Like an architect who holds the blueprints for buildings, God holds the blueprints of our lives. So I remind myself that while things may seem to be in shambles from the outside, God is carefully creating a new and improved version of me. I've gained patience, smoothed out the rough edges that were once in the relationship with my father, and learned to trust God's process. I'm still a work in progress and hope that I always will be.

Lord, I thank You that all things are working together for my good. I'm grateful for the ways You've equipped me with the tools I need to build not just for me but also for Your church. —Tia McCollors

Digging Deeper: Psalm 51:10; Jeremiah 30:17; Romans 8:28; 1 Peter 5:10

Wednesday, October 2

And pray in the Spirit on all occasions with all kinds of prayers and requests. With this in mind, be alert and always keep on praying for all the Lord's people. —Ephesians 6:18 (NIV)

A friend asked me to pray for a family that her daughter, a physician, was treating. The mother had delivered healthy twins but was seriously ill with Covid-19. The father was overwhelmed with work and care of an older child. Since I didn't know the family, I wasn't sure my prayers would help, but I prayed daily for the family and medical staff. A few weeks later, I learned that the mother had recovered and was home with her family.

Then several counties in northern Kansas were ravaged by wildfires fueled by sixty-mile-per-hour winds. Many families lost everything: houses, barns, cattle, and hay. One family lost valuable Clydesdale horses. I prayed again. My church also prayed.

Healing scarred land and rebuilding herds take years, but help arrived from many sources and recovery efforts are well underway.

I've been asked to pray for a person contemplating divorce; a woman dying of cancer; a child in an unhealthy family situation; and a teenager in a coma following a horrific accident. Sometimes I know names; other times I have only the prayer request. Some prayers have been answered; I don't know about others. I do know that my faith in the power of prayer has steadily grown. And I'm confident that God sees each heart, understands each hurt, and will answer every prayer in His perfect time.

Let these words of my mouth and this meditation of my heart be pleasing in your sight, Lord, my Rock and my Redeemer. —Penney Schwab

Digging Deeper: Isaiah 65:24; John 17:20–23; Philippians 1:3–6

Thursday, October 3

Now may the Lord of peace Himself continually grant you peace in every circumstance.
—2 Thessalonians 3:16 (NASB)

The tree had to have been over a hundred years old—a massive red fir towering over the corner of the house just outside my daughter's bedroom window.

I loved the fir most of the time. But I definitely didn't love it when the wind blew hard from the west and the thing would bend like a reed, becoming a hundred-foot club. If it snapped, it would reduce our old farmhouse to sticks.

"Everybody up," I'd say. "We're sleeping in the basement tonight."

My daughter would groan. "With the spiders?"

"Spiders are better than hospitals." I'm fairly sure she adamantly disagrees with this statement to this day.

I knew the tree had to go. My family's well-being took precedent. Still, I hated to remove something so old and beautiful.

I've found it's much the same in my life. Sometimes there are beautiful things, happy things, things I've had forever, but if I'm honest, I know they can be dangerous when the winds of my flesh kick up. Way too many times I've hardheadedly ignored the weather report and allowed unchecked metaphorical firs to crush my life to rubble. But after a lot of years and crash landings, it's starting to sink in—peace is more beautiful than any tree.

Peace with God, peace with men, peace in my soul.

And it turns out red fir burns great in the fireplace. So I'll leave the basement to the spiders and enjoy the night. But I'll definitely keep the chainsaw handy.

Because I've found I really love the sound of the wind.

Lord, please give me eyes to see the danger and the strength to act. Rock me to sleep on the winds of peace! —Buck Storm

---

Friday, October 4

In the same way, let your light shine before
others, so that they may see your good works
and give glory to your Father who is in heaven.
—Matthew 5:16 (ESV)

I drove past the old, closed farmstand today and
saw a "Farm for Sale" sign. The owner died a little
over a year ago. I didn't know him by name, but I
recognized his picture in the obituary. I went to his
stand regularly to buy flowers for my sister's grave. He
strongly resembled my father, and because of that, I
felt as if I knew him more than I actually did.

He had funny signs that he wrote and placed
around the farmstand. "Please take me home"
and "Take better care of me" on plants that were
struggling. "Better than your mother's" was above
the apple pies; "Buy one for a prickly friend" was
by the cactus.

After my dad died, I went to the farmer's stand
more often. I lingered as he talked about growing
apples. Once I told him he looked like my dad,
and he shrugged it off, until my jaw tightened. His
voice softened, as he called me "dear," handed me a
small pot of daffodils, and said, "Have this. There's
nothing better than growing flowers. Flowers make
people happy. Simple as that."

I pulled into the driveway and thought about him meeting my dad in heaven, shaking hands, two doppelgangers, strangers connected by my love. Walking up the steps, I noticed the daffodils that border the side porch were opening. I went closer to see the first blooms of spring and I smiled, feeling close to heaven, if only for an instant.

Lord, thank You for the beautiful people You place in my path who shine with Your light here on earth.
—Sabra Ciancanelli

Digging Deeper: Psalm 37:23; Ephesians 4:32

Saturday, October 5

Then saith he unto his disciples, The harvest truly is plenteous, but the labourers are few.
—**Matthew 9:37** (KJV)

I knew no one at the out-of-town wedding reception, so I found an isolated table where I could enjoy my plate in peace...until the minister—the one who had performed the service—asked if he could join me.

"Sure," I said, though I kinda *did* mind, but what was I going to say? He seemed like a nice guy and had given a mercifully short sermon at the wedding. What's not to like?

"These events must be a perk of your job," I said. "Free food."

"Not really," he said. "I'm never sure what to do at these things, and I'm always under the microscope."

His candor intrigued me. "Guess I hadn't thought of that," I said, and for the next few hours, we had a breathtakingly deep conversation about…well, about everything, but especially about the pressures on those who are called to the cloth.

At the end of our talk, he thanked me. "I don't get a chance to talk like this too often, but since you're not from around here and we probably won't see each other again, I figured I could trust you."

He could, and luckily he was wrong about a one-time encounter: we visit each other regularly. Our conversations always leave me with a deep appreciation for the people who serve God—and maybe "people" includes us too. We can't hide our light under a bushel. We can't hide *ourselves* under a bushel. We need to follow the example of our ministers and bring light to the world.

Lord, have mercy on those who heed Your call and let us, who benefit from the hard work of your disciples, be forever grateful for their selfless service.
—Mark Collins

Digging Deeper: Psalm 139:15

Sunday, October 6

He gives power to the faint and strengthens the powerless. —Isaiah 40:29 (NRSV)

One bright fall day, I dusted off my bike and pumped air into the tires. I'd biked to our library many times, so, halfway there, why was I winded? Walking in, I noticed a wobble in my balance. And hadn't grocery bags been getting heavier?

When was the last time I exercised? *Oh.*

I used to get in lots of exercise with my friend Karen. She and I met through our elementary-age kids. After putting them on the yellow school bus, we walked two miles through our neighborhood. We rode stationary bikes and lifted weights at the Y. We talked about everything from quilting to faith. Our routine continued for years, without effort.

Then Karen's husband, Randy, retired, and I lost my exercise partner as they began walking and going to the Y together. That day at the library, I realized I needed to renew my strength, just like those bike tires needed air.

When was the last time I prayed for strength? *Dear Lord, please help me find my next exercise partner.*

Ginny called as she was dusting off her treadmill, wanting to know if I'd be interested in working out with her. I nearly shouted, "I'll join you in my basement!" As we walked, we talked over the phone about everything from caregiving to faith. Then we lifted weights and stretched. We agreed to "walk and talk" twice a week.

I texted two friends in my neighborhood. Joan meets me to walk on Wednesday afternoons. On Sunday afternoons, Joyce and I walk. The topics are wide-ranging but always include faith. I often wave to Karen and Randy.

My faith muscles feel stronger too!

Dear Lord, You are the Source of my strength, in body and spirit. —Leanne Jackson

Digging Deeper: Isaiah 35:3; Galatians 6:2

Monday, October 7

Bear one another's burdens, and so fulfill the law of Christ. —Galatians 6:2 (ESV)

October 7, 2021, was my first time back in my New York City office since March 2020. I was unnerved by the commuter train ride, breathing through two masks while being around strangers. For most of the pandemic, I had remained at home with my husband and sons, venturing out only to visit my dad or to sprint through the supermarket, gathering groceries as quickly as possible. I even grew to like online church services, especially when our church could offer no other way for us to worship together.

But on this first day back, as I approached my office building, it was the sight of Mohamed standing by his coffee cart near my office that brought unexpected tears. Throughout the pandemic, I had wondered about Mo, from whom I bought coffee daily, as we shared pleasantries and asked about each other's families. I had prayed for him and his family, asking the Lord to keep them healthy, fed, clothed, and housed, as Mo is the family's breadwinner and without office workers coming to buy coffee, his business was at risk. While I wasn't able to be in direct contact with Mo, my thoughts about him and prayers for his family kept me tied closer to Christ.

I was so happy to see Mo smiling, greeting his customers, as he always did. He told me that his family was fine, and he actually remembered how I take my coffee (vanilla creamer with a splash of half-and-half, no sugar). It was a perfect start to my day and certainly flipped my anxiety to joy!

Lord, I thank You for Your protection of Mo and all the many workers who suffered a loss of business during the pandemic. —Gayle T. Williams

Digging Deeper: 1 Thessalonians 5:11; James 5:16

Tuesday, October 8

Open my eyes, that I may see Wondrous things from Your law. —Psalm 119:18 (NKJV)

For several weeks, I have been my wife's "eyes" while she waits for trifocals to arrive following cataract surgery. I hold her hand when we walk, and I read product labels for her.

Sharon was in the seventh grade before she knew she was not seeing well. Back in the 1950s, they didn't always prescreen schoolchildren for vision problems.

One day, Sharon's teacher taped an eye chart to the chalkboard, then went around the room, asking students to read it. When she got to Sharon, she gasped, and students burst into laughter because Sharon couldn't even read the big letter E.

"How my parents missed this, I don't know," Sharon recalls. "I could read by holding a book up to my nose, but the rest of the world was hazy."

When she finally got glasses, she was astonished that she could see individual leaves on trees and the eye color of her friends.

Sadly, until that day, Sharon thought that "hazy" was how the world looked to everyone.

I suppose that's the worst kind of blindness—when I think I'm seeing clearly, but I'm not. It reminds me that when it comes to the big issues of life, I may need the help of others who can see things I missed.

Above all, I need to check with God's Word, to see how the world looks through His perfect eyes, untainted by modern culture and personal prejudice.

Help me, Lord, to see the world as You see it, through eyes of love. —Daniel Schantz

Digging Deeper: Isaiah 6:9–10; Hebrews 4:3

Wednesday, October 9

Do to others as you would have them do to you. —Luke 6:31 (NIV)

Coming up the driveway after a hike with Gracie, I noticed a couple of boxes at the front door. "Look," I said, "maybe Chewy came."

My golden retriever popped up from the back of the Jeep. She knows the word *Chewy*, recognizes her food boxes, and adores the driver who delivers them.

Alas, these boxes weren't from Chewy. They weren't even for us.

I bristled at the prospect of trying to untangle the delivery service's mistake. I had calls to return and a deadline to meet. I dragged the packages inside. Sooner or later, someone would figure out the problem. As I started up the stairs to work, a little voice in my head said, "Do unto others..."

I ignored the nudge but not for long. I couldn't concentrate with those boxes downstairs. What if their contents were urgent? Finally, I examined the address. It was for a woman who was staying at an inn two towns over. She'd gotten the zip code wrong. How the delivery service had messed up, I couldn't tell you.

I called the inn, and they agreed to give the guest my number. The next morning, Gracie and I stood at the window, my dog erupting with a woof as the woman drove up our driveway to collect the boxes that I left outside for her. She had been quite relieved to hear from me. I was relieved too.

A few hours later, Gracie leapt off the couch and ran to the window. It was her Chewy box, right on time.

God of goodness, I am not always as quick as I should be to do the right thing. Help me always to remember to do unto others. —Edward Grinnan

Digging Deeper: Matthew 5:15–17;
1 Timothy 5:24–25; Hebrews 10:24–25

**Your word is a lamp to my feet and a light to
my path. —Psalm 119:105** (NRSV)

It kind of surprised me when I noticed it: I tend to
stare down at the ground when I walk. Working at
home, I'd go out for a stroll, just to break up the day,
and for much of that time I'd stare at the sidewalk.
Even in the park, I'd be looking at the path and the
flowers that bordered it or the twigs crunching under
my footsteps.

Look up, Rick, I'd tell myself. *Notice that pine tree.
Take in the view of the river. Isn't it marvelous? See the
light on the hills. Watch the birds take wing and float
on the breeze.*

And then a squirrel would dart along the path,
and I'd watch it scurry into the leaves, searching
for food, pausing to come up and check me out, as
though I might offer him a peanut.

The long view and the short view. Aren't they
both manifestations of the Creator's goodness? Yes,
that hawk in the sky might take my breath away as
does the sunlight on the palisades beyond, but then,
I see the most curious patterns on a path. The fallen
leaves, stuck to the ground, can take on shapes that
mirror what's in the heavens.

"God is in the details" is an old truism. I can
feel a huge presence filling me up as I stare at a
panoramic view of the sun setting over the Hudson
River, the clouds rimmed with light. And then I'll

look down and discover a ladybug sitting on a leaf and imagine God noticing it, just as God never stops watching out for me.

Open my eyes, Lord, to the wonders of Your creation. —Rick Hamlin

Digging Deeper: Genesis 1:10–12; Psalm 1:2; Ephesians 2:5

Friday, October 11

Two are better than one.... For if they fall, one will lift up the other. —Ecclesiastes 4:9–10 (NRSVUE)

The first time I walked into Ed's hardware store, I accidentally opened the door into his knees. I apologized. He said, "It's OK," but pushed past me. The second time I was there, I attempted to chat with Ed, but he didn't seem to have time or wasn't interested.

It took a crisis in both of our lives for Ed and me to discover what we shared. I was in the store one day, and even though Ed had never shown any interest in connecting, this day, for some reason, he said, as I laid out a five-dollar bill for a bag of birdseed, "You OK?"

I looked up at him, shocked at his intuition. "Not really," I said.

He waited. Again, I was surprised. But there was no one else around. I went on, "It's my wife. She's not happy with me. You know?"

"I do," he said and smiled. I'd known Ed for maybe six years by that point, and this was the first moment I think I had ever seen him smile. And it wasn't so much a smile as it was a sort of kinship.

I then started popping by the store on days when I didn't really need hardware. I would poke around the aisles and finally say hello to Ed. On one of these occasions, he asked if I wanted some coffee. I joined him in the office. We talked some more.

We finally discovered what we shared: a need for a friend who would listen and understand.

Help me, Lord, to be a friend, and find a friend, today.
—Jon M. Sweeney

Digging Deeper: 1 Peter 4:8–10

Saturday, October 12

I wait for the LORD, my whole being waits, and in his word I put my hope. —Psalm 130:5 (NIV)

"Ready?" my dad asked.

We began to ease the table out of my parents' minivan. Together, we carried the table into my garage. We lowered it onto two legs, then four. The table had been a fixture in my family's dining room for most of my life. It was strange to see it in a garage.

"Are you sure you want this table?" my dad asked.

"It needs to be refinished," I said. "But it's solid."

"Yes," he said. "But this will be a big project."

He was right. The table was large. It had seated our family of seven.

I only needed a table for one. While I had hoped to be married by now, that hadn't happened yet. I was still waiting to find the right woman.

I looked down at the tabletop. It was rough from two decades of family dinners. There were tine marks from rogue forks. Bare oak showed through in places. I planned to strip the rest of the table down by hand.

And I intended to spend the hours of sanding, staining, and varnishing in prayer. Asking the Lord to someday surround this table with a family of my own. And praying that I would trust His plans for me, even if those plans were different from my own.

I looked back up at my dad. "I know this will take time," I said. "But it's worth the wait."

Lord, give me patience as You reveal Your plans for me. —Logan Eliasen

Digging Deeper: Isaiah 40:30–31; Micah 7:7

Sunday, October 13

Again I will build you, and you shall be built, O virgin Israel! Again you shall adorn yourself with tambourines and shall go forth in the dance of the merrymakers. —Jeremiah 31:4 (ESV)

The Swiss Guards broke rank and did a little dance.

I wouldn't have believed it if I hadn't seen it with my own eyes—after all, the Swiss Guards usually stand guard over the Vatican with steady, stoic vigilance. But it happened—two uniformed guards turned to us and did a quick happy dance before returning to their guarded posture.

I don't blame them—we danced too.

In December 2019, my son had tried out for—and made—a traveling soccer team. We had much excitement (and a whole lot of money) invested into a fun family trip to Europe for spring break 2020. I'm sure you can guess what happened to that.

They postponed the trip to June 2021—and as the date approached, we wondered if once again our trip would be canceled. It wasn't. Instead, the day Italy opened to American travelers, we were on that plane. We were among the first Americans into Rome after months of isolation. And oh, what a welcome we received.

Every single one of us had struggled together. We had been isolated and alone. We had lost family and friends. We had plans canceled. We lost a lot, collectively. And nothing would ever be the same, but that day standing in front of St. Peter's Cathedral, we collectively seemed to understand that life was coming back.

It was a moment that warranted a little dance. After all, our collective struggle deserved a collective celebration. At that moment, we connected, human to human, with people from across the world who were so different from us yet exactly the same.

Dear Lord, we praise You for blessing us with each other and the joy to gather once more.
—Erin MacPherson

Digging Deeper: 1 Samuel 18:7;
Jeremiah 31:13

Monday, October 14

For God so loved the world that he gave his one and only Son, that whoever believes in him shall not perish but have eternal life. —John 3:16 (NIV)

I knew Sister Dot for many years, starting from my time in a Catholic seminary where she was one of my faculty advisors. Her beautiful faith, lovely sense of humor, and great commitment to social justice made us instant and lifelong friends.

We stay connected even though we lived in different states. On a trip back to Texas, she told me that her cancer had returned.

Shocked, I failed to find words. My pain must have shown on my face because Dot took my hand and said, "I love you too." Tears ran down our faces. She smiled and said, "All my life, I've been getting ready for this moment, to finally see God face-to-face. When I'm gone and you think of me, just know I'll be thinking of you too."

Two weeks later, I received a call informing me that Sister Dot was now with the God whom she loved. For weeks afterward, I was filled with memories not only of her but also of all the people I had loved who were now gone. Why does life have to include death?

When I returned home, I was sorting through old paperwork. Soon, I opened an envelope that was unfamiliar. Inside was a photo of Sister Dot along with my seminary classmates. She looked so happy. As I held it in my hand, I remembered Dot saying that when I thought of her, she would also be thinking of me.

Those words gave me great solace. To me, they meant that while death is a part of life, love endures, and the final word is God's. Although I still miss her, I am sustained by the thought that one day we will all be reunited and that all things finally will be well.

Lord, give us the courage to keep facing whatever comes knowing that only You have eternal life. Amen.
—Adam Ruiz

Digging Deeper: Psalm 16:11; John 4:14, 5:24

Tuesday, October 15

Sing and make music from your heart to the Lord, always giving thanks to God the Father for everything, in the name of our Lord Jesus Christ.
—Ephesians 5:19–20 (NIV)

I rushed out of work early one Tuesday afternoon, hurrying to get my son to his weekly piano lesson. I prayed that his teacher, who specialized in teaching children with various needs, would be able to connect well with him. My son was diagnosed with autism when he was three years old. We can't always clearly predict what will upset him.

I sat off to the side in the lesson room, always alert to any early signs of his frustration rising. But this day, for the first time, I began to recognize the melody he was playing. His little fingers stretched intentionally to reach each note. My heart leapt for joy.

I often wrestle with the thought that I don't recognize what God is doing. I question why things have to be a certain way. I might hear and see only a small piece of the song and assume God's got it all wrong and must not hear my prayers. I focus on my frustration. Sometimes, I feel like giving up. But when I am sensitive to listening to God, I begin to notice the heavenly music emerging. It fills me and all those who hear it with encouragement.

God, help me to see that when I see only the messy parts, You see so much more. Help me to remember that You are the wonderful conductor of the music in my life. —Nicole Garcia

Digging Deeper: Psalm 71:23; Isaiah 30:21; Acts 16:25

Wednesday, October 16

Stop pointing your finger. —Isaiah 58:9 (NLT)

"It was the gnats!"

I'm a competitive person. When I'm losing, or have lost, in some form—*any* form—of competition, my husband still likes to kid me with those words. Their origin was years ago, when we were dating.

We were playing tennis and clouds of irritating gnats kept circling my head.

When I lost the match, I had a ready explanation: "It was the gnats!" Somehow I felt better when I placed the blame for my inferior tennis skills on those pesky insects.

I still too often turn to blame. When my son-in-law beats me at ping-pong: "It's your table; I'm not used to it." When I leave a pot on the stove until it scorches: "I got a phone call and they just kept talking and made me forget." I've looked for some reason, any reason, that what occurred was not my fault. It allows me to feel better about myself.

Why do I do this? I asked God during my quiet time. What I heard in my heart is this: *Blaming is a form of pride, and we all know what pride comes before.*

So, this morning when my husband told me he'd woken up at 4 a.m. to a beeping oven, indicating I'd forgotten to turn it off after dinner last night, I said, "I'm sorry. That's completely my fault. I should have remembered." This evening, when he creamed me in foosball, I said, "Great game. You beat me fair and square!" And you know what? I felt better about myself than when I've made excuses.

Lord, when I'm tempted to point my finger, please remind me to point it at myself.
—Kim Taylor Henry

Digging Deeper: Proverbs 16:18, 29:23; Matthew 23:12

Thursday, October 17

The LORD is close to the brokenhearted;
he rescues those whose spirits are crushed.
—Psalm 34:18 (NLT)

When my mother had a stroke, her condition deteriorated quickly, and in a matter of days she was gone. Dad was heartbroken and lost without her. During their marriage of sixty-two years, they leaned on each other for support and strength. I was worried for Dad. Would he have enough companionship without Mom?

At the end of our telephone calls, he choked up and cried. He shared how going home to an empty home was painful and heartbreaking. Some nights, he got up and thought my mom was lying next to him on the bed and felt her loss all over again. He was lonely and missing Mom. My heart ached for him. Due to the distance (he was in New York and I am in Florida), all I could do was call him several times a week and pray daily for him.

My two siblings, who live in New York, visited him and looked out for him. His sister called him several times a day. However, it was his church family and friends who came alongside him and offered companionship. Johnny, his longtime buddy, drove him to church and into town to run errands. He made sure Dad was not always alone in the apartment. His church family checked on him and offered support. Slowly, he got stronger and gained confidence in his new reality without Mom.

Many people rallied around him in his time of grief and helped him face his loss with hope and faith. Their companionship to my dad was an answer to my prayer.

Lord, comfort those who are grieving and surround them with a caring community. —Pablo Diaz

Digging Deeper: Genesis 23:1–2; Psalm 73:26

Friday, October 18

"For I know the plans I have for you," declares the LORD, "plans to prosper you and not to harm you, plans to give you hope and a future." —Jeremiah 29:11 (NIV)

One of my husband, Jim's, favorite shows is *The Joy of Painting* on PBS. "It's almost meditative," he'll say as he watches Bob Ross layer paint onto the canvas. I love it, too, and will often watch with him. It always feels rewarding to see empty white space transformed into something beautiful.

One day, though, as Jim and I enjoyed an episode together, Mr. Ross did something that took me aback: he dipped one of his broadest brushes into a dollop of midnight-black paint and proceeded to pull it across the middle of what had been a lovely forest scene. I'd thought it had been nearly finished. But now it looked ruined—bisected by an ugly, black gash.

"Why'd he do *that*?" I asked my husband, as I stared at this new, ruinous flaw. I could not imagine how it would be made to belong within a painting that had been so pretty. Bob Ross didn't seem worried though. Clearly, he could see something here that I could not.

And, sure enough, as I watched, brushstroke by brushstroke, he transformed that black stripe into an incredible river. Vibrant and realistic, it tumbled its way through what, just moments ago, had been a nice—but much less interesting—painting.

I smiled, impressed. That black stripe had never been a flaw at all. Bob Ross had a plan, but instead of telling us up front, he'd waited for us to discover the beauty as it unfolded. And just like God's plans, because I trusted, when the time came, I saw it too.

One needs to look no further than Calvary to know that where You are at work, God, what might appear calamitous at first does not remain that way.
—Erin Janoso

Digging Deeper: Genesis 50:20; Proverbs 3:5–6; Mark 8:31; John 11:4

Saturday, October 19

The harvest is plentiful, but the laborers are few.
—Matthew 9:37 (NRSV)

Last year, I noticed a few local trees that had shed a goodly crop of nuts. I could identify what they weren't—hazelnuts, chestnuts, black walnuts. Though curious, I left the mystery meats for the squirrels.

This October, when I passed that way, the ground was littered with the light-brown balls. I brought several home. Determining that they were small Japanese walnuts, I returned and collected a passel. And then a peck more when neighbor girls joined me. (The squirrels hadn't shown interest.) *What a gift to enhance my winter baking!* The foraging was quick compared to the nut cracking, the shells so hard we resorted to hammers on the sidewalk. The girls caught on quickly and came back to smash more.

Tenaciously picking out the meats fell to me and presented an all-fall challenge. The edible sections, more tightly packed than English walnuts, didn't readily release their hold. Evening after evening, as I watched the news, I poked at crevices and chipped off morsels that eventually equaled one cup, a pint. By winter, a quart?

An hour ago, as I set aside the prolonged but oddly satisfying task, an old aphorism came to mind: "The gift becomes the work." In spiritual terms, our salvation is an "indescribable" gift of God (2 Corinthians 9:15). And yet God asks that we work with that beneficent harvest to amplify its effect, through our faithfulness to Him and service to others. I can foresee the fruition: a bountiful kingdom supply.

Lord, each of us has a unique role in enhancing Your gifts to the benefit of our homes, neighborhoods, even the world. Show me what that work means in this autumn season. —Evelyn Bence

Sunday, October 20

Happy is the man that findeth wisdom.
—Proverbs 3:13 (KJV)

Hey, Brock, look what I found in my desk drawer," my
mother says, handing me an envelope. It is made of a fine
paper that texting and emails have pretty much made
extinct. The handwriting is old-school beautiful. "Mr.
Brockwell Kidd" is written there. I touch the embossed
name on the back flap, Madison S. Wigginton.

I suppose I was a pushy kid when I decided,
about halfway through high school, that I needed
a mentor and chose Mr. Wigginton. Maybe
being a preacher's kid like me caused him to say
yes. Whatever his thinking, he granted me an
appointment.

Mr. Wigginton was one of Nashville's preeminent
businessmen, now retired. He lived in an elegant
house in a posh neighborhood, widowed and alone.

The first time I knocked on his door, a butler
answered. "Mr. Kidd?" he asked. I stopped myself
from turning around to see if my dad was standing
behind me. I sat in a wingback chair, drinking
tea, munching on a macaroon, waiting for Mr.
Wigginton to appear. He was around ninety, tall,
and spry. His voice was deep and his eyes told me his
heart was young.

I asked for advice. He talked of the importance of friendship and of loyalty to others in business. And so our visits went, sound advice offered to an eager kid. The last time I saw Mr. Wigginton, he was standing on the sideline of the football field at my high-school graduation. Earlier, we had enjoyed one last visit. His parting advice: "Love people and try to understand them." I carry his words with me even now.

Father, You send messengers to impart your wisdom. Help us to be wise enough to listen. —Brock Kidd

Digging Deeper: Ecclesiastes 2:26; Colossians 3:10

Monday, October 21

Take delight in the LORD, and he will give you the desires of your heart. —Psalm 37:4 (NIV)

When I was single, I enjoyed taking walks with my neighbor Helen. Walking and talking with her made the time pass quickly and was more fun. Often, we'd walk too long because we got so caught up in conversation. But when Chuck and I got married and moved away from that neighborhood, I lost my walking companion.

Chuck went to work, so I walked alone. I prayed, listened to music, or called friends to pass the time. But I still missed the fellowship from walking with another person.

After Chuck retired, I hoped he and I would walk together. But I preferred walking in the mornings, kicking my day off with exercise that energized me for the rest of the day. Chuck, on the other hand, wanted to walk after supper, a time I didn't like. We tried to compromise until other things interfered with one of our schedules. So I resumed my walks alone.

I prayed for another walking partner, even asked a few people who lived nearby if they'd like to join me but didn't find anyone who could. *If only Helen lived in this neighborhood,* I wished, knowing how ridiculous my desire was. After all, she and her husband had lived in the same lovely home for years.

Imagine my surprise one day when I ran into Helen on the nature trail in my neighborhood.

"What are you doing here?" I asked.

"We downsized and moved," Helen said. "I was going to call to see where you lived."

Soon we resumed our walks together, and I thanked God for caring about my little wish.

Thank You, Lord, for hearing and fulfilling the desire of our hearts. —Marilyn Turk

Digging Deeper: Matthew 7:11; Philippians 4:19

Tuesday, October 22

Then my people shall dwell…in untroubled places of rest. —Isaiah 32:18 (JPS)

About five months after my husband's funeral, the head of the synagogue's Cemetery Committee told me that the funeral home had buried him in the wrong grave. "I didn't want to tell you right away," she said. "I thought you had enough to deal with."

One of the first things Keith and I had done after moving to Bellingham had been to sell our gravesites in Los Angeles and buy new ones here. We'd chosen a pair of sites in a new row, some distance from the other graves, hard up against the fence that fronted a tree-filled public park. Then we had ignored them, until Keith died.

I learned that Keith now lay in one of four graves owned by a synagogue family, an older couple and their son and daughter-in-law. The man of the couple had been interred several years before; Keith was in the son's grave. I was offered a choice: they could move him to the correct grave, or I could swap our chosen sites for the one he was in and the one next to it. I recoiled with horror at the idea of digging him up; as long as I could end up beside him, I would be OK with it.

But I couldn't understand why it had happened—until the first time I visited the cemetery and saw the graves without all the trappings of the graveside service around them. Then it made perfect sense. More than anything, Keith had hated being left alone. Now he had company, and it was another man waiting for his wife to join him. God had arranged everything better than I could have done myself.

Sometimes it takes me longer than it should to figure out that You're right again, Lord of Surprises.
—Rhoda Blecker

Digging Deeper: Psalms 16:10, 36:13

Wednesday, October 23

I will be your God through all your lifetime,
yes, even when your hair is white with age.
—Isaiah 46:4 (TLB)

It was a record-breaking year. The latest recorded
date for the season's first snowfall had come and
gone weeks ago, but the skies remained clear and
the mornings warm. Yet what I appreciated most
wasn't the mild weather. It was the leaves. Our
extended Indian summer had kept the foliage on the
trees long after it usually would have been swept away
by blustery winds or blackened by the icy grip of an
overnight frost.

This year, every tree was clad in technicolor.
The sunny yellows and ochres of the aspens and
cottonwood were subtle compared to the "burning
bush" reds of the maples and scrub oak. I'd never
realized how many trees grew in Colorado Springs
until all of them seemed to be shouting at once,
"Look at me! Look at me!"

The leaves were so breathtakingly vibrant it was
easy to forget they were dying. This explosion of
beauty was their fond farewell, as their time came to
an end. Day after day, as I marveled at their radiant
hues, I pleaded with God to make me just like them.

I'm not quite ancient, but I'm in the waning
season of my life. Unlike the trees that surround me,
the red in my hair has faded and my cheeks have lost
their glow. But that doesn't mean God's glory can't
continue to shine through my life, as He shows me

how to add a bit of color to the lives of those He's invited me to love.

Please, Lord, teach me how to live fully, mirroring Your beauty through every season of my life, until You call me home. —Vicki Kuyper

Digging Deeper: Psalms 71:18, 73:26; Proverbs 16:31; Ecclesiastes 3:1–22

Thursday, October 24

REMEMBERING GRATITUDE: Nothing Is Impossible

Jesus looked at them and said, "With man this is impossible, but not with God; all things are possible with God." —Mark 10:27 (NIV)

Six years after my deliverance from pain and prescription opioids, you'd think my miracle would've lost a little luster. But there's no trip back in time like revisiting old journals. When life was its hardest, I'd named them Learnals. Yearnals.

How well I remembered the cheerful spiral book with hearts sprinkled on its cover. A bud of hope lived in my heart awaiting winter's thaw. But an unexpected tumor surgery took care of that.

I was almost afraid to crack it open, to return to days I'd tried to forget. Yet something compelled me. Its pages were devoid of entries. A chill came over me. I'd been in so much pain I couldn't even jot in a journal.

As I closed the cover, I noticed a single entry I'd missed before. The words were dated and in quotation marks, but no author was cited. A snippet of conversation or a comment on the radio?

"What would you dream that is so impossible, if it came true, you would know for certain it was from God?"

Fourteen years before, I'd scrawled in a shaky hand, the most fragile of faith: "I'd dream of no more tumor pain. But everyone knows that's impossible." These days, I give away journals so struggling others can dare to believe. Miracles aren't always borne of faith that moves mountains. Only of a God who does.

Things thought impossible? Your specialty, Lord!
—Roberta Messner

Digging Deeper: Jeremiah 32:27; Matthew 19:26; Luke 1:37

Friday, October 25

CELEBRATE!! God's Nudges
My sheep hear my voice, and I know them, and they follow me. —John 10:27 (RSV)

My dog, Zeke, and I were walking through our neighborhood on a perfect autumn morning. We live on a street with large spaces between houses, so we don't lean over backyard fences to catch up with neighbors. Takes more effort to engage with our neighbors. Some say that's why they live on a street like this. They like their privacy.

That's what I was thinking as I neared the Barneses' house and saw the elderly couple sitting together on a bench, enjoying the sunshine. My immediate response was that I should walk down their driveway and offer to take a picture of them. Then I started arguing with myself.

"You might be intruding. Don't do it."

"Yes, do it."

"Just keep walking."

"What if God is nudging you to take a picture?"

I was almost past their driveway when my feet suddenly turned and headed toward them. *What if they don't remember who I am?* I haven't seen them for years.

"Hi, I'm Carol. I live down the street. You look so sweet sitting here together. Would you let me take a picture of you?"

They both smiled and Frank said, "Sure!" So I snapped several pictures with my phone.

We talked while Frank petted Zeke. Before leaving, I got their email address so I could send the pictures to them. Later that day, I got this message: "Thanks, Carol, for such nice pictures and stopping to visit. You made our day. I'm forwarding the pictures to our son. Hope we'll have a chance to visit again when you're out walking. Cheers, Frank."

Lord, let me always hear and respond to Your nudges.
—Carol Kuykendall

Saturday, October 26

The generous will themselves be blessed, for they share their food with the poor. —Proverbs 22:9 (NIV)

Will Lonny and the boys be home tomorrow?" our longtime church friend Jim asked over the phone. "Your fireplace is finished. If they'll lift, I'll deliver."

There was joy in Jim's voice, and my heart beat fast. A few years earlier, when my husband, Lonny, and I purchased our new house, I'd asked Jim if he'd build a mantelpiece. The one in our new home was minimalistic and modern. I'm an old soul.

Jim said he'd be happy to help. He'd recently left the home he'd raised his boys in too.

So Lonny and I designed an Arts and Crafts mantel with an upper panel and layered oak sides.

Then Jim had a knee replacement. Shoulder surgery. And surgery on his back. When it was finally time for the fireplace, I worried. All that sanding, staining, and standing at the saw. "We'll wait," I said. "The fireplace will be nice. But we value you."

Jim persisted. When he drove his truck over, we waited at the curb. Then we carried pieces to the living room and lifted as Jim anchored wood to the wall. It was stunning. Where things had been blank and barren, golden oak gleamed.

But I've had back surgeries too, and I noticed Jim's gait when he headed for our door.

"We could've waited," I said.

"I wanted to help."

Jim's smile spoke that this giving had gifted him too.

When the fire in the fireplace burns brightly, I'm reminded of love.

Lord, thank You for blessing those who bless others. Amen. —Shawnelle Eliasen

Digging Deeper: Hebrews 13:16

Sunday, October 27

...singing and making melody in your heart to the Lord. —Ephesians 5:19 (KJV)

My sister-in-law Alithea has the most beautiful singing voice. Our church doesn't use musical instruments, so my favorite spot to sit in is whichever one is in front of Alithea! Then I can hear her clearly. It's not just that she can hit the notes; her voice has a special, rich quality, one of those "velvet voices" people speak of. What a gift!

If Alithea's voice is velvet, mine is...well, maybe cotton. It's not terrible, but pretty common, I suppose. Nothing special about it. Oh, how I would love to be able to raise my voice to the Lord and have such a beautiful sound emerge!

In spite of my average voice, I began several years ago singing to the Lord as I start each morning.

It's amazing what it does for my headspace the rest of the day; it helps me focus on how praiseworthy God is and reminds me of who gave me this day in the first place. My singing might sound average to anyone else, but I believe that because God loves me so much, it sounds as beautiful to Him as Alithea's voice sounds to me—maybe even more so. If human love can be blind, maybe God's love is not exactly deaf, but perhaps willing to transform a plain old cotton voice into a velvet one.

I'm told it helps to sing from one's diaphragm, but I'm sure it can't compare to how we sound to God when we sing from our hearts.

Father, I will praise You with my voice, such as it is. Please accept my offering of song.
—Ginger Rue

Digging Deeper: Psalms 95:1, 100:1

Monday, October 28

The kingdom of heaven is like a grain of mustard seed that a man took and sowed in his field. It is the smallest of all seeds, but when it has grown it is larger than all the garden plants and becomes a tree.
—Matthew 13:31–32 (ESV)

My son reached over and touched my windshield with his pointer finger, and it immediately shattered—like a spiderweb of glass exploding out from the center point where his finger sat.

"Mom! I hardly even touched it!"

We were baffled, until I took the car into the shop to be fixed. There, they found a tiny pebble that had hit my windshield and embedded itself into the glass, ready and waiting for one tiny touch to cause an explosion of shattered glass.

Jesus called the kingdom of heaven a mustard seed—the tiniest of all seeds that grows into the largest and most beautiful plant in the garden.

But there is an opposite truth, as evidenced by my windshield. A teeny, tiny pebble can wiggle its way into our lives and embed itself in us. This tiny pebble may seem small and insignificant, but it can cause a lot of damage.

Aside from teasing my son for weeks about having superhuman strength, my family has also started talking about mustard seeds and pebbles.

We nurture those mustard seeds—those Godly conversations with friends, those quiet moments in the Word.

And the pebbles? The little white lies, the feelings of discontent in our hearts, the grumbling that seems to seep into our conversations. Well, we dig those out of our hearts and toss them aside before they turn into shattered glass.

Dear God, we thank You for sending Jesus to teach us about the kingdom of heaven. Grow the tiny mustard seeds of faith in my heart. —Erin MacPherson

Digging Deeper: Ecclesiastes 11:6; Zechariah 8:12

Tuesday, October 29

Do you not know that your bodies are temples of the Holy Spirit, who is in you, whom you have received from God? —1 Corinthians 6:19 (NIV)

Sometimes it's just best to avoid the mirror, I thought. My aging had moved from a slow process to an outright sprint, the once barely discernible facial lines having turned into little valleys. While I had no inclination to argue with Paul's description of our bodies as "temples," the image staring back at me looked anything but.

I thought of Westminster Abbey. Since I was reared in a church no larger than many bedrooms, my tour of that edifice had been riveting—not to mention my long-held idea of the beautiful temple to which David referred in his sweeping desire to "dwell in the house of the Lord all the days of [his] life" (Psalm 27:4, NIV). The figure in my mirror simply couldn't compare.

Pausing to consider my assumed definition of "temple," I grabbed the dictionary to affirm what I was certain temple meant. But there in the final entry was this: "a place devoted to a special purpose." As was consistently his Spirit-led way, Paul had been spot on.

Though there is nothing quite like entering a lofty space dedicated to worship, it's far more awe inspiring to know that I, an ordinary servant, am also a temple devoted to housing the Holy Spirit. No matter the harsh mirror, I would continue to let the Light shine—through the wrinkles, the thinning hair, the bad knees. After all, my purpose is to carry the Spirit. You can't get any more riveting than that.

Jesus, I'm so grateful that You have accepted my flawed body as a place where Your Spirit not only works through me but lives in me. —Jacqueline F. Wheelock

Digging Deeper: Psalm 27:4; 2 Corinthians 4:7, 16–18

Wednesday, October 30

I am perfect in beauty. —Ezekiel 27:3 (NIV)

I lost my appreciation for Halloween pumpkins ever since Andrew, my last child, was no longer interested in carving them. I haven't purchased one in thirty-five years. But recently, when visiting my brother and sister-in-law, they talked about the pumpkin extravaganza in their town of Louisville, Kentucky. I wasn't sure I even wanted to go on that chilly October evening, but I said yes, wondering what I was getting myself into.

That amazing display of more than 5,000 hand-carved pumpkins had me saying "holy cow!" and "holy moly!" more often than I'd like to admit during our mile-and-a-half walk. I was stunned when I saw how many artists had carved lifelike portraits of stars like Lucille Ball, Oprah, Judge Judy, Sonny and Cher, Prince, E.T., Beauty and the Beast, Smokey the Bear, Rosa Parks, Hank Aaron, and hundreds of others. Imagine 5,000 carved pumpkins of faces, butterflies, fish, flowers, and hundreds of other designs.

The display in the dark of night, with each pumpkin lit up and music playing, created something that quite honestly shook my soul. As I watched hundreds of families of all ages walking hand-in-hand, some in strollers, wheelchairs, walkers, or carrying canes, all oohing and aahing, some singing along with the piped-in music, I noticed that all of us were totally gobsmacked. Those 5,000 pumpkins filled each of us with the wonder of God's gift to us in the form of artistic expression. That night, I learned that I am never too old to appreciate a new experience and that I should always say yes to every opportunity. I can't wait for next Halloween.

Father, open my heart to experience and appreciate the talents of others because all those talents come from You. —Patricia Lorenz

Digging Deeper: Psalm 107:8–9; Romans 12:2

Thursday, October 31

You will be enriched in every way so that you can be generous on every occasion, and through us your generosity will result in thanksgiving to God. —2 Corinthians 9:11 (NIV)

Our church had what I thought was a brilliant idea that October—cartoon-looking cards to invite children and their parents to attend Sunday services. The pastor suggested we hand them out or perhaps drop them in trick-or-treat bags.

I've never been a big fan of trick-or-treating. I don't like scary costumes. Groups of kids running around in the dark can be dangerous. Getting candy from neighbors you might not know well seems unsafe. Too much sugar is unhealthy. Plus, I didn't want to celebrate the potentially evil origins of the holiday that some anti-Halloween parents warned me about. *Yes, these cards were a good idea.* I grabbed several stacks on the way out of the church lobby.

My husband, Michael, eyed me suspiciously. He had fond memories of the holiday. He's always wanted to be the house that handed out full-sized candy bars on Halloween, but I wouldn't consider such an expense.

"You're not thinking about giving those cards instead of candy, are you?" he asked, warily.

I explained the church cards promoted Jesus and were free. I told him we could spread the Gospel instead of tooth decay.

"If we hand out those cards, they'll need to be attached to full-sized candy bars," Michael said with a nod, "so kids can taste the generous goodness of God."

A sweet idea that satisfied us both!

May I always be bighearted, openhanded, and extravagantly generous in whatever I do in Your name, Lord. —Stephanie Thompson

Digging Deeper: Psalm 34:8; Proverbs 11:25; Luke 6:38; 2 Corinthians 9:6–10

YOU WERE CALLED TO PEACE

1 _____

2 _____

3 _____

4 _____

5 _____

6 _____

7 _____

8 _____

9 _____

10 _____

11 _____

12 _____

13 _____

14 _____

15 _____

16 _____

17 _____

18 _____

19 _____

20 _____

21 _____

22 _____

23 _____

24 _____

25 _____

26 _____

27 _____

28 _____

29 _____

30 _____

31 _____

NOVEMBER

In peace I will lie down and sleep, for you alone,
LORD, make me dwell in safety.

—Psalm 4:8 (NIV)

Friday, November 1

Where can I go from your Spirit? Where can
I flee from your presence? —Psalm 139:7 (NIV)

My son, Solomon, is studying music in film at
college. We were on the way to the store when he
told me about his latest class where they focus on the
intersection of music and its role in movies.

"So diegetic sound is when the characters hear the
sound or music," Solomon explained. "Nondiegetic
is when it is added as part of the experience, like
background music, but the characters don't hear it
and aren't aware of it."

I turned off the radio so I could focus on the
conversation.

"So, listen, Mom, my favorite is when it's sort of like
a trick. Like when you think the character doesn't hear
the music, that it's for background or effect, but then
the character takes off his headphones and the sound
stops, so you realize he heard the music all along."

That night, as I was falling asleep, I thought
about how these terms, diegetic and nondiegetic,
could be applied to faith—the times when God is
present and I know it, and the infinite times He
intervenes, adding His beautiful music, yet I go
about my life completely unaware. But my favorite,
like Solomon, is when I suddenly recognize His
glorious presence has been there all along.

**Lord, thank You for the moments when I hear
and recognize Your music in my life.**
—Sabra Ciancanelli

Saturday, November 2

My sheep hear my voice, and I know them, and they follow me. —John 10:27 (ESV)

The leaves have fallen in the woods surrounding the house. Farmer Doug has picked the corn in the field next door. The air is crisp and cool. Because of these things, I hear sounds that had long been muffled by the foliage. Far-off train whistles. Cars and pickup trucks booming along the county road in front of the farm. Coyotes yipping in the woods. Geese squawking as they float on the lake behind our place.

Those sounds were always there. It's just that I didn't hear them very much during the growing season. Which made me wonder how much of the Divine voice I miss because it's obscured by all the things I have growing. Family concerns. Projects to do. Places to go. God speaks to me all the time, but I'm not hearing. My deafness is despite the plea in a hymn I've been singing in church ever since I was kid:

> Open my ears, that I may hear
> Voices of truth thou sendest clear;
> And while the wave notes fall on my ear,
> Everything false will disappear.*

---

*"Open My Eyes, That I May See," music and lyrics by Clara H. Scott

Ah, voices of Divine truth are all around me. When I listen to God speaking, I find strength for the living of my days. Beauty that feeds my soul in the natural sounds. Love in the voice of my wife that reminds me to be loving in turn. Direction from the God who guides and walks with me all the days of my life.

Oh God Who Speaks, help me be one of Your people who listens to Your voice no matter where it's coming from or who or when. Teach me attentiveness. Amen.
—J. Brent Bill

Digging Deeper: 1 Samuel 3:1–10

Sunday, November 3

Jehoram was thirty-two years old when he became king, and he reigned in Jerusalem eight years. No one was sorry when he died. —2 Chronicles 21:20 (NLT)

Amy and her two younger sisters were my babysitting charges when I was a teenager. All three of them were beautiful, sweet girls, and I adored them. Their dad told me once that Amy had said they liked me because "she talks to us just like we're real people." I've held that in my heart for decades, and it helped me as a middle-grade teacher and a writer of children's books.

When I moved away to start college, I lost touch with Amy and her family. I was rocking my first baby when I got the call with the terrible news: Amy, a recent college graduate, had been killed in a car accident.

Even though I hadn't seen or talked to Amy in years, I felt her loss tremendously. I grieved not only for her family but also because such a light had been extinguished in this world.

Amy's family started a scholarship fund at her alma mater, and more than twenty years later, it's still going strong. Everyone who knew Amy loved her. Her life was too short, but she lived it well.

When I came across the passage in 2 Chronicles, I thought of Amy and also of my own life. Do I want to be like that king and squander my opportunities to show God's love? Or do I want to spend my days—however many there may be—like Amy and leave a legacy of such love and kindness that my absence will be felt as a loss?

Lord, help me to honor You while I live on this earth!
—Ginger Rue

Digging Deeper: Psalm 90:12; 1 Corinthians 15:55

Monday, November 4

Fear not. —2 Kings 6:16 (KJV)

"Mimi, I have a birthday wish," says sixteen-year-old Abby, our dream of a granddaughter.

"Mama said I couldn't get a tattoo until my eighteenth birthday, and when the time comes, I want all three of us to get a tattoo, together."

"OK." I smile, sure that her request would be forgotten in two years.

Seeing tattoos as forms of expression, I often asked their wearers to share their meanings. But I certainly didn't want one. Then, along about age seventeen, I realized Abby was holding tight to my commitment.

"It has to be small," I said, "and mean something important to me."

Abby began throwing out suggestions. Keri found a renowned tattoo artist, famous for his ability to create tiny tattoos.

"I've decided on my tattoo," I announced, finally, as the time drew near. "I choose 'fear nothing.'" These were the words my husband, David, said at the end of every church service.

"Hmm," said Keri.

"Hmm," said Abby.

"Mimi, Mama and I have decided that we will get the same tattoo as you," Abby announced later. Then, as an afterthought, she added, "And we will get them in Big Dad's [the name our grandchildren chose for David] handwriting."

So, there you have it, tiny and inconspicuous on my inner wrist, "Fear Nothing," as if David scrawled it there. Both Keri's and Abby's are the same, always reminding us of David's ending to every benediction: "Christ is risen. Christ is with you. Go out into all the world...and fear nothing."

I hope and pray that through the years my girls will find strength, courage, and comfort in the message that I cling to now.

Father, You hold our world in the palm of Your hand. I will fear nothing. —Pam Kidd

Digging Deeper: Psalm 23:4; John 14:27

Tuesday, November 5

See what love the Father has given us, that we should be called children of God, and that is what we are. —1 John 3:1 (NRSVUE)

Decades ago, I wrote a ream of poetry—not anymore. I used to plan dinner parties, sit down or buffet—now neither. Such changes have recently prompted me to mull over an age-old question: who am I? I wasn't expecting the answer I found this morning.

A neighbor teen who is developmentally delayed and speaks Spanish at home accompanied me to my polling site. She waited quietly as I cast my ballot. We both said "no, thank you" to free stickers—"I voted" or "future voter"—and walked out, she slightly ahead of me. Before we reached the car, a well-dressed man rather rushed toward her. She understood his fast-talking Spanish, though I didn't. Even so, I perceived the question. As she responded in Spanish, I cut in, "She didn't vote! She's a child!" In my protective mode, that last word just slipped out.

As the man backed away, the teen, suddenly animated, named him as a reporter for a local Spanish-language TV station. In the car, when the conversation finally died down, I ventured an apology. "I'm sorry I called you a child. I spoke so quickly. I wasn't thinking."

"I'm *not* a child. You know that!" She paused. "Except I *am* a child of God." She suddenly burst into song, one she'd learned years before in vacation Bible school: "We are the children of God!"

By the time I dropped her off, I was singing her refrain. *Child of God.* For today, that's all I need to know.

Father God, no matter what my age or season of life, help me remember my baseline identity— as Your child. —Evelyn Bence

Digging Deeper: Romans 8:12–27

Wednesday, November 6

If we confess our sins, he is faithful and just and will forgive us our sins and purify us from all unrighteousness. —1 John 1:9 (NIV)

Those exhaustive-seeming alphabetical lists of phobias online always omit one of mine. Librarians call it "library anxiety" and have strategies for alleviating it. However, library-phobes like me rarely enter physical libraries to be helped. If we must use one, we do so virtually, which only intensifies the problem.

My library-phobia goes like this. I'm looking for an article my students can read without hitting a paywall. On our university library homepage, I put in the author and title and get...nothing. I try advanced searches and consult "Resources on All Subjects" and get... "Try your search again."

An hour later, I give up and send my students an email with the article probably illegally attached as disassociated pics of my screen. By then, I'm apoplectic with library loathing.

In one such collapse, I emailed one of my favorite colleagues: the easy-going librarian who always soothes me by expertly populating my fruitless searches. This time, though, instead of simply requesting help, I described the preceding hour and ended, "Please don't read this that I'm mad at you. I'm not. I'm just *so* frustrated."

It being the start of the semester, when everyone's inboxes are overwhelmed, my email bomb went unanswered. Weeks later, I found a seat beside my colleague at a meeting and begged forgiveness, and she huge-heartedly granted it, reminding me of my daily, hourly need for forgivenesses of all sorts and of our long-suffering God, who sees all and instantly grants them.

Father God, forgive my explosions of frustration. Better yet, defuse them before they happen. Most of all, though, thank You for Your constant and unmerited forgiveness. —Patty Kirk

Digging Deeper: Mark 11:22–25; Hebrews 8:7–13

Thursday, November 7

I will sing, will sing to the Lord, Will hymn the Lord, the God of Israel. —Judges 5:3 (JPS)

"Pick three songs," said my friend Laura. She and I both loved musical theater and often told each other what was happening to us by choosing which Rodgers and Hammerstein or Cole Porter or Lerner and Loewe song was playing in our minds at that moment. Now she was upping the program by asking me which three I'd pick for my whole life (so far).

I thought back to my childhood memories. I still had PTSD from being molested by a medical professional, a friend of my father's, because some pain never leaves. "The first one would be from *Kiss Me Kate*," I said. "'I Hate Men.'" That one worked until I met my husband, Keith.

The next choice would have to cover the thirty-six years that Keith and I were together, and there were lots of love songs, so this was a harder decision to make. Ultimately, however, none of them exactly fit, so I had to range further afield than just Broadway. "Not a show tune," I said. "I'd have to take Brian Wilson's 'God Only Knows.'"

Laura nodded. "And now?"

And then what could I use for the sorrow of my life after he died? I didn't want Howard Shore's "Into the West." We had played that at his funeral, and the grief was too raw then. It had to be a song I could resonate with now. The answer finally came to me with such force that I marveled I hadn't thought of it immediately. "It would have to be from *Carousel*: 'You'll Never Walk Alone.'"

You are to be honored greatly, Lord Who Inspires Music, for knowing what songs will give to our souls.
—Rhoda Blecker

Friday, November 8

**Now when Jesus saw the crowds, he went up on a mountainside and sat down. His disciples came to him, and he began to teach them.... Blessed are the merciful, for they will be shown mercy.
—Matthew 5:1–2, 7 (NIV)**

"Sally" came to the hospital after overdosing on heroin.

Luckily, prompt medical care saved her life. When I visited with her, she remembered "floating in the air and looking into the kitchen of a house where a woman lay on the floor." Soon, she sensed a Being of Light next to her. She didn't feel judged by the Being of Light; only loved. The Being directed her to look at the woman, who was apparently near death. When Sally looked, she realized it was her but, strangely, she felt totally detached from herself. The Being encouraged her to be as compassionate to the woman on the floor as the Being was with her.

She then woke up in the hospital. When I asked her who this Being was, she said she didn't know. I was disappointed that she didn't say Jesus. That would have been my answer. After our conversation, I went to the chapel to pray.

But soon, my disappointment turned to peace when in prayer I realized that the Being of Light (Jesus) was asking me to be as compassionate toward the woman as He had been. I also felt Jesus asking me to realize there have been many times when I didn't recognize Him either. And even then, God had been merciful and accepting of me. As I sat in silence, I prayed for the gift to see clearly and to recognize God in the many ways He comes to bless me.

God, open my heart so that my eyes can see You more clearly. Amen. —Adam Ruiz

Digging Deeper: Exodus 33:19; Psalm 6:2

Saturday, November 9

One generation shall commend your works to another, and shall declare your mighty acts. —Psalm 145:4 (ESV)

While sorting our parents' estate, my siblings and I discovered a toy wooden barn in a corner of the garage, tucked under the workbench. Dad had built the barn in 1963 for Phil's fourth Christmas, an event documented by an old black-and-white photo in the family album. My brother ran his hand over the faded red wood, drawing our attention to the variety of screws and nails that held the structure together, little bits of this and that, which Dad had kept in an old coffee can on his workbench. Raising a family of six on a teacher's salary had not allowed random trips to the hardware store.

Phil lent me the barn for eight years. My grandchildren created stories with farm animals, plastic dalmatian puppies, and an occasional Star Wars battle in the haymow against the Empire.

This past spring, my sister, Renae, and I drove from Arizona to California to return the barn to its rightful owner. Again, Phil ran his hands over the handcrafted plywood, as he lifted it from the car and carried it inside.

That night, stories of Dad and Mom flowed round the table while we sat and drank coffee and tea—tales of life on that little hobby farm when we were children. As Phil excused himself to do the evening chores on *his* hobby farm, I realized I had not just delivered a barn but a container of love and childhood. We, too, were transported to a time far, far away. And yet not so distant at all.

Lord, when all I have is a little bit of this and that, may I create structures of love to last generations.
—Lynne Hartke

Digging Deeper: Deuteronomy 7:9; Proverbs 13:22

Sunday, November 10

Yet you, LORD, are our Father. We are the clay, you are the potter; we are all the work of your hand.
—Isaiah 64:8 (NIV)

I've loved coloring since I was a child. There is something special about being able to transform plain black-and-white pages into something colorful, unique, and beautiful. As a child, I was particular about my coloring books and didn't like to share.

Some years ago, when adult coloring books became popular, I jumped on board. I snatched up a collection of books, colored pencils, and a vivid set of markers. Coloring was an ideal way for me to unwind and destress at the end of the day.

Once, my daughter jumped on my bed, excited to see me coloring. It was one of her favorite pastimes as well.

"I love coloring, don't you, Mommy? Can I color with you?" she asked.

She didn't wait for a response but grabbed a marker and set to work on the adjoining page. *Please don't scribble outside the lines,* I thought. *I should buy her another one so she doesn't have to color in mine.*

My selfish thoughts dissolved as we spent time together. I thought about how out of the nearly eight billion people in the world, no two are created exactly the same. My daughter's creation and mine, very different, reflected our personalities and distinct tastes. She'd colored out of the lines and that was OK. Hers was a one-of-a-kind masterpiece.

God has made all of our lives beautiful, and our experiences are a reflection of His handiwork.

Lord, thank You for a life that was fashioned just for me. All the things in my life are working together for my good, and what a beautiful picture it will be.
—Tia McCollors

Veterans Day, Monday, November 11

It is for freedom that Christ has set us free.
—Galatians 5:1 (NIV)

On this Veterans Day, I remember my maternal
uncle, Robert Braswell Mathews. Uncle Bob was
seventeen when the United States was thrust into
World War II. He joined the United States Army
and was assigned to the Signal Corps. He spent
three rugged years in India, Burma, and China. He
entered the war a naïve teenager from Georgia and
returned home a grizzled veteran in 1945.

After the war, Uncle Bob was able to attend
the University of California School of Architecture
due to the generosity of a grateful nation and the
creation of the G.I. Bill. Upon graduation, he spent
the next forty years designing some of the tallest
buildings in the United States and was the "architect
of note" for the restoration of the California State
Capitol building.

However, what impressed me most as a teenager
was hearing his stories of the sacrifice of his friends
who gave their lives during the war for my freedom.
As Uncle Bob grew older, I watched tears escape
down his creased cheeks as he recalled "the boys who
did not come home" or "the nurses who cured my
malaria."

Bob died three years ago at age ninety-six. As his only nephew, I was the minister at his graveside service. As "Taps" was trumpeted and six young soldiers in dress uniform snapped to attention, my sister and I were presented with the flag of the United States that draped his coffin. I will never forget that moment. And we should never forget all the men and women of every nation who have sacrificed for world peace and unification.

Dear God, on this Veterans Day, may we honor those who have sacrificed for our liberty and freedom. Amen. —Scott Walker

Digging Deeper: Joshua 1:9; Isaiah 41:10

Tuesday, November 12

Dress in the wardrobe God picked out for you: compassion, kindness, humility, quiet strength, discipline. —Colossians 3:12 (MSG)

Those who know me well wouldn't describe my fashion preferences as understated. I've been known to dress as an elf (complete with green, curly-toed, bell-laden shoes), not only for my grandchildren on Christmas morning but also on the sales floor when I sold designer shoes. I've also donned a sparkly narwhal sweater simply to add a bit of creative zing to a snowy, stay-at-home day when I had a busy writing schedule. So, when the rose-colored, denim patchwork pants I'd ordered finally arrived, I was understandably excited. Then I opened the package.

Instead of drawstring joggers, I found a silver and gold sequin sheath dress. Not quite the outfit I'd purchased to wear for babysitting the grandkids. Appropriate for a New Year's Eve party or an Academy Awards acceptance speech? Perhaps. But for changing dirty diapers and running school carpools? Not so much.

I had to laugh at how impractical this beautiful dress would be for my current stage of life. That's when Colossians 3:12 came to mind. In this verse, God talks about choosing to dress myself in qualities like compassion, kindness, and quiet strength. Now, there's an outfit that's appropriate for caring for my grandkids, as well as for every situation and season of life.

Father, please help me worry less about how I dress my body and more about how I choose to clothe my heart and mind. —Vicki Kuyper

Digging Deeper: Proverbs 27:19; Ezekiel 36:26; Romans 14:19

Wednesday, November 13

Now faith is the assurance of things hoped for, the conviction of things not seen. —Hebrews 11:1 (ESV)

There is a massive incline just up the street from us. It falls somewhere between a hill and a mountain. Your ears pop as you go up, the car strains, and you can feel as if you're going straight into a cloud, especially on foggy mornings like this one.

Beau and I were headed up the hill to the grocery store. He started to get scared. "Mama, I can't see the road up there. Where are you going?"

I reminded him that this was the same road we traveled every week; it just looked different because a cloud was hanging out a little too low. "It is so sad that the sun is gone," he said, looking mournfully out the window.

"The sun isn't gone," I told him. "It's always there! Sometimes clouds come down and block it so it feels like it's gone, or very far away, but the sun is exactly where it has always been, just like Jesus."

During that five-minute drive to the store, Beau and I talked about how sometimes things we love feel very far away. But behind the clouds, they're still there, waiting to see us again.

Now Beau isn't afraid of the fog; he knows the sun is right behind it always.

Lord, help me remember that You are always there, always watching, always loving, even on days when it seems like I am alone. —Ashley Kappel

Digging Deeper: Jeremiah 29:11; Mark 11:22–24

Thursday, November 14

Day after day they pour forth speech; night after night they reveal knowledge. —Psalm 19:2 (NIV)

Today I would like to discuss *Hamlet.*

You must be mad! Not really.

I hadn't read it in years, and I don't know what made me reach for it today. Possibly it's the gray, blustery weather, or the ad for cheap airfare to Copenhagen I saw online.

Who knows? But skimming though this archetypal revenge tragedy, I couldn't help thinking what a horrible collection of human beings these characters are (except, possibly, Horatio). Why then are we so drawn to them?

They roar to life on a swell of language, sometimes tedious and verbose, more often rich and poetical, ambiguous and ambivalent, bawdy and numinous. The language of the play itself can drive you mad interpreting it.

The key to *Hamlet* can be found in another of the Bard's masterworks, *The Tempest*, a kind of revenge comedy, specifically in the relationship between the exiled duke, Prospero, and his fettered servant, Caliban. Prospero's speech is refined and civilized, as befits royalty, while Caliban spews some of Shakespeare's most inventive invective. Yet prior to Prospero's arrival on the desert isle, its sole inhabitant, Caliban, did not speak a word at all. He learned from the duke.

Therein is the brilliance of Shakespeare. He uses his relationship to our most precious gift, language, to capture the beauty of our God-given humanity, the vulgarity of our base desires, and the redemption that comes from reconciling the two in the timeless fluency of poetry. He uses the miracle of language itself to change us, to turn even the vengeful Hamlet into a person who begs our understanding— reminding us of the forgiveness that God shows us throughout our lives.

> **Among the gifts of the garden was the language You gave us, Lord, to explain ourselves to ourselves. But let us always use it to praise You. Always.**
> —Edward Grinnan

Digging Deeper: John 16:25; Acts 2:6–21

Friday, November 15

He who loves his brother abides in the light, and there is no cause for stumbling in him.
—1 John 2:10 (NKJV)

My brother, Kevin, and I were very close growing up. We'd often hug each other…well, *hug* isn't the right word. *Wrestle* might be a better word. *Engaged in mortal combat* would be the most accurate. True story: our sainted mother would hear Kevin and me…um, hugging, and she would call up to us, "Brothers don't fight!"

We couldn't respond because, you know, mutual chokehold.

Over time, we became actually close, sharing moments of both solitude and outrageousness. The time we nearly drowned at Ohiopyle State Park (not funny); the time we towed Kevin's pickup home using a six-foot rope through rush hour (kinda funny now);

the time he found a water hose in the produce section of the local supermarket and squirted me in the back (funny for him); the time a policeman asked Kevin for his driver's license and Kevin confidently handed over...a three of clubs (not funny for either the cop or Kevin but absolutely hilarious to me).

There are other times—not meant for public consumption—where "funny" was nowhere to be found. Some were desperate times when we weren't sure we'd make it. We did. We weathered those times, and we weathered them together.

Today is Kevin's birthday. It's a significant one, ending in a zero. I'm not sure why I was chosen to have the best brother ever. Writing about Kevin leaves me with a catch in my throat, and this time it's not a chokehold.

Lord, You gave me the gift of a lifetime blood-friend. Your bounty is without end. —Mark Collins

Digging Deeper: Genesis 33:4; Luke 15:32

Saturday, November 16

Therefore, having such a hope, we use great boldness in our speech. —2 Corinthians 3:12 (NASB)

My friend Isaac is attending barber school. I love him. He's funny, open, and the most guileless person I know. When he invited me to be a guinea pig on which to practice his burgeoning skills, how could I say no? "Only five bucks," he said.

I'd never been to a barber school. It was big, packed with tattooed and pierced students. Isaac led me to one of a zillion barber chairs and draped a cape around me. I eyed a nearby mannequin that looked like it had run headfirst into a fan. "Did that guy pay five bucks?"

Isaac just laughed and started in with the clippers. "So I heard this sermon the other day," he said.

Then he talked about Jesus.

I've stood on a thousand stages. I can't remember a single time in front of a crowd I've found it difficult to vocalize my faith. But—and I bet I'm not alone in this—in a public setting I can get a little uncomfortable openly talking faith. It's true, and it makes me truly ashamed.

But not Isaac. He talked on in perfect, wonderful Isaac-ness. No one looked our way, but I know they listened. And what they heard was a man who knew Jesus not only as Savior but also as Friend.

I heard too. I was convicted but also encouraged and uplifted and emboldened. You know what? By the time we were done, I'd also gotten a darn good haircut. I can't wait to see what God does with Isaac. And just maybe He'll do something with me too.

Forgive me, Lord. Please make me bold so the world might know Your bottomless, unending love!
—Buck Storm

Digging Deeper: 1 Corinthians 16:13;
2 Timothy 1:7–8

Sunday, November 17

Praise the LORD! Praise God in his sanctuary; praise him in his mighty heavens! —Psalm 150:1 (ESV)

I usually receive powerful messages at worship on Sunday, but this week I felt detached. Not feeling truly present, I stood up for praise and worship, but my eye was drawn to the far-left side of the chapel. There I found a young mom with the absolute cutest one-year-old on her hip. My initial thought was, *Oh I remember those days. Good for you, Momma.* As the praise band began, the mom lifted her free hand and worshipped. *Praise Him even when your hands are full*—good message.

Then a few moments later, her one-year-old also lifted her hands. The vision of this young mom and baby praising together struck my soul, immediately attaching me to community and centering my presence in worship. It was beautiful to watch and inspiring to my heart. *The priorities of parents are often reflected in the actions of their children*—powerful message.

I was grateful to the Lord for calling my attention to this young mom and her baby. Too often I am too full, full of things to do and thoughts to sort, and I sometimes do not pay attention to the messages around me. Ah, but *this* Sunday, God surprised me through a message in this young mom's example. My prayer this Sunday was, "Momma, may you continue to be a shining example of living faith to us all!"

Father, may I strive to praise You through all the circumstances of my life. May my eyes continuously be fixed upon You. —Jolynda Strandberg

Digging Deeper: Deuteronomy 10:20–22; Psalm 34; Isaiah 12:4–6

Monday, November 18

You will be enriched in every way so that you can be generous on every occasion, and through us your generosity will result in thanksgiving to God. —2 Corinthians 9:11 (NIV)

Out for lunch with a friend at a local steakhouse, we enjoyed truly exceptional service. When we both complimented our server, she shared that she would be leaving her job soon to become a paralegal. Talking further, she mentioned some upcoming challenges. The paralegal school was in a different city, so she will have to relocate. She is a single mom with a young son and they live with her dad. Upon moving, they will be far from her dad, who helps with his grandson's care.

After we finished eating, my friend and I remained at the table catching up. Our server continued checking in with us and refreshing our drinks. Finally, we both signed our bills. Returning with our credit cards, she graciously thanked us both for our tips and, turning to my friend, said, "You don't have to do this." He responded, "I know, but I want to help you." Before we left, she thanked him two more times—he must have left quite a sizable tip!

Walking to the car, I said, "You really warmed my heart with your generosity." He smiled and said, "When I see people as committed to developing themselves as she is, I figure they need the money more than me, and I give it to them."

Lord, You tell us to generously bless others from what You give us. Thank You for putting people in our lives who demonstrate this so well and inspire us with their kind and giving hearts. —John Dilworth

Digging Deeper: 1 Chronicles 29:14; 2 Corinthians 9:6; 1 Timothy 6:18

Tuesday, November 19

If you are sensible, you will control your temper. —Proverbs 19:11 (GNT)

I received a flyer about a local event that I thought was edgy, if not immoral, and I was irritated. I grabbed a yellow tablet and slapped it down on my desk. "I will write the director of this event and give him a piece of my mind."

Throughout the day, I jotted down my objections with a bold, black pen. At the end of the day, I had three pages of handwritten rage. *This is good stuff,* I thought. *Tomorrow I will fire this off and see if I can get this event stopped.*

The next morning, I looked over my work and I could see that the last page was too strong. *They will think I'm a crackpot when they read this.* So, I tossed that page. Two of my paragraphs were repetitious, so I eliminated one of those, and several of my opinions were unsupported by evidence, so I scratched those.

At last I was down to one magnificent ballistic missive that easily rivaled the 1941 declaration of war on Germany.

But by now I was emotionally drained. As I reviewed my work, reality set in. *Nobody gives a rip what an old man like me thinks about this. They will just laugh at me.* I tore up the letter.

That night in bed, I felt at peace. I had clarified my beliefs in writing, a valuable exercise, but God had saved me from making a fool of myself. I slept well.

I thank You, Father, for the gift of temper and for helping me to use it wisely. —Daniel Schantz

Digging Deeper: Ecclesiastes 7:9; Colossians 3:12–14

Wednesday, November 20

In this world you will have trouble. But take heart! I have overcome the world. —John 16:33 (NIV)

My heart leaped at the email. A dream come true, a prayer answered—a publisher had accepted my proposed book for publication.

"Yes! Thank God!" I couldn't wait to tell my husband the good news. For a year, I'd been hoping for this answer, trying to prepare myself if it was rejected. But now I could rejoice and celebrate God's goodness. My spirit soared and my confidence rose a few decimal points. I planned to ride this high for a long time.

But a short time later, I received a text from my son telling me my grandson had gotten into trouble at school. Immediately my heart sank, and anxiety set in. My focus shifted to my grandson's situation and my prayers for the outcome.

Life is like that, you know. One minute you're on a mountaintop of emotions, enjoying good news and celebrating. Then all of a sudden, you slide down that mountain into the valley of worry, anxiety, and depression. As much as we don't like it, we have to face life's ups and downs.

In the Bible, Jesus acknowledged this human state of "trials and tribulations." But He offers hope. We don't have to be knocked down by trouble; we can tolerate it by knowing He is with us and will get us through it. We don't have to sink under the weight of our emotional burdens because He will help us carry them.

No, we won't be able to avoid life's pitfalls. But by keeping our trust in Jesus, we'll make it to the next mountaintop, strengthened for the journey.

Dear Lord, thank You for being with me on this unpredictable journey of life.
—Marilyn Turk

Digging Deeper: Psalm 59:16; Nahum 1:7; Matthew 11:28–30

REMEMBERING GRATITUDE:
Open Heart, Open Hands
Every good and perfect gift is from above.
—James 1:17 (NIV)

When my upholsterer delivered the chairs he'd re-covered, he couldn't take his eyes off the old radio on a shelf in my antique cupboard. "That Philco, Roberta!" Pete exclaimed with a faraway gleam in his eye. "My boy and I are taking a repair class at the radio museum. It's the first thing we've found we like to do together." Pete stroked the marbled brown Bakelite with something resembling reverence. "My son could fix this. How much would it take to buy it?"

Buy it? My retro radio wasn't for sale. I had loved it since forever, right down to its little red knobs and dial pointer.

I thought of how Pete had driven an hour to fetch his nine-year-old son at his ex-wife's house. How, showing more promise than any adult in the group, the boy had been awarded the voltage tester for the week. But my heart refused to budge. That radio was mine. *Mine.* Not. For. Sale.

Pete had just closed the door on the driver's side of his pickup when I caught sight of his boy beside him. A scene reappeared from seventh grade. My home economics teacher had noticed me ogling her sewing-machine brooch and pinned it onto my sweater. "For you, my dear," she whispered. "We must always know when to give something away."

I flagged down the father and son in the truck leaving my driveway. I'd nearly traded a little boy's grin for a silly shelf-sitter.

Giver of all gifts, as I walk through Your world, keep my heart and hands open. —Roberta Messner

Digging Deeper: Luke 6:38; 2 Corinthians 9:7

Friday, November 22

Happy are the people to whom such blessings fall; happy are the people whose God is the LORD. —Psalm 144:15 (NRSV)

After crawling out of bed, I stumbled into the kitchen and saw coffee stains, a squished blueberry, and small green leaves crushed into the floor tile. My husband, Charlie, rises before I do, and this was not an unusual morning experience. But last night while he slept, I'd scrubbed the floors and now felt frustration rising.

The dirty little secret about the kindest man I know is that he's not neat, to put it mildly. Fortunately, this usually isn't a big issue because it's not deliberate. His sloppiness comes with a blissful innocence and absence of malice that makes my spousal transgressions look much worse. He's told me he didn't notice the Ben & Jerry's footprints because he couldn't feel ice cream on the soles of his feet; he couldn't see the sesame seeds scattered from his toast because he's tall with eyes far from the floor. And he means it. He is dumbfounded that such things happen.

But this morning, I was in no mood. Mouth opened, breath drawn, I looked up to catch his eye. That's when I saw the flowers he'd bought me in a vase and knew he'd trimmed the leaves to make them last. That's when I remembered he was making coffee at home to save money and eating blueberries for brain health.

That's when I thanked God for sending me a living reminder of His many blessings to me. And of all the things I needed to let go of to better appreciate the good.

Gracious Father, thank You for Your great generosity and all the reminders You give me of it.
—Marci Alborghetti

Digging Deeper: Ecclesiastes 11:7–9; Matthew 7:3–4

Saturday, November 23

Sing for joy to God our strength; shout aloud to the God of Jacob! —Psalm 81:1 (NIV)

For as long as I've played music, I've struggled with rhythm. Fast-moving beats, subdivided into even smaller, split-second intervals? Yeah, impossible. For me, anyway.

My trumpet teacher consistently pushes back on this, though. "You *can* feel the beat," he insists. But I've always been sure I knew otherwise.

A set of rhythmic exercises during a recent lesson was proving my point. They were relatively simple, yet—try as I might—I couldn't get them right. With each failure, my anxiety grew, and my brain's thinking gears ground closer to a halt.

Finally, I gave up. In frustration, I tried to describe this frozen and fearful short-circuit in my mind to my teacher.

"Were you afraid when we were playing through that?" he asked in reply, pointing toward a duet book we'd worked out of earlier. It was still open to the last piece we'd played together, and I looked at it now with new eyes. The page was peppered with complex rhythms, so much trickier than the exercises I'd just been bombing. Yet, I'd played these at least mostly correctly or the duet wouldn't have worked. And it *had*. It'd been such a delight, fear hadn't even crossed my mind.

And that, I realized suddenly, was the difference. It's the fear that can't count, not me. The music on the stand proved it. When I'm playing from a place of joy rather than fear—letting myself be immersed in the good things that God wants for me instead of my own insecurities—not only can I subdivide and play rhythms correctly, but I can feel them too. What fun!

Thank You, God, for this joyful reminder that fear separates me from You and from the joy You would bestow upon my life. —Erin Janoso

Digging Deeper: Genesis 43:23; Isaiah 41:10

The LORD is my light. —Psalm 27:1 (KJV)

Years ago, I became enamored with *The Alchemist*, a novel by Paulo Coelho. It's the story of a young boy who sets out on a journey of discovery, only to find that God had already laid out his path and left omens to guide him along the way.

Now, granted, I never considered riding a camel across a desert or digging for treasure in the shadow of a pyramid like the boy in the book. But I have come to believe that, as Coelho suggests, we are all writing our "personal legends" as we follow the life path God has set for us. The good and bad omens along the way, well, I'd guess God offers them as learning opportunities.

Along my path, I encounter a teacher who gave up a lucrative career to pass on a love of literature to her students and a woodworker who hired me as a gangly kid, showing me the pride that comes from hard work and a job well done. I see letters of hope in my old Aunt Kate's careful handwriting and hear shouts of encouragement from my high-school coach.

On the darker side, I pass people intent on disparaging others, a cheating husband, a dishonest clerk. Distractions happen. I've been taken in by the "shiny" people who flaunt "Christianity" as they diminish others with their judgments. I've been momentarily impressed by people who use vast wealth or Ivy League degrees to make themselves seem superior.

Now, as I travel my path, I finally see that the "personal legends" of the finest people aren't marked by facades of riches or walls of fancy plaques, but by kindnesses shown to others and good deeds given freely.

Father, as I travel on, guide my path with omens of Your light. —Brock Kidd

Digging Deeper: Ephesians 5:8; 1 John 8:12

Monday, November 25

In peace I will lie down and sleep, for you alone, LORD, make me dwell in safety. —Psalm 4:8 (NIV)

I stood in the foyer of my daughter's home, marveling at the stacks of door deliveries. No more two-week Sears, Roebuck & Co. waits as when I was a child. Yet how easily one could overlook something crucial—an unexpected gift, perhaps?—among these packages.

Not until months later, long after I'd returned home to the to-do list that often upended my rest, did the Holy Spirit—so often His way—send my thoughts back to my daughter's entryway. What priceless package from the Savior might I be overlooking, hidden behind the relentless day-to-day duties?

Peace, whispered the Spirit. Jesus Himself had gifted me with peace, so where was it? Why did life's routine sometimes have me awake in the wee hours? The Lord declared, unequivocally, "My peace I give unto you" (John 14:27, KJV). But if I allowed that peace to remain hidden—in unexplored trust in Jesus, in unprayed prayers and unread scripture—it was of little use. Though I may outwardly behave in positive ways, peace, lost in the anteroom of my soul, is but a hidden treasure inherently mine.

I turned to Psalm 4:8, where David says his sleep *will* be peaceful. No debate. He would rest because he keeps the gift of peace always at the fore. How many more peaceful nights could I have had if I'd regularly opened David's scriptural gift and clung to its power? Soothed, I opened the chambers of my heart and rediscovered the priceless peace that was always there.

Lord, thank You for reminding me that peace is already mine if I but pursue it.
—Jacqueline F. Wheelock

Digging Deeper: Psalms 34:14, 119:165; John 14:27

Tuesday, November 26

About midnight Paul and Silas were praying and singing hymns to God, and the prisoners were listening to them. —Acts 16:25 (NRSVUE)

When your kid decides on what to call your grandkid, you just go with it no matter what, exclaiming, "Oh, that's charming. What a great name." But I was a bit flummoxed when Tim and Henley decided on Silas. Why Silas?

The first thing I thought of was the nineteenth-century English novel by George Eliot, *Silas Marner*—which I've never read (English major that I was). But then I recalled something vaguely biblical about it, maybe from the book of Acts. I thumbed through a couple pages, with the help of Google, and there Silas was, Paul's companion in prison. They even sang hymns together. Then there was an earthquake, and all the prison doors were opened.

"We'll have to do that with you," I told the infant Silas. He responded with an enthusiastic, "gagagagagagaga."

The first opportunity came when he was one year old, and his parents were attending a wedding in Vermont. Gramps and Minnie—our grandparent names—were in charge. We took him to church, not sure how long he'd last.

To my amazement, he hardly peeped throughout the service, gazing at the stained-glass windows, the mosaics, listening to the music, looking at the people looking at him. When the organist launched into the final hymn, I urged him to burst into song, like his biblical namesake. He satisfied me with a quiet hum. And a drool.

The Bible is full of names, some better known than others. Maybe they're meant to remind us of how we measure up to our biblical counterparts. But for us, now, Silas is a name that opens the doors of our hearts.

Help me sing hymns of praise. Like Silas.
—Rick Hamlin

Digging Deeper: Psalm 95:1; Colossians 3:16

CELEBRATE!! Re-Celebrate!

Taste and see that the LORD is good; blessed is the one who takes refuge in him. —Psalm 34:8 (NIV)

I love weddings. They are one of the most joyous of celebrations. I love the unique settings, the bride's dress, and her face as she walks down the aisle toward her groom. Most of all, I love to hear the bride and groom voice the promises of their vows. I always reach for my husband, Lynn's, hand because I like to get remarried at other people's weddings.

I also like to re-celebrate the joy of a new baby. Especially at baby showers. I recently cohosted a shower for a young couple who brought their month-old, first-born baby to the celebration. Their joy was obvious and contagious. I re-celebrated the births of each of our children as I watched them, still giddy and filled with wonder. I re-experienced the sacred wonder I felt that God had allowed me to coparticipate in one of His miracles: the creation of a new life. So precious! So powerful!

I'm also a birthday person. I believe that God, who chose the date of our birth, intends us to re-celebrate that day every year. Our birthday begins a new year for us, and I like to pause to think about who God made me to be and where I am in the process of "becoming." It's a day to remember how much God the Father loves us, His children. I also know there's still a little girl inside me who loves birthday celebrations with singing and cake and candles.

Lord, so many of life's celebrations give us
opportunities to re-celebrate and remember Your
goodness, which strengthens our faith. May
I never grow numb to the joy of celebrating.
—Carol Kuykendall

Digging Deeper: Psalm 16:5–11; Ephesians 2:10

Thanksgiving, Thursday, November 28

Rejoice always, pray without ceasing,
give thanks in all circumstances; for this
is the will of God in Christ Jesus for you.
—1 Thessalonians 5:16–18 (ESV)

I dreaded how quiet Thanksgiving would be with
just me and my boys, but the pandemic made it
difficult to gather. The holiday always bustled with
the chaos of family. This year, the boys would likely
stay in their room playing video games, leaving me
to wallow alone in self-pity.

Making the holiday worse, the absence of family
would also mean the absence of their amazing dishes—
the American tradition of turkey and sweet potato and
the Puerto Rican flavor of pigeon peas with yellow rice,
pasteles, empanadas, and the Latino way of cooking
pork called *pernil*.

Reading in 1 Thessalonians, I was reminded to
give thanks in all circumstances—even these. *I can't
have my family,* I thought, *but I can still have my feast!*

The week before Thanksgiving, I called family
and gathered recipes. Surprisingly, my boys were

excited to help prep our Thanksgiving meal the day before. Together we washed, peeled, cut, seasoned, and stirred.

Thanksgiving morning, we watched the parade as we always did, then continued to cook until our home was filled with the aroma of tradition. I made the table pretty, lit candles, and used real plates, instead of the paper ones we usually use for big family meals. I enjoyed the company of my children, who are usually at the kids' table or off playing away from the adults.

After our bellies were full, we snuggled on the couch to watch movies, with ice cream and cookies. I had nothing to dread. What I thought would be the worst Thanksgiving ever ended up being the very best—filled with love, thankfulness, family, and good food.

Lord, in this world of constant change, give me the strength to adapt, the joy to move forward, and the willingness to embrace something new.
—Karen Valentin

Digging Deeper: Psalm 118:1; Ecclesiastes 3:13

Friday, November 29

But the wisdom that is from above is first pure, then peaceable. —James 3:17 (ASV)

Willow, my German shepherd pup, whined from the back of the blue Subaru. I glanced over my shoulder and said, "We'll be there in a little bit. Lie down." Willow sighed and dropped into a heap as we wound through the mountains on the way to the veterinary clinic. With every curve, my mind did mental gymnastics over a decision I faced. I could see pros and cons; each list was long. By the time I pulled into the veterinary clinic, I was no closer to a decision than I had been forty-five minutes earlier.

After checking in, Willow and I made our way to the waiting room inside the rustic log-cabin building. I settled into a comfy chair, puppy lying at my feet, and continued to juggle thoughts. Suddenly, Willow growled, stood up, and started barking ferociously at something over my head. I looked up and laughed. It was a mounted elk head. She hadn't noticed it when we walked in because she was focused straight ahead. Its head was tipped back as if it were bugling, its long antlers swept back toward the wall. She'd never seen an animal like that and never one that looked as if it were walking through the wall.

After calming the pup, I shook my head. I'd been just like her—focused straight ahead, when I should have been looking up. On our drive home, I chatted with God about what I was facing, and He guided me to a decision.

Lord, thank You for arranging circumstances in my life to remind me to search for Your answers. Amen.
—Rebecca Ondov

Digging Deeper: Psalm 25:5; John 16:13

STAR WORDS: Surprise—Hannah

Every good gift and perfect gift is from above.
—James 1:17 (NIV)

Thanksgiving had already passed, yet I had not begun Christmas gifts. Worse, I had no ideas, not even for my generous granddaughter, Hannah, whose tastes at twenty-four so much resembled mine. Both of us liked to make things instead of buying them. Both of us had way too many houseplants, yet *squealed* at each new bud. Both of us preferred yard sales and flea markets to the mall. Surely I could find some eclectic, cottage-themed item to show my love.

That chilly Advent Sunday, while the sun gleamed pale as milk, I had forced myself to walk a loop around the park. By the sweet house on Beacon Street with the grapevine trellis, bird feeder, and fresh paint, I had once found a pile of early readers, ideal for my granddaughter in kindergarten. Today—surprise—I found another "free" box, this filled with recent home decorating magazines. I scooped up two *Country Living* holiday issues, Thanksgiving and Christmas. When was the last time I'd indulged with a glossy magazine?

Back home, I curled up with hot tea and pages of homey crafts, comfort-food recipes, houseplants . . . and then it hit me. Of course! A Christmas subscription for Hannah would delight all year.

(Seriously now, is a magazine a surprise from God? Absolutely! I know He gives good things to those who trust Him to provide.)

Lord, all good gifts come from You, even little ones.
—Gail Thorell Schilling

Digging Deeper: 1 Corinthians 2:12; 1 Timothy 6:17

LET US SING FOR JOY

1 _____

2 _____

3 _____

4 _____

5 _____

6 _____

7 _____

8 _____

9 _____

10 _____

11 _____

12 _____

13 _____

14 _____

15 _____

16 _____

17 _____

18 _____

19 _____

20 _____

21 _____

22 _____

23 _____

24 _____

25 _____

26 _____

27 _____

28 _____

29 _____

30 _____

DECEMBER

*Peace I leave with you; my peace
I give to you. Not as the world
gives do I give to you. Let not
your hearts be troubled, neither
let them be afraid.*

—John 14:27 (ESV)

First Sunday of Advent, Sunday, December 1

A CHRISTMAS OFFERING: My Time

Let each of you look not only to his own interests, but also to the interests of others. —Philippians 2:4 (ESV)

"Sorry about this mess," my oldest son, Logan, says. "I wish the ride back were shorter."

Empty brown boxes, flaps open like yawning mouths, clutter the living room. Tinsel glints on the rug. Leftover lights lie in gnarled knots. All five boys had gathered to help decorate our new home for Christmas, and Logan is the last to leave. The weekend had been rich with family and fun, but he knows I missed placing vintage ceramic trees and metal-winged angels in their places-of-old in the home he grew up in.

"Daddy and I will clean up," I say. "You get going."

Logan heads toward his own home, and I slip onto a chair. I slip off to sleep, too, and wake an hour later to the jingle of the bells we'd hung on the door. Logan strides back in.

"We forgot your crystal mistletoe," he says. He roots through boxes until he holds it in his hand. Every Christmas past, he'd hung it from the chandelier in our Victorian. "I'll get the ladder," he says now.

Soon an old treasure dangles from our new chandelier.

"You'll be driving until midnight," I say.

"I pray about how to use my time, Mom, and tonight I needed to care for you."

What a beautiful way to begin Advent season. I hold my son close as his sacrifice pulls me from the past to the present, where I understand that time is an offering.

A holy offering that brings the Lord's comfort and love.

Lord, I offer my time. In Your hands, may it be used to care for others. Amen. —Shawnelle Eliasen

Digging Deeper: Romans 12:10; Galatians 6:10

Monday, December 2

Enter his gates with thanksgiving and his courts with praise; give thanks to him and praise his name. —Psalm 100:4 (NIV)

As Christmas approached, before starting my prayers one morning, I paused to turn on the Christmas tree lights. Watching the ornaments sparkle as they reflected the lights, I was glad for a tradition Pat and I had kept. During our honeymoon in Boothbay Harbor, Maine, we bought a glass sailboat Christmas ornament. Placing the sailboat on the tree our first Christmas, we decided we would add ornaments to highlight significant events from the coming years.

Sipping coffee, I lingered by the tree, realizing the only ornaments on our tree this Christmas are the special ones. I started recalling memories from the ornaments—a rice basket from weekly community runs through Indonesian rice fields, a pontoon boat from years of lake fun, a cap and tassel from our son's college graduation, handmade olive-wood ornaments from Bethlehem. My mind flooded with great memories of people, adventures, places, and experiences. I was focused that morning on happy times, but the backstories of some ornaments reminded me of difficulties too—financial struggles early in our journey, challenging obstacles with our son's adoption, family health issues complicated by living overseas.

I never made it to my morning prayers— our Christmas tree became a prayer of immense gratitude. We had no idea the little glass sailboat selected to commemorate our life together started something that would transform a Christmas tree forty years later into the story of our voyage— through both good and difficult stretches.

Dear Jesus, immersed in a lifetime of memories, Your faithfulness—the one constant throughout our journey—fills me with praise and thanksgiving for Your abiding love. Thank You, Lord! —John Dilworth

Digging Deeper: Deuteronomy 7:9; Psalm 105:1; Colossians 4:2

Tuesday, December 3

Go tell the king what you have seen.
—2 Samuel 18:21 (NLT)

Hi," the young man said. "We'd like to interview you for the newspaper." He placed a voice recorder in front of me. My heart lurched. I am a lousy self-promoter. It's too much like bragging. But this was perfect timing for Christmas book sales. Silently I prayed, "Lord, protect me from pride. Let this glorify You." But openly talking about my faith is something I sometimes struggle with as well.

The reporter and a photographer sat across the table from me, my illustrations strewn between us. "How did you transition from cattle rancher to children's book illustrator?" he asked.

I took a breath. "Get ready to be in church for a bit." *Here goes.* I held nothing back. I told them how I asked God to use me. Then I was physically broken to the point of having to give up my first love of ranching. How I had to submit back to Him everything that made me who I was. "I don't care if I never walk again, Lord, I still choose You."

The reporter looked stricken. The photographer was openly crying. I went on. "At that point, God took over. He opened doors that had been shut. He healed me. He gave back all that had been taken from me."

Peace as I'd never known before came over me. I had shared what God had wanted me to. Even if these were the only ones meant to hear it, I did exactly as He asked of me. And to my amazement, God made the front page of our local paper because of my testimony.

Lord, help me to remember that my testimony is simply the love story You've written in my life.
—Erika Bentsen

Wednesday, December 4

**Honor everyone. Love the brotherhood. Fear God.
—1 Peter 2:17 (ESV)**

For years (and years and even more years), we hired a babysitter every week so we could go to our church Life Group.

I admit: it was hard. It's hard to leave toddlers with a babysitter. It's hard to find the money to pay for childcare. It's hard to summon up the energy to get showered and dressed and look presentable. It's hard to focus on God and community when you need sleep. It was hard but worth it. We grew in community, finding a group of like-minded friends who we could live life with.

Then, something incredible happened: someone made the suggestion that we start bringing our kids. By that time, we no longer had a gaggle of toddlers running about, but among the families in the group, we had nine (yes, nine) strong, smart, and opinionated teenagers.

On the first day, we had dinner (nothing gets a group of teenagers more excited than a whole bunch of home-cooked food) and then settled around the living room for a discussion. Two questions in, one of the teenagers interjected with a question about the text that I hadn't thought of. A few minutes later, another teen brought up a point that really got me thinking.

By the end of the night, not only had every single kid involved shared some idea, some insight, but also each one had shared something of themselves. I had learned from them.

These kids are so smart and insightful, but what's more, they love Jesus. They want to serve God. And they need Christian community as badly as I do.

I'm so grateful they get a head start on living in fellowship.

Lord, thank You for the blessing of living life within community. —Erin MacPherson

Digging Deeper: Zechariah 9:7; 1 Peter 5:9

Thursday, December 5

Our love for others is our grateful response to the love God first demonstrated to us. —1 John 4:19 (TPT)

There were eleven of us, squished together on the wooden steps. Between work schedules, Covid-19, pregnancies, and living in three different states, it had been a couple of years since we'd all been together: two grandparents, our two children, their spouses, and five grandchildren. But finally, here we were together again...family.

Trying to get five children ranging in age from one to eight to smile, let alone all look at the camera at the same time, wasn't easy, but the finished photo was everything I'd hoped it would be. It was a visual keepsake of those I loved most in this world.

Looking at the photo, it dawned on me that the reason we were all here was because I'd said two words forty years earlier: *I do.* It was love that brought us to this moment. However, my love story doesn't fit the usual mold. Two of my grandchildren were born into another family and adopted out of foster care. Eight years ago, my husband revealed he was gay, and our marriage ended. But our love and care for each other continues.

So much thought and prayer had gone into my decision to marry. When I ended up suddenly single, I asked God if I hadn't heard Him correctly. If I'd made a mistake. But if I had, it would mean faces would be missing, not only from this photo but also from this world. I realized that when it comes to love, I have no regrets. Only blessings.

Lord, thank You for my family. Help us continue to love each other in a way that honors You. —Vicki Kuyper

Digging Deeper: Psalm 127:3; Isaiah 43:18–19; John 15:12; Romans 8:28

Friday, December 6

Peace I leave with you; my peace I give to you. Not as the world gives do I give to you. Let not your hearts be troubled, neither let them be afraid. —John 14:27 (ESV)

Christmas music filled my living room as I opened one of the storage containers that housed decorations. "Peace on earth, goodwill to men," the singer belted out.

But I felt anything but peace. It was the sixth of December in a month that always sped by too fast. I usually put up my tree and decorations immediately after Thanksgiving so I can savor every moment of the too-brief Christmas season. That year, the halls still weren't decked and only eighteen days remained until Christmas.

I reached into the container for the Christmas countdown calendar. A keepsake from my childhood, the calendar features a little plush mouse that we place in a numbered pocket of the calendar every day of December through the twenty-fourth. I sighed as I lifted the calendar, my heart heavy. It would be displayed only a short time this year, and I would have few days to savor Christmas.

I froze as my gaze locked on the calendar. Each year, when I put the calendar in storage, I always left the mouse in the twenty-fourth pocket or moved it back to the first.

But the mouse smiled at me from the sixth pocket—the sixth of December. There was no reason the mouse should have been in the sixth pocket. No reason but God, who had known which day I would take out the calendar that year. Wonder and the peace only the omniscient and loving God can give flooded my soul.

Lord, thank You for giving me Your special peace all year through. —Jerusha Agen

Digging Deeper: Luke 1:78–79; 2 Thessalonians 3:16

Saturday, December 7

So let's keep focused on that goal, those of us who want everything God has for us. —Philippians 3:15 (MSG)

A recent Guideposts ministry visit took me to Marine Corps Base Hawaii's Kaneohe Bay Chapel. The facility is inspiring, a tribute to the importance our nation places on spiritual readiness and support.

While touring the grounds, I spotted a small bronze plaque. The inscription "Korea…November/December 1950" hooked my attention.

The bronze inscription related the story of the "Star of Koto-ri." In late November 1950, First Marine Division personnel were moving south under minus-forty-degree conditions. Allied air assets needed to drop bridge sections near the Chosin Reservoir so the Marines could get out. On December 7 and 8, clouds, snow, and a windchill of minus sixty degrees prohibited flights.

Then, according to the accounts of the "Chosin Few" survivors, a small star appeared. That star inspired hope. Bridge work took place. The Marines pulled through.

I was being shown around by Marine Lance Corporal Camden. Normally a mechanic for aircraft maintenance equipment, he was on temporary duty as a chaplain's assistant. He pointed out a star in stained glass that commemorated the "Chosin Few" experience. Then, he showed me handcrafted, native wood altar furnishings and described the richness of the congregation and his gratitude to worship God in that space.

I left the chapel grounds inspired, knowing that the "Star of Koto-ri" spirit continues in a young Marine's heart.

Sustaining God, may we all focus on the light of Your presence that so sustains our day. Bless the Armed Forces members stateside and abroad who now answer our nation's call. Amen. —Ken Sampson

Digging Deeper: Exodus 13:21; Philippians 3:12–14; Revelation 22:5

Second Sunday of Advent, Sunday, December 8

A CHRISTMAS OFFERING: My Home
Offer hospitality to one another without grumbling. —1 Peter 4:9 (NIV)

The doorbell rings as I'm baking cookies. Gingerbread boys, awaiting frosting, cover the counters. The sink is piled with bowls. The rest of the house is tattered too. Life is December-wild, and today we have just a few hours between morning service and evening plans.

My husband answers the door. We're surprised to see a young couple from church.

"My parents are in town and our kids are napping," the mama says. "Is this OK?"

We open the door wide.

But as the husbands head for the garage, I'm self-conscious. As we walk toward the kitchen,

I notice boots and gloves under the piano bench and abandoned books on the rug. "I'll frost cookies while we visit," I say. When my friend offers help, I'm humbled. As we pipe frosting on gingerbread, I worry about the flour on the floor.

Conversation is light as we get started. Holiday activities and plans. But soon things take a turn to the deeper, and my kitchen becomes holy ground. The mess no longer matters. I have the opportunity to listen to a brave, unadorned soul.

While she shares, I ask the Lord for wisdom. He hears and fills my mouth with encouragement and truth from His Word. And later, when we stand at the door again, my arms go around her and she whispers in my ear. "I needed to be here today," she said. "In this kind of calm."

The Lord can use the imperfect to bring His perfect peace. On this second Sunday of Advent, I offer Him my home.

Lord, may my home be used to love others for Your glory. Amen. —Shawnelle Eliasen

Digging Deeper: 1 Timothy 5:10

Monday, December 9

Repent, for the kingdom of heaven has come near. —Matthew 3:2 (NIV)

One Saturday evening last July, as I washed my dinner dishes, two neighbors from Morocco, a young mother and her mother, knocked on the door. They were gussied up, wearing what I would call their Sunday best, sleeves sparkling with embroidered sequins. "We're having a birthday party. Adam is six today," the young woman said. "Can you come?"

I gestured toward my work-a-day Saturday clothes.

"It's OK," she said. I expected her to continue with a typically American response, "You can come as you are." Rather, she smiled and kindly urged, "It's OK. You can change."

Her high expectation nudged me to up my game. From my closet, I pulled my brightest and best summer shift, turquoise with golden embroidery.

Four gathered women soon welcomed me with smiles, hand claps, and high fives. Their acknowledgment of my effort set the tone of the evening. Though I'd already eaten, they served me— and I ate portions of—a festive four-course meal. The birthday boy blew out his candles, twice. I briefly joined a joyful dance. I brought home leftover cake.

Months later—now in Advent when the liturgical calendar emphasizes preparation for God's kingdom come—I reflect on the hostess's invitation. Changing my outfit that evening to show respect involved a simple physical action. In Scripture, I see a challenge—repent, turn, about-face—that goes to the heart of more significant thoughts and habits. My impatience. My prejudicial stereotypes. My procrastinations. With God's help, I—and you also—can change.

Lord, You challenge me to be my best self. What does that mean for me today? —Evelyn Bence

Digging Deeper: Luke 3:1–6

Tuesday, December 10

Run from anything that gives you the evil thoughts that young men often have, but stay close to anything that makes you want to do right.
—2 Timothy 2:22 (TLB)

Here in Largo, Florida, we have one huge neighborhood that goes bonkers with holiday lights every Christmas season. The homeowners have been collecting money for hospice for over twenty years, so people flock there to enjoy the lighted wonderland and donate to hospice. Every house for miles is decorated with thousands of Christmas lights from the top of the roof to the ground. All the trees and shrubs are covered in lights. Manger scenes, inflated cartoon characters, Santa, reindeer, elves, dinosaurs, candy canes, superheroes, wise men, plastic snowmen, carolers, and angels fill the yards. Many have music playing. There are Hanukkah decorations: blue lights, menorahs, and six-pointed stars of David.

One year, after passing a house that was off the charts with lights and decorations on every square foot of the property, the next house was dark without one decoration except a big arrow pointing to the previous extravagant home. Inside the light-framed arrow, it said DITTO in huge letters.

I couldn't stop laughing. That creative genius not only made every passerby laugh out loud, but he also made a good point. Sometimes we just have to find someone or something to emulate. That's the joy of Christmas. We get to choose who we want to be like. For me, it's about noticing someone on their knees in front of the manger scene inside the church at midnight mass. That's when I say, "Ditto. I want to be just like that person."

Baby Jesus, help me to feel like Mary did the night You were born: awestruck, safe, holy.
—Patricia Lorenz

Digging Deeper: Psalm 48:12–14;
Matthew 8:19; Luke 9:57

Wednesday, December 11

About midnight Paul and Silas were praying and singing hymns to God, and the prisoners were listening to them. —Acts 16:25 (NRSV)

Our first grandson—our first grandchild—was born on July 3 to our son Tim and daughter-in-law Henley and was given a nice biblical name, Silas. Remember Silas? He was imprisoned with Paul, and the two of them prayed and sang hymns until there was an earthquake that opened all the doors of the prison.

Opening doors. That's exactly what a grandchild does. All that love and affection that's been harboring in you, waiting to be let out so you can sing those silly songs you sang to your own kids and play the games and hug and nurture this new gift of life.

When holding Silas in my arms and hearing him sing, like Silas in the Bible sang, the name seemed just right.

But what would be the name of that second grandson, scheduled to arrive in December? How could you top this? What would his parents, our son William and daughter-in-law Karen, decide? What sort of expectations would they signal by the name they gave?

Before I give you the answer, let me tell you how moved I was by their choice. How touched beyond all reason. No, they didn't pick from the Bible but from their own family. The middle name, Peter, because that was Karen's brother's name. The first name—Rick.

On December 11, this new Rick Hamlin entered the world, and, like his cousin, he rocked our world.

God's blessings are multiple. God's surprises come in ways you can't guess. I don't expect Ricky or Silas to be anything like their Gramps. They come with gifts of their own. As do we all.

Thank You for the gift of children. —Rick Hamlin

Digging Deeper: Psalm 127:3; Matthew 19:14; James 1:17

Thursday, December 12

You set the boundaries of the earth, and you made both summer and winter. —Psalm 74:17 (NLT)

Chestnuts roasting on an open fire
Jack Frost nibbling on your nose…

That's how my grandson Ashton used to sing "The Christmas Song" by Mel Tormé and Robert Wells. Regardless of whether Mel was right ("Jack Frost nipping at your nose") or Ashton, today I was on Ashton's side—it feels like Jack Frost is nibbling *on* my nose.

It's cold today in Indiana. Colder than Juneau, Alaska, even!

The touch of the cold reminded me of the warmth of God's love. That's because the bitter cold feels so much like absence of warmth that it literally takes my breath away. If there is anything about God that I know, it is that God's love is warm and life-giving. When I relax into God's great love, I can breathe deeply and warm my soul.

As I thought of that, I gave thanks today. I have a warm house and the love of God warms me as well. As I drove into town on errands, though, I thought of my brothers and sisters who are less fortunate than I—who live with the bitter cold in their bones. And I wondered, what am I called to do for them? Surely it is not just enough for me to rejoice in my warmth.

What *would* Jesus have me do?

And once I hear the voice of Jesus instructing me, would I dare leave my warm surroundings to do it?

O God who melts my heart with tender love, thank You for encompassing me with Your warmth. I pray, too, for those who are physically cold. Show me how to bring some warmth into their lives. Amen.

—J. Brent Bill

Friday, December 13

**Be kind to one another, tenderhearted, forgiving
one another, as God in Christ forgave you.
—Ephesians 4:32 (ESV)**

Beau, four, is my most empathetic child. He is quick to
apologize and feels genuine grief when he has hurt you.
So it was no surprise that when he came home from
school refusing to wear his beloved winter coat that
looks like a shark, I knew something had happened.

"Buddy, you love this coat," I said. "Why won't
you wear it anymore?" He beckoned me to bend
closer so no one else could hear. "Heart at school
thinks my jacket is a real shark," he whispered. "And
now I'm afraid I'm going to go to jail for scaring
her." I held back my giggle as I stared into his eyes,
already overflowing with tears. "There is no jail for
four-year-olds; you're still learning about life," I told
him. "And I don't think Heart really thinks you are
wearing a shark."

But my words fell on deaf ears. It took one more
day of him refusing to wear his coat in freezing temps
for me to realize I had better find another coat. As
I was digging in our closet, I found other items of
Beau's, all shark, dinosaur, or monster themed. "Did
you hide these?" I asked.

"They scare people," he said.

Beau and I had a long talk that day. Though he loves dinosaurs, friendly monsters, and sharks, he was no longer willing to wear them around his friends, for fear they truly did frighten them. I learned a lesson that day about taking care of those most vulnerable. Maybe Heart really was scared, maybe she wasn't. Either way, Beau wasn't willing to risk hurting his friend.

Lord, give me a childlike heart so that I may care deeply for those around me. —Ashley Kappel

Digging Deeper: Romans 12:15; 1 Corinthians 12:26; Galatians 6:2

Saturday, December 14

No misfortune is seen in Jacob, no misery observed in Israel. The Lord their God is with them.... —**Numbers 23:21** (NIV)

I'm calling this past holiday season The Revolt of the Machines.

The uprising began on December 24. Our oven failed. We'd planned several meals involving the oven. Good luck finding someone to repair it on Christmas Eve. We managed most of the menu with a toaster oven and the microwave.

A few days later, while Gracie and I were hiking a snowy Berkshire trail, I got a call from my wife, Julee. The power had failed, so no water or heat. We rushed home to find a lineman high on a pole working on a sick transformer.

We have an emergency generator. I tried to remember how to start it. I called Stephen, our electrician. "The battery is dead," he said.

"I've never used it. How can the battery be dead?"

"Because you never used it. You should start it occasionally. I'll go look for a new battery."

I ran down the driveway and called up to the lineman. "They're bringing out a new transformer. Hope it gets here today," he said, glancing at his watch.

I went over and sat dejectedly on the woodpile. At least we had the woodstove. So why such a feeling of desperation? Control. I felt out of control. The more we rely on machines and technology, the more control we give up. Wasn't my faith supposed to be the answer to loss of control?

A new transformer arrived. Stephen showed up with a new battery. All was well. And I said a prayer I should have said when the machines first revolted.

Today, Lord, grant me the serenity to accept the things I cannot change, change the things I can, and the wisdom to know the difference. —Edward Grinnan

Digging Deeper: Job 37:14–16; Psalm 59:16–17

Third Sunday of Advent, Sunday, December 15

A CHRISTMAS OFFERING: My Gifts
As each has received a gift, use it to serve one another, as good stewards of God's varied grace. —1 Peter 4:10 (ESV)

When my two youngest sons learn that my parents aren't going to put up a Christmas tree, they make a plan.

"We'll do it," twelve-year-old Isaiah says.

"Let's go tomorrow after church," says Gabriel, who is fourteen.

The next day, we burst through my parents' door in a wild rush. Gabriel retrieves boxes from the garage, and soon he and Dad unbend branches and tether them to the tree's trunk. Isaiah works on ornaments and Mom joins in, pulling paper cut-out angels and baked cinnamon snowmen from a tin of treasures. Each one has a story, and Mom shares them while Isaiah threads hooks through the ornaments to prepare them for the tree. Then we hang lights and decorate.

When it's finished, it's glorious. But the boys have a further plan.

"Nana, do you still have that skinny tree in the bedroom?" Isaiah asks.

She does. Mom has an assortment of faux pines. One in the bedroom. Two in the garage.

"Let's get them all!" Gabriel says.

There are enough decorations to adorn all the trees, and the living room window fills with festivity. When the day goes long, the room is dark. Except for twinkling lights. We sit quietly and admire.

"We weren't even going to have a tree," Dad says, smile wide as wilderness. "And you've given us a forest."

But God is the giver of gifts. Today, He whispered and my boys used theirs. On this third Sunday of

Advent, with Christmas joy like arms around us, I offer Him my own.

Lord, I offer my gifts to You. May they be used to bring peace, joy, and love. Amen.
—Shawnelle Eliasen

Digging Deeper: Romans 12:6–8

Monday, December 16

Let them do good, that they be rich in good works, ready to give, willing to share.
—1 Timothy 6:18 (NKJV)

While rummaging through my cupboards, I inventoried what I would need to make the Christmas cookies I was planning to give a dozen friends. *What am I going to use for trays this year?* I wanted them to be something special, not just plastic. I opened another cupboard and spotted the beautiful china plates on the top shelf. At a thrift store years ago, my heart flew over the moon when I found the set of white plates with the two-inch-wide dark blue rims. Fourteen-karat gold stars gleamed from the blue rims. *They would make gorgeous cookie plates.* Instantly, I stuffed that thought. *But those are some of my favorite plates.*

Over the next week, I shopped our small town, trying to find trays—nothing. Instead, each time I opened the cupboard door, I saw those plates on the top shelf, collecting dust. I hadn't used them in a couple years.

After an evening of making peanut brittle, I stood on my tiptoes and reached for a plate. As I looked at the golden stars twinkling from the dark blue rim, I knew why I was struggling with giving them away. I didn't own these plates—they owned me. What happened to sharing everything that we have (Acts 4:32)? *When I give them away, many will be able to enjoy them.*

Of course, my friends were thrilled with their gifts, but my greatest surprise was when a friend brought a cake to a birthday party on her favorite plate, one that twinkled with gold stars.

Lord, help me to balance owning things until I don't use them anymore—then sharing so others can enjoy them too. Amen. —Rebecca Ondov

Digging Deeper: Luke 3:11; Hebrews 13:16

Tuesday, December 17

A new command I give you: Love one another. As I have loved you, so you must love one another. —John 13:34 (NIV)

When I was driving through billowing snow on the interstate in central Massachusetts, my car began to sputter. I needed to pull over and, though I was unfamiliar with this town, took the next exit.

There were just three houses on the road abutting the highway, and I picked the one with the light in the front window. Knowing it was risky, I rang the doorbell and stood back from the door so that the homeowner could see that I was a twenty-something

Black woman in this mostly White town, allowing them to choose whether to answer.

An elderly White woman opened the door and looked at me with a small smile. Barely taking a breath, I said, "My car broke down and is parked over there, but if you would please let me use your phone to call my fiancé to come get me, I would be so grateful. You can even pass the phone to me outside and I'll stay right here."

The woman chuckled and waved me in and handed me her corded phone. I made the call, thanked her profusely, and started toward the door.

"It's too cold for you to wait out there," she said. She left the room and returned quickly with a cup of hot chocolate. We chatted for about fifteen minutes, when my fiancé arrived to take me home.

That encounter has lived with me for nearly forty years because I was so grateful that the woman didn't see a Black woman at her door; she saw a member of God's family. And based solely on that, she was led to help.

Lord, I thank You for all the members of Your Earthly family. —Gayle T. Williams

Digging Deeper: Deuteronomy 10:18; Ephesians 4:32

Wednesday, December 18

Don't be impatient for the Lord to act! Keep traveling steadily along his pathway and in due season he will honor you with every blessing, and you will see the wicked destroyed. —Psalm 37:34 (TLB)

Today, we cut the cord on our cable service and went completely to streaming. I explained to my sons—who don't watch TV, preferring their phones and laptops for entertainment—that I have now lived to see the beginning and end of an era.

I feel old telling them that when I was six, we had only four channels of TV to choose from, one with a snowy static that we learned to ignore. As the youngest, it was my job to stand to the side and twist the dial while the rest of my family voiced their opinions.

By the time we made the leap from a rabbit-ear antenna to cable, my parents had divorced and my siblings were off and about. My mom was working full time and attending college at night, so I spent most of my weekdays from the bus to bed home alone, watching family show reruns of *Little House on the Prairie* and *The Brady Bunch*. I hadn't thought about that lonely time in years.

With our new streaming set up and ready to go, my sons and husband gathered beside me as I navigated the virtually limitless streaming possibilities. My focus shifted inward, and I felt a knot of emotion grow in my throat. God had taken me full circle from a kid, sitting alone seeking the company of family on a screen, to now, surrounded by love, so much love, we could barely squeeze on the couch.

Heavenly Father, thank You for times like this when I recognize Your love and my blessings, greater than I ever imagined. —Sabra Ciancanelli

Digging Deeper: Genesis 28:3; Galatians 6:9

Thursday, December 19

You should remember the words of the Lord Jesus: "It is more blessed to give than to receive."
—Acts 20:35 (NLT)

"Presents can be stolen twice during the gift exchange," Judy, the organizer, explained to the group of cancer survivors at the party. "After that, the gift is out of circulation."

Familiar with the rules for white elephant gift-giving parties, I resigned myself to an awkward hour of watching strangers open boxes of chocolates and restaurant gift cards.

However, the added twist of only purple items—the designated color for all cancer survivors—had stirred everyone's creativity. Festively wrapped packages contained a violet scarf, a lavender coffee mug, and a purple lap quilt. At first, the gathered women were polite, not "stealing" gifts from other players, until a spa day certificate was taken from the initial recipient, and then the inhibitions ended. Radiation, chemo, and cancer side effects were momentarily forgotten as laughter and purple items flowed around the room.

Mary, wearing a long-haired wig, reluctantly parted with the hand-beaded purple bowl she had opened, when Shelly requested it—but Shelly didn't keep her selection for long.

"I decided I like my gift best," Joann declared, as she took the bowl *she had brought* from Shelly, putting the item out of circulation.

"She chose her own gift! Why did she do that?"

Joann simply smiled at the gentle ribbing, tucking the bowl under her chair, out of sight. Later, I saw Joann quietly return the bowl to Mary. Only then did I realize, she had chosen her own gift for the sole purpose of gifting it back.

Champion Giver of All, show me ways to gift back. —Lynne Hartke

Digging Deeper: Deuteronomy 15:10; 2 Corinthians 9:7

Friday, December 20

Take delight in the LORD, and he will give you the desires of your heart. —Psalm 37:4 (NIV)

Because I'm dyslexic, I was in the fifth grade before I learned to read. I never did well in school and feel fortunate to have graduated from high school. My school years were marked by negative voices that said I would never do well.

It was only after I asked Christ into my life that I found the courage to pursue my dream of writing novels. I believed God had given me the gift of being a storyteller, but I had to learn to be a writer. My English, grammar, and spelling skills were lacking, but I trudged on, pouring my heart onto the page. Each day I would quote Norman Vincent Peale. *I believe I am divinely guided. I believe I will always take the right turn in the road. I believe God will make a way where there is no way.*

After five years, I'd completed four manuscripts and had yet to sell a single word. I needed something. Some small hope. I decided to submit an anecdote based on something that happened to our five-year-old son.

Dale was in the church Christmas program. His entire role was to step forward and recite a Bible verse, which he did flawlessly, only, in a moment of panic, he forgot the reference. Looking to me for help, I mouthed *Luke*. Dale's eyes lit up, he squared his shoulders, and shouted out: "Luke Skywalker!"

The anecdote sold for five dollars. I was elated and encouraged. And I learned a valuable lesson. Celebrate the small successes and believe—God will make a way where there is no way. He did for me.

Lord, help me to not get ahead of Your perfect timing and trust that You have purpose in all Your pauses.
—Debbie Macomber

Digging Deeper: Proverbs 3:5–6, 16:9; Jeremiah 29:11

Saturday, December 21

REMEMBERING GRATITUDE:
When Christmas Wouldn't Come
Neglect not the gift that is in thee....
—1 Timothy 4:14 (KJV)

It was the third week of December, but a surgical complication had me barely leaving my chair. In a fit of despair, the memory returned to me of a long-ago patient I'd met as a nurse. She was paralyzed, in a wheelchair, and unable to speak. Her world had shrunk to her caregivers, delivery workers, and the people she watched on TV.

But when Christmas was coming, Margie found a way to give. We came up with a shopping list that included the postal carrier, the weather girl, the star of her favorite show, a national newscaster. I did the shopping, wrote the letters she dictated. When the grateful responses poured in, I had a front-row seat at the magic.

Oh, Margie, how did I forget you? She'd given me the perfect model for how to get past my own self-focus. I picked up some pinecones from my yard and made pomander balls from oranges studded with cloves, then hauled myself to my vehicle and drove to the brick rancher on my road. In past years, their Christmas decorations had always been pitch-perfect, but I'd noticed on my way to the doctor that their twinkling white lights had stopped at the middle of the porch. I had a feeling something was amiss.

When a weary woman answered the door, I heard myself say: "I've missed the oranges and pine in your window boxes. You folks need anything?" I learned the couple had Covid-19 and were trying to take care of each other. As the wife closed the door, she called over her shoulder: "I can't believe somebody did that for us."

The memory of Margie changed everything. I hadn't bought a single Christmas present. Didn't mean I didn't give any.

Thank You, Lord, for those who bring us back to ourselves. And to You. —Roberta Messner

Digging Deeper: James 1:17; 1 Peter 4:10

Fourth Sunday of Advent, Sunday, December 22

A CHRISTMAS OFFERING: My Praise
For you make me glad by your deeds, Lord;
I sing for joy at what your hands have done.
—Psalm 92:4 (NIV)

I'm dusting when the middle layer of my vintage ceramic Christmas tree slips from my hands and hits hardwood. My youngest sons come running.

I'd wanted a tree like this for years. My boys and I had searched antique shops like long-ago pirates searched for treasure. I'd given up. Then, one snowy evening, we saw it lighting the window of a tiny, red-brick antique shop, colors bright and warm against the hard blue-gray of night. It was Christmas magic. We went back the next day. For years, the tree sat on the buffet in our old home. I'd planned to pass it down one day to a son.

"I am so sorry, Mom," fourteen-year-old Gabriel says now. His green eyes are wide with sorrow. "Let me clean this up."

Only when I sit in another room, I don't hear the vacuum. When I look around the corner, Gabe is placing pieces in a box. "I can fix it, Mom," he says. "I know I can."

This boy is my fixer. He finds ways to bind the broken. When he spends days fitting fragments, filling spaces, and covering cracks with coats of paint, he's fixing a part of me too.

Gabriel, with hands that brought wholeness, places the tree back on our bookcase right before Christmas. When it glows with light, it's lovelier than it had been in the antique store window.

The Lord is compassionate. In His hands, the broken becomes beautiful, and scars sing songs of grace. On this fourth Sunday of Advent, I offer Him my praise.

Oh Lord, You sent Jesus to make us whole. I praise You! Amen. —Shawnelle Eliasen

Digging Deeper: Psalms 71:8, 103:1

Monday, December 23

...I have called you friends, because all things that I have heard from My Father I have made known to you. —John 15:15 (NASB)

Friends pray for each other. At least Jorge, Ginny, and I have ever since we were together in the church youth group and high school plays. These days, we're separated by thousands of miles, but through texts and emails, we stay in touch, sometimes about the most mundane matters.

A few days before Christmas, I sent a photo to Ginny and Jorge of our two sons and their two sons. My friends responded with "hearts" and hugs and words of congrats. Then Jorge apologized for his run-on sentences because, as he explained, he was dictating his texts while driving. He was on an urgent errand. What errand? we asked.

His wife, Maggie, woke up that morning realizing they didn't have any cranberry sauce to go with the turkey dinner she was cooking (for that son who hadn't been able to make their Thanksgiving dinner several weeks earlier). "We've got to have some cranberry sauce," she said.

Jorge was in his car, looking for a parking place at the supermarket full of last-minute shoppers. He found a place and darted inside. "You have a cranberry emergency on your hands," Ginny texted.

"Cranberry prayers," I texted.

"I'm praying too," Ginny wrote.

After a few tense moments, we heard from Jorge: "Prayers answered. I literally got the last tub of cranberry relish."

"See?" Ginny said. "Prayer changes things!"

"Nothing is too big or small when there is a need," Jorge said, putting the final word on things, as usual. But then isn't that what you get from old friends? God's honest truth flavored with love.

The friends You've put in my life, Lord, are a godsend.
—Rick Hamlin

Digging Deeper: Job 6:14; Proverbs 17:17;
1 Thessalonians 5:11

Christmas Eve, Tuesday, December 24

A CHRISTMAS OFFERING: My Hope
The Word became flesh and made his dwelling among us. —John 1:14 (NIV)

It's Christmas Eve, and our home is rich with anticipation.

There's a coming together of family. Our five boys are here. A fire burns bright and warm, and the hearth holds an invitation. We've gone to church. Shared a meal. Now it's time to gather around.

We've read the same book on Christmas Eve since our sons were small. Back then, their daddy and I read. Boys jumbled on our laps and turned pages with tiny fingers. Now everyone reads, and *Mary's First Christmas* is small in our sons' hands.

Into the stillness, story is spoken. A young man reads about Mary and Joseph. A stable and a stone manger. The book passes brother-to-brother. I listen to voices. Study faces in the soft, warm light. Tonight all is peaceful, but I know of slumbering struggles. Life brought hard circumstances. Some of my sons strayed from faith.

The book changes hands and the voice changes too. We hear of angels and a babe in Mary's arms. And I think of how the Son in her arms will stretch His own arms.

Jesus was born in a stable but was bound to the cross. He became flesh to seek and save. Dwelling among men meant that men could dwell in heaven. His purpose is deeply personal. Tonight I understand that it's for these young men gathered by the fire.

Words on pages point to the Word that brings life. Holy hope is born in me.

"It's your turn, Mom," says a son. I'll read to the book's end, but there's a new beginning.

On this Christmas Eve, I offer my hope.

Jesus, You are my hope. Amen. —Shawnelle Eliasen

Digging Deeper: Luke 15:3–7; John 1; Hebrews 10:23

Christmas Day, Wednesday, December 25

A CHRISTMAS OFFERING: Jesus

From his fullness we have all received, grace upon grace. —John 1:16 (NRSV)

Dawn breaks on Christmas morning. I meet my oldest son, Logan, in the living room. It's the time of transformation.

When my boys were tiny, they'd fly down the stairs in wide-eyed wonder. There were sleds propped in doorways. Dinosaurs grazing in potted plants. Orange Hot Wheels tracks crisscrossing carpet and pirate ships sailing wool-rug seas. Things were bigger. Brighter. Colorful plastic filled our space.

Now things are smaller and simpler as Logan and I place packages under the tree. We fill stockings with fruit, nuts, and trinkets. He sets the stage for battle with vintage Star Wars figures and planes.

I slide cinnamon rolls into the oven. As coffee perks, our family wakes. Tousle-headed young men, their daddy, and I gather. Christmas morning will be savored; it's not a wild rush. And as the boys pull paper from packages, I notice something significant.

These gifts are intentional. Given with sensitivity and sight. There are favorite books. Vinyl albums. An established terrarium for our green-grower. There's intimacy in the giving. Like the birth of Jesus. Savior King in a stable. Simplicity swathed in complexity. Jesus brought salvation. Restoration. Life to the fullest.

"Mom?" a son says. He hands me a package. Typeset blocks and a tray. He knows my affinity for printed words, and this gift stirs my soul. It's an intimate offering.

Suddenly, I consider the intimate offerings I've lifted to the Lord this Christmas season. My time. Home. Gifts. Praise. Hope.

And I'm humbled when I compare Jesus's offering with my own.

The gift of the Christ-child is infinitely intimate. Because of this gift, I can spend eternity with Him. And that is an offering greater than any other.

Father, thank You for Your Son. Amen.
—Shawnelle Eliasen

Digging Deeper: Romans 5:8

Thursday, December 26

"For I know the plans I have for you," declares the LORD, "plans to prosper you and not to harm you, plans to give you hope and a future."
—Jeremiah 29:11 (NIV)

The first week of winter came with a snowstorm and high winds. I was scheduled to drive from my home in Vermont to an office in Massachusetts, south of Boston, for an important meeting. I didn't feel I had much of a choice. I really had to go.

My car had four-wheel drive. I've driven in snow all my life. I wasn't worried, and the driving wasn't a big deal. Until I reached Boston traffic.

Suddenly, there, surrounded by people in cars without four-wheel drive, apparently unaccustomed to driving in snow, traffic slowed to a crawl. My blood pressure began to rise. I think I said some unkind things.

This went on for an hour or more until I realized I was going to be late for my appointment. This was before cell phones. I pulled off the road and went to a pay phone, dialing my contact, prepared to apologize and say I'd be there soon. He answered and quickly said, "Where are you? I've been trying for hours!"

"I know, I'm sorry," I began to say, but he cut me off: "We changed the meeting from in-person to a phone call and have been waiting to talk since this morning."

It was only then that I realized how my ego sometimes obscures my judgment—and my relationship with God. It hadn't occurred to me to consider another plan or to pause to ask for God's guidance. I'd only thought, *You've got this.* In fact, we don't.

Remind me to turn to You every morning, every day.
—Jon M. Sweeney

Digging Deeper: Psalm 32:8

Friday, December 27

A soft answer turns away wrath, but a harsh word stirs up anger. —Proverbs 15:1 (RSV)

I felt wilty as I drove my husband, Lynn, to his first physical therapy appointment one afternoon. He was recovering from a minor stroke and needed to learn to navigate life. I helped him out of the car to a bench at the front door.

"I'll park and be right back," I said, then pulled into a handicapped parking spot. As I paused to gather my things, I noticed an elderly lady sitting in the passenger seat of the car next to me. I smiled and opened my car door, then saw a woman pulling a walker out of the trunk of that car. Obviously she was ready to help the passenger waiting in her car. "How do you like that walker?" I asked in a friendly voice because we were in the market for a good walker.

"We need to get to an appointment!" she said with angry impatience because my open door was stopping her progress.

"Sorry," I mumbled and hurried on. When I helped Lynn back to our car a couple hours later, I saw there was a note on the windshield. *Probably from the lady apologizing for being unfriendly,* I thought. I turned the paper over and saw only two shockingly unkind words with three exclamation marks. Weary from the realities revealed in Lynn's physical therapy, those words cut deeply. I stuffed the paper in my pocket. Later, as I pulled into our garage, I considered keeping the message as a reminder of what I hoped to learn...but instead I crumpled it up and threw it in the trash on my way through the garage.

Lord, thank You for reminding me not to carry others' unkind words too far. —Carol Kuykendall

Digging Deeper: Micah 7:18; Ephesians 4:29

Saturday, December 28

I have tried hard to find you—don't let me wander from your commands. —Psalm 119:10 (NLT)

My husband, Michael, and I were toasty warm in our upstairs television room, despite the wintry weather conditions. It had been an extremely windy day, even by Oklahoma standards, with gusts up to sixty-five miles per hour and temperatures in the thirties.

As I stepped onto the staircase to go down to the kitchen, frigid air startled me. The wind whistled, and the howl of coyotes was louder than usual. *What's going on?* I hurried downstairs and followed the loud, cold breeze to our foyer.

The front door had blown wide open. Our obedient dog, Missy, stood staring into the inky darkness. "Good girl," I said, slamming the door.

"Where's Mr. Whiskers?" asked Michael, who had followed me down.

Our pets lived inside, but lately our aging, long-haired tuxedo cat has been prone to wander. He waits at the screen door when Missy goes out to do her business. He jumps on the windowsill and meows to sit close to the screen. He darted into the garage last week and it took hours to catch him.

We searched Mr. Whiskers's favorite hiding spots—under the beds and deep in closets. There was no sign of him. *Had he escaped?*

I opened the front door to call "kitty, kitty." A strong blast of air blew back my hair. In dashed Mr. Whiskers. He bolted through the foyer and ran under the master bed.

Like Mr. Whiskers, I'm prone to wander too. Thankfully, the Lord never closes the door on me.

Thank You, Lord, that my bad choices don't leave me out in the cold. Help me to stay safely near You the next time I'm prone to wander.
—Stephanie Thompson

Digging Deeper: Psalm 139:7–10; Romans 8:35–39; Galatians 5:7

Sunday, December 29

But he that shall endure unto the end...
—Matthew 24:13 (KJV)

Football. Growing up in the South, it was almost like religion. You had your team, and, good seasons and bad, you stuck with them. My family orbited around the Tennessee Volunteers, and autumn was football time in Tennessee. I can still remember the glory of Neyland Stadium as my grandfather hoisted me high in the air, when *the* coach of our lifetime,

Johnny Majors, took the field. The timbre of the crowd was electric.

Through the years, no matter how near or far we were from Neyland Stadium, life stood still on game day. "Go, Big Orange" was our rallying cry.

Not surprisingly, I ended up as a student at the University of Tennessee, and every game day I was there, again cheering my team on through wins and losses, highs and lows. But now, in the midst of one of the low seasons, Coach Majors's career was winding down.

The weather was relentless for his last game, and people left the stadium in droves. The buddies I had come with deserted the stands one by one, until I was left alone high up in the student section. Drenched, I sat there thinking about Coach Majors's legacy. His lessons in loyalty, in perseverance, and enduring tough times with grace. Far beyond a game, he had shown me a way of life, where being tough is sticking with your friends, your family, your faith, in good times and bad.

It would be unthinkable to walk out on Coach Majors now. As the clock ticked those final seconds, I stood with respect as one of life's teachers left the field. I was grateful for the cold rain that washed away my tears.

Father, You used a game I loved to make me strong. I am humbled by Your lessons. —Brock Kidd

Digging Deeper: Matthew 24:13; Acts 13:43

Monday, December 30

You hypocrite, first take the log out of your
own eye, and then you will see clearly to
take the speck out of your neighbor's eye.
—Matthew 7:5 (NRSVUE)

Nowadays, I grade my students' writing using my
university's course management app instead of with
a pencil, as I've graded for decades. I hate online
grading: having to sit at my computer, type out every
word instead of scribbling quick abbreviations, and
figure out—again—how to enlarge their documents
and diminish or, better yet, render invisible the other
junk that invariably takes up the screen.

There's one good thing about virtual grading,
though. Instead of writing out the same feedback
over and over, I can type it into a document from
which to copy-and-paste it onto papers endlessly.
I've made grading banks for each assignment and
can just scoop whatever I need to say from previous
years' comments.

I can also preempt errors. Today, for an
assignment on how various cultures have influenced
modern English, I sent out this instruction in
advance: "Don't refer to people as *Blacks*, *gays*,
or *females*, etc. Use such terms only as adjectives.
Even adjectives can sound discriminatory—e.g.,
an autistic person vs. *a person with autism*. Just
remember this underlying principle: a person's
entire identity ≠ one of their attributes."

As I typed, a news story featuring a close-up from a funeral for opioid crisis victims distracted me, conjuring the many drug addicts I've known. Even in that pious moment of conviction, I referred to them in my mind exactly as I just wrote them: as addicts, not people worth my genuine love or respect. With His usual perfect timing, God showed me just what I needed to see in this moment. Clearly, I needed a refresher course in practicing what I preach.

I want to see people as people, but the impulse to automatically pigeonhole them is hard to resist. Please help me, God. —Patty Kirk

Digging Deeper: Mark 5; Luke 6:37–42

Tuesday, December 31

Shew me thy ways, O LORD; teach me thy paths. Lead me in thy truth, and teach me....
—Psalm 25:4-5 (KJV)

"What are you doing New Year's Eve?"

We hear those lyrics by Frank Loesser a lot this time of year. And, despite it being a love song, it's a good question. One that I've answered differently throughout my life.

As a kid and young adult, it was often spent at our Quaker church, which held a "Watch Night

Service"—games and refreshments leading up to a worship service at midnight. Then, for about twenty years, we celebrated with our daughter Laura and her husband, Michael, and their growing family.

These days, the celebration is quieter. Just Nancy and me at home with a nice dinner and watching old movies and going to bed and sleeping in the new year.

As I drift off, though, I often do a personal "year in review." I look at the highs and the lows. The joys and sorrows. The new life born into our family...and the dearly departed.

And then I think of the year ahead. *What will it bring?* I wonder. Or I make plans for the new year—and remind myself that it is impossible to predict. A pandemic. A year of joy and reconciliation? And I think, *Do I stick with fear? Or move forward with hope?*

My faith tells me to move forward with hope. To trust in the living Word of God—and let Him be a light unto my path.

O God of the Past, Present, and Future, it is in You that I put my trust. Walk close with me in this coming year so that I might always keep my eyes of faith on You. Amen. —J. Brent Bill

Digging Deeper: Psalm 16:8–11; Romans 13, 15:4–6

YOU WERE CALLED TO PEACE

1 _____

2 _____

3 _____

4 _____

5 _____

6 _____

7 _____

8 _____

9 _____

10 _____

11 _____

12 _____

13 _____

14 _____

15 _____

16 _____

17 _____

18 _____

19 _____

20 _____

21 _____

22 _____

23 _____

24 _____

25 _____

26 _____

27 _____

28 _____

29 _____

30 _____

31 _____

FELLOWSHIP CORNER

As a teacher and student of God's Word, **Jerusha Agen** is awed by the letters of love the Father writes into every moment of our lives. Writing devotions is a special opportunity to sit down and focus her attention on this evidence of God at work. Jerusha loves to interweave such displays of God's providence into her suspense novels too. Her stories are infused with the hope of salvation in Jesus Christ. When Jerusha isn't writing, you'll often find her sharing irresistibly adorable photos of her big furry dogs and little furry cats in her newsletter and on social media. Get a free suspense story from Jerusha and find more of her writing at jerushaagen.com.

After spending much of the past year frantically searching for God's peace, **Marci Alborghetti** is finally coming to realize that it is not so much something to be grasped at but something to believe in. In facing her mother's final days after years of dementia and her own ongoing health challenges, she often found herself desperate for the Lord to take away her anxiety and pain and replace it with His peace. But this desperation only increased her anxiety and fear; with the calm help of her husband, Charlie, she is coming to understand that she needs, now more than ever, to place her faith in His faith, her hope in His hope, her love in His love. She has experienced great comfort in the kindness of friends and family members who reached out after her mother's death and during her own illness. She has enjoyed corresponding, both by old-fashioned letters and new-fashioned texts, with folks near and far.

 **Evelyn Bence** of Arlington, Virginia, writes: "What? I see I've been writing Guideposts devotionals for twenty years. I wonder if readers have been blessed by the anecdotes and their spiritual 'takeaways' as much as I have been, composing them. The children in my ethnically diverse neighborhood are growing up around me. One girl—now an older teen—looks to me as I help her interpret her world, which now includes vocational training and a part-time restaurant job. A highlight of this year was my hosting Easter dinner for a few friends. Yes, I've written a book about table hospitality—*Room at My Table*—but after Covid-related isolation, I'd lost my lifelong vision for welcoming guests. I like to think that I'm back. Maybe not with polished cutlery but with a welcome and smile."

The call to peace resonates in **Erika Bentsen's** crazy, unpredictable, wonderful life. Ambulance driving was a calling she didn't see coming. "My whole life changed because I accompanied my husband to the meeting! I figured if I can drive a stock trailer, I can handle an ambulance. Next thing I know, we're training as emergency medical responders. Now I'm considering becoming an EMT." Erika has a new appreciation of the first-responder network. "All throughout my ranching career, we had a 'grab-n-go' philosophy when it came to medical emergencies. From our training, I understand the value of pre-hospital care. This team I get to work with is amazing." Erika makes time to illustrate books in the midst of the chaos. *The Finest Gifts: A Christmas Story* about Jesus's birth has been translated into Spanish. Currently, she is collaborating with her niece, Haley, on a bedtime story for littles.

J. Brent Bill is a photographer, retreat leader, and Quaker minister. He's also the author of numerous books, including *Holy Silence: The Gift of Quaker Spirituality*; *Beauty, Truth, Life, and Love*; *Hope and Witness in Dangerous Times*; and

Life Lessons from a Bad Quaker. Bill is a graduate of Wilmington College and the Earlham School of Religion. He is recognized as one of the most important communicators of the spirituality of the Quaker tradition today. He is a member of *Spirituality & Practice*'s Living Spiritual Teachers Project. Of Bill's writing, one reviewer said that he's ". . . a substantial spiritual guide, but never in a flashy way. Think of, oh, perhaps something like Mister Rogers meets the Dalai Lama." He has been a local church pastor, a denominational executive, and a seminary faculty member. He lives on Ploughshares Farm, about forty acres of former Indiana farmland being converted into tall grass prairie and native hardwood forests.

"I have been busy," says **Rhoda Blecker**, "thanks to programs that put people together online rather than in person. I was already doing much of my work at home, but I had been missing the services and the committee meetings at the synagogue, so I was delighted when a virtual option became available there too." While the pandemic seclusion was a burden to some, Rhoda found it not very different from her usual life and appreciated it. "I never had to find a reason to say no to an invitation if I was really busy or tired. I didn't need to worry about hurting anyone's feelings when I just wanted serenity and quiet. It was actually a good year."

"This year has been busy with lots of extra projects, new friends, and new hobbies," says **Sabra Ciancanelli** of Tivoli, New York. "I rediscovered my love of painting this winter, taking an online class that rekindled the magic of getting lost in the creative process. My sons and husband are all doing well, and we are blessed with five healthy cats and a very sweet and tolerant blind dog. The other day when all of our kitchen appliances conked out, most likely sparked by a power surge, amazingly, I knew it wasn't worth getting stressed over. I said a prayer, not about the appliances, but one of thanks and grace for God's patience teaching me over the years, that despite the chaos or challenges life throws my way, I can calmly persevere if I take a deep breath and focus on my faith."

"I can readily attest to the mysteries of faith," notes **Mark Collins** of Pittsburgh, Pennsylvania. "Problem is, sometimes it really *is* a mystery—a genuine page-turner—but I can't skip the middle part to see how it ends." Mark's wife and three grown daughters keep him (mostly) grounded and present-tense, as does his part-time teaching job at the University of Pittsburgh. "Semi-retirement has taught me to accept the 'peace that passeth all understanding,'" says Mark, "but, at my age, my understanding gets passeth by a lot."

 "Interim pastoral ministry in Florida continues to be a rewarding and enjoyable experience," says **Pablo Diaz**. "We get a chance to make new friends and worship with different faith communities. The ministry and tradition of each congregation enriches us in many ways. We experience the presence and mission of God in places we never imagined living or serving. My wife, Elba, and I also appreciate the gift of discovering the history, landscape, shops, restaurants, and, of course, the beaches of each town. We are never alone because our adult children and extended family like coming to visit us, especially when it's cold back home. Moving every two years has it challenges. Packing and unpacking is not fun. Saying goodbye to people we have come to know and love is never easy. Yet the blessings outweigh the challenges. We don't know where our next place is going to be. God does, and that gives us peace."

"This was a road trip year for us," says **John Dilworth** of Massillon, Ohio. "Visiting Kentucky to experience the Ark Encounter and Creation Museum, exploring caves in Ohio's Hocking Hills, and an autumn trip around Lake Ontario to Watertown, New York. We drove from there through the Adirondack Mountains to Plattsburgh, New York, where I had served my first Air Force assignment. We left Plattsburgh on an early morning, fog-shrouded Lake Champlain ferry ride to Vermont. The drive across Vermont and New Hampshire thrilled us with fall color. While in New Hampshire, we visited family we hadn't seen in ages, and we also enjoyed a side trip to Portsmouth, where we had gotten married and I had completed my military service. We also stopped in Durham to see our first home. A lot had changed, but other things remained the same. The chapel where we married was torn down. The two Air Force bases where I served my first and last military assignments were both closed. But our first home was still painted the same color! And fall in New England is still radiant with magnificent colors. We are thankful for memories from new adventurers, time with family, and countless memories enjoyed from the past."

"This has been a year of reflection," says **Logan Eliasen**. "In the past, God has taught me to rely on Him in times of change. This year, I have learned to trust God when life remains the same. I often wish He would reveal His plans for me. But I am learning to wait, seeking Him in the stillness. I am grateful that the Lord is the One who both parts seas and leads His people beside quiet waters. And I desire to follow Him wherever he may guide me."

"Anchoring. It's been the year for our family to anchor down and thrive in our new home," says **Shawnelle Eliasen** of LeClaire, Iowa. "After two and a half years, we got an offer on our Victorian. The sale stretched over months and seemed uncertain, but once it went through, I knew that it was time to settle. There was a freedom. Our memories came along with us, and our new home has filled with fresh blessing." Shawnelle's husband, Lonny, spent a great portion of the year working in Europe. "We missed him like crazy," she says. "But it was dear to see the boys step into new roles and responsibilities. The Lord provided for everything we needed, and we all grew in faith."

"Holding onto joy. This has been one of the hardest things for me in the midst of many life changes and several experiences of loss," says **Nicole Garcia**. "However, God has been faithful. He has provided a reason to smile, even on the hardest days. He has blessed me with friends and family who have prayed me through. He has showed me beauty in both the starry and the sunny skies. I look for him and He is there, making a way where I thought there couldn't be one. Depending on Him more than myself has been my biggest challenge and reward. I am grateful for this season of life and the transforming moments that have been woven into my story. I've been mom, daughter, and wife, but I've also found some time for me. I have hurt, I have grown, and I have known His healing love. In every ending, there is also a beginning of something new."

Edward Grinnan is saddened to announce the passing of his wife of thirty-four years, Julee Cruise, whose love and humor supplied so much inspiration for his writing…and will continue to do so. "She's keeping an eye on me from heaven," he says. "I am certain of that." Edward, who is editor-in-chief of *Guideposts* magazine and vice president of strategic content development for Guideposts as an organization, recently finished his latest book—about his family's experience with Alzheimer's and his own susceptibility to the disease—and is at work on his next book. You can catch his blog at guideposts.org and listen to his meditative sleep stories on the Abide biblical meditation app. He and his golden retriever, Gracie, split their time between Manhattan and the Berkshires of western Massachusetts. "Life never slows down, even in tragedy," says Edward. "And that's a blessing."

"Different stages of life offer new challenges and new joys," writes **Rick Hamlin**, "and we certainly have experienced the latter as we've been launched into grandparenthood, with two grandsons born five months apart coast-to-coast. We've got Silas, a good biblical name, only half a block away, and Baby Ricky—can the world cope with another Rick Hamlin?—in San Francisco. Silas's dad, our younger son, Tim, is in his third year at Union Seminary in his call to become an Episcopal priest, and Ricky's dad, our older son, Will, works for Pinterest. Their spouses, Henley and Karen, respectively, are great moms, dedicated career women, and matchless daughters-in-law. Honoring and seeking the peace of God is certainly at the center of my spiritual life. I start each day with half an hour of meditative prayer, a practice I've been able to share in many church talks and in my book, *Even Silence Is Praise*. Indeed, 'practice' is the operative word. Carol and I continue to sing in the choir and worship at the church where we were wed some forty years ago."

Lynne Hartke often hears the Sonoran Desert, where she lives, described as a desolate, godforsaken place. After three decades of exploring desert trails with her husband, Kevin, and rust-colored mutt, Mollie, Lynne has encountered the beauty found in barren places, a beauty enjoyed by the couple's four grown children and four grandchildren. A breast cancer survivor, Lynne was named a Voice of Hope with the American Cancer Society in 2018. She anticipates more adventures near the hundred-year-old cabin they purchased in an old-growth forest in northern Arizona. Lynne is a pastor's wife, speaker, and author of *Under a Desert Sky: Redefining Hope, Beauty, and Faith in the Hardest Places*. Connect with her at lynnehartke.com.

"This has been quite the year," says **Carla Hendricks** of Franklin, Tennessee. "I celebrated the first anniversary of my career as a social worker, serving and advocating for foster children in juvenile court. I support the nonprofit my husband, Anthony, cofounded that exists to educate our community on racial justice, equity, and healing. My oldest son continues to write Christian music and work in the field of video production. My youngest son recently left home with dreams of an acting career in Los Angeles. My youngest daughter is preparing to enter her first year of high school, while my other daughter will enter her senior year. I continue to pursue writing opportunities to encourage and inspire readers every opportunity I can, including contributing to *Walking in Grace*. Add to this equation parenting and attempting to maintain a decent household, and I'm exhausted just sharing all this!"

"*Daily Guideposts'* new title, *Walking in Grace,* is a beautiful summation of how I see my life," says **Kim Taylor Henry**. "God has blessed me richly—so much more than I deserve. While the pandemic put a (hopefully temporary) halt to the international travel my husband and I love to do, it provided us even more time to spend with our adult children and their spouses and our grandchildren—an even greater blessing than travel! We cherish every moment with them. We spent a lot of time playing games, watching the kids' games (especially ice hockey and soccer), taking walks, hiking, family dinners, going to our daughter Rachel's jumper horseshows, and just enjoying everyday life with all fifteen of us (eight adults and seven children!). Times in the world are hard, but life is still good, so incredibly good, as I walk each day in His grace. Please say hi through my website at kimtaylorhenry. com, or my email, kim@kimtaylorhenry.com."

 **Leanne Jackson** of Fishers, Indiana, says, "My first prayer every day is 'thank you.'" This year, Leanne has been thankful for the physical therapist who figured out the cause of her hip pain. And the surgeon who replaced her "bone-on-bone" hip joint. And her family and friends, including *Walking in Grace* readers, who pray for her. And those who gently taught her to be the care recipient for a while, after her lifetime of being the caregiver. "While waiting for surgery, I wrote these devotions. Stories about walking and gardening reminded me that I would get back to those activities, without pain, and I did!" Leanne looks forward to meeting you at leannejacksonwrites. com.

This past year has been a season of transitions for **Erin Janoso's** family. After spending her K–2 years as a homeschooler, Aurora joined a "regular school's" third grade this past September. She's thriving there, and especially enjoys her art and music classes. Jim has continued his microscopy work, as well as his involvement with the Interior Alaska Wilderness Search and Rescue. Jim's parents made the big move from the Allentown, Pennsylvania, home where they'd lived for 50+ years and raised their three children, to central Montana, so they could live closer to their grandchildren. "We've enjoyed getting to spend more time with Jim's parents," says Erin, "gardening, visiting, and doing puzzles." Erin continues to love playing her trumpet in various community groups. She has added substitute teaching and volunteering with a Fairbanks music education advocacy committee to her list of favorite activities. "As a family, we are happy to get to spend the school year in Fairbanks and the summers in Montana with family now that Jim's parents have moved. It truly is a situation that allows us to enjoy the best of both worlds."

This year has been one of contentment for **Ashley Kappel**. She finds joy in the everydayness of raising children, working full time, loving an aging dog, and spending time with her husband, Brian. The blessing of feeling at peace in her home isn't lost on Ashley; she is grateful for it every day and prays that it continues as long as the Lord wills. When she catches a moment, she enjoys daily walks with Brian, reading Jodi Picoult novels, and cooking with her kids. But mostly she's reading chapters before bedtime, making the forty-fifth meal of the week, and setting new records for loads of unfolded laundry. And that's OK, because there's glory in the ordinary, and she's more than happy to savor a little boring in the bustle of this phase of life. She prays you, too, find your glory in the ordinary this year.

 **Jenny Lynn Keller** is an award-winning author who transforms her family's rowdy adventures into stories filled with hope, humor, and plenty of Southern charm. On her website, jennylynnkeller.com, she highlights Southern folklore and places of interest through a weekly blog. Her beloved true animal stories appear in Callie Smith Grant's compilations *The Horse of My Dreams*, *The Dog Who Came to Christmas*, and *The Cat in the Christmas Tree*. Follow her on facebook.com/jennylynnkeller.

"Life continues its joyous ride," reports **Brock Kidd** from Nashville, Tennessee. "While my hometown continues to rapidly grow around us, so do our children." Brock's oldest son, Harrison, graduated from George Washington University last spring. "As Harrison enters the real world, our youngest son, David, is entering kindergarten! As busy as my wife, Corinne, and I are, we still manage a little prayer time at the dinner table together most nights and are reminded of the value of being called to peace."

"Early in our marriage, my parents were frequent visitors to the defunct coal-mining community where David and I chose to serve," says **Pam Kidd** of Nashville, Tennessee. "I'll never forget one old coal miner's description of them as 'the most joyfullest couple 'mongst one another.' I'd like to think that David and I have inherited this distinction, because life for us is joyful indeed. Together, we build upon the remarkable project that began as 'saving a few AIDS orphans' in Zimbabwe. With the support of many Guideposts readers, we are even building a school on our Village Hope farm, adding a grade a year. Already at grade eight, we have fed, clothed, and educated more children than we can count. Together, we also run a progressive organization in Nashville that meets monthly, featuring great speakers who introduce us to new ways to serve our brothers and sisters in a hurting world. And then there's our son and daughter, who have connected us to a struggling black university, American Baptist College, where some of the great civil rights accomplishments took root. Happiness exudes from our focus there. Add our family and our six grandchildren, and, well, joy flows 'amongst one another' and life is good."

After running injuries and bike accidents, **Patty Kirk** started exercising this year on her husband Kris's elliptical. Without birds, flowers, and trees to admire and nothing but an iPad on the elliptical's shelf to motivate her, her exercise regimen was not as fun or spiritually uplifting as all those years of running and bicycling had been. There was one good outcome, though. At first, Patty gave in to her lifelong temptation to binge on true crime shows as an enticement to spend an hour on an indoor exercise machine. Combatting this temptation was the sole reason she's never subscribed to TV. There was plenty of true crime to be had online. Soon, though, she found such shows too sickening to watch first thing in the morning, and—as if in answer to a lifetime of "lead us not into temptations"—the desire, magically, vanished. Instead, one game of spider solitaire per workout motivates her, leaving the day blessedly free for writing, grading papers, gardening, cooking, sewing—in short, everything she'd prefer to spend her time doing.

 **Carol Knapp** of Priest River, Idaho, is loving life amid the forested mountains. She and her husband, Terry, woke one morning to a small herd of elk among the trees out their window. They are grateful for the firefighters who contained a wildfire near their town last summer. They lost a beloved brother-in-law to cancer—but took heart in his unwavering faith. Carol was overjoyed with a floral bouquet Terry presented her on their fiftieth wedding anniversary—two yellow roses for them, four red for their children, and twenty white carnations representing their grandchildren! A wonderful opportunity to trust the peace of Christ arose when their son Phil and his family were told their local rental home was being sold. Housing was scarce. Carol got to participate in the answer to her own prayer through finding a rental ad she would not have ordinarily seen and contacting the owner. Their son moved into the new

home within two weeks! An exciting upcoming event is the graduation of grandson Caleb from Bible school—at least the sixth generation in the family to "carry the call" of bringing God's Word to others.

"I'm living in a season with greater perspective of all of life's seasons," says **Carol Kuykendall** of Boulder, Colorado. "Most recently, my husband, Lynn, suffered a minor stroke, which is shaping our lives because he no longer drives. He's turned in his car keys and passed his car down to our son's family of six, with four who have driver's licenses. They are so appreciative, which helps Lynn with his memory of the day that car drove out of our driveway. I'm faced with questions about whether to do all I've always done. At the same pace. How do I retire from being involved in leadership of the MOPS group at our church? I don't. How do I cut back on writing or speaking because the 'doing' can take more time? I don't. How do I let others host some of the family gatherings because the 'cleanups' are challenging? I don't because I love having the 'homestead house' filled with the chaotic sounds of three generations of people who enjoy being together. This is a precious season of life, and Lynn and I thank God for the gifts He continues to give us."

"Although this year I've continued the writing career I began over thirty-five years ago, it's taken a back seat to caring for my three granddaughters, Taylor, Lula, and Shea," says **Vicki Kuyper** of Colorado Springs, Colorado. "I never imagined I'd be busier in my Medicare years than back when I had young children of my own, but God always has surprised me with the unexpected. On occasion, travel is still on my agenda, but more times than not, it's to visit my two grandsons, Xander and Oliver, who live a couple of states away. Of course, writing for *Walking in Grace* continues to be part of my abbreviated freelance schedule. I so enjoy putting into words the ways I see God at work throughout the changing seasons of my life. It's like keeping a very public journal. Having the opportunity to share my firsthand experiences with other members of the Guideposts family serves as a daily reminder to keep my eyes and heart open, expectantly ready to catch a glimpse of God's hand at work in the world."

"Seems like the older I get, the more determined I am to get even older," says **Patricia Lorenz** of Largo, Florida. In October of this year, Patricia will be turning seventy-nine.

"In order to live longer than my dad, who made it to ninety-eight, I want to protect all the delicate systems of my body that God created. So I continue to swim in the big pool across the street and do the water aerobics class for at least two hours a day, six days a week. From May through October, I'm jumping in the waves of the Gulf of Mexico, praising God with all the joy that overcomes me when I'm in the ocean." Patricia enjoys the occasional bike ride, tries to walk at least a mile many days, takes a good nap four or five days a week, drinks lots of water, and, most important of all, socializes with friends four or five times a week. "Having a group of friends I can laugh with makes getting older even more joyful. Traveling to California, Wisconsin, and Ohio to see my four kids and nine grands is another joyful thing that puts a spring in my step. I am blessed indeed."

 **Debbie Macomber** is a #1 *New York Times* bestselling author and one of today's most popular writers, with more than 200 million copies of her books in print worldwide. In addition to fiction, Macomber has also published three bestselling cookbooks, an adult coloring book, numerous inspirational and nonfiction works, and two acclaimed children's books. Celebrated as "the

official storyteller of Christmas," Macomber's annual Christmas books are beloved, and five have been crafted into original Hallmark Channel movies. She serves on the Guideposts National Advisory Cabinet, is a YFC National Ambassador, and is World Vision's international spokesperson for their Knit for Kids charity initiative. A devoted grandmother, Debbie and her husband, Wayne, live in Port Orchard, Washington, the town that inspired the Cedar Cove series.

Instead of summer-camp drop-offs and teddy bear picnics, **Erin MacPherson** now spends her time sitting in coffee shops sipping espresso milkshakes, visiting colleges, and cheering the team on at high-school football games. With two teenagers (and one pre-teen), trusting God in every detail has become the only way to survive. Erin lives in Austin, Texas, with her husband, three kids, and two golden retrievers, and can be found on Facebook at Author Erin MacPherson.

Tia McCollors continues to enjoy being a part of the Guideposts family and appreciates the many emails she receives from the devoted readers who grew up with Guideposts and now continue the rich traditions with their own families. As a wife and mother of three, she challenges her family to try something new each year and to push themselves out of their comfort zone. One of her proudest accomplishments was recently learning to swim at the age of forty-eight. Tia still enjoys Mexican food, fresh flowers, movie marathons on rainy days, and novels. She expresses her creative side through writing, speaking, and trying new recipes and DIY projects that she finds on Pinterest. You can connect with Tia online at tiamccollors.com, through her "Fans of Tia" Facebook page, or follow her on Instagram @TMcCollors.

Colossians 3:15 (NIV), "Let the peace of Christ rule in your hearts…" became especially meaningful for **Roberta Messner** this year as she traveled while recovering from surgery. "Walking was really difficult," she says, "but the driver who transported me from my hotel to the airport was the kindest, most peaceful man. It was early morning, and I hadn't had my coffee. We had the best time of fellowship while sipping our delicious drinks." Before Roberta left his sedan, he asked God to give her a future of wonderful health. At her connecting flight, there was a text from the

faith-filled driver, assuring her of his prayers for safety. Back home, Roberta mailed him the best thank-you present she could think of: his very own copy of *Walking in Grace* to keep him company on the job.

 **Gabrielle Meyer** grew up above a carriage house on a historic estate near the banks of the Mississippi River. Her father was the caretaker and her mother homeschooled her and her siblings. Her parents instilled in her a deep faith and appreciation for family. Gabrielle went on to work for the Minnesota Historical Society, where she fell in love with the rich history of her state. That love inspired her to write fiction and nonfiction inspired by real people, places, and events. She currently resides in central Minnesota on the banks of the upper Mississippi River, not far from where she grew up, with her husband and four children, including teenage daughters and twin boys. By day, she's a homeschool mom and a small business owner, and by night she pens fiction and nonfiction filled with hope. Her work currently includes historical and contemporary romances, cozy mysteries, and home and family devotions. You can

learn more about Gabrielle and her writing by visiting gabriellemeyer.com.

 "It's been a time of change," says **Rebecca Ondov** of Hamilton, Montana. "The chickens are gone (a raccoon ate them) as well as my cat, Stealth (I think he was an appetizer for the mountain lion before the lion ate the goat next door). I also said goodbye to my constant companion for nearly a quarter of my life—my golden retriever, Sunrise. Yet with the goodbyes come opportunities for new beginnings. My German shepherd, Willow, is growing out of her puppy brain and into an amazing companion. And I decided to foster Paco, a six-pound poodle, for friends who are between homes and living in a rental that doesn't accept dogs. Yes, a seventy-six-pound German shepherd and a six-pound poodle—let the circus begin! On evenings and weekends, I love to garden, hike, kayak, and horseback ride. I'm also hosting Biblical Citizenship and Constitution classes through Patriot Academy. And still working my job of brokering lumber. Life is exciting as every day we get closer to the end-of-days. And the best is yet to come! I love it when you connect with me on social

media or by email. You can find out how through my website, rebeccaondov.com."

Shirley Raye Redmond has sold articles to such publications as *Focus on the Family Magazine*, *Home Life*, *The Christian Standard*, and *Chicken Soup for the Soul*. Her writing has appeared in multiple Guideposts devotionals as well as two Guideposts mystery series—*Savannah Secrets* and *Secrets from Grandma's Attic*. Her children's book *Courageous World Changers: 50 True Stories of Daring Women of God* (Harvest House) won the 2021 Christianity Today Book Award in its category. Her most recent book is *Courageous and Bold Heroes of the Bible* (Harvest House). She has been married for forty-seven years to her college sweetheart, Bill. They are blessed with two adult children and their spouses, plus five adorable grandchildren. They all live in New Mexico, where they enjoy chicken-stuffed sopapillas with green chile.

Ginger Rue is starting to feel old. "Our oldest child is now a college graduate, and our other two are in college," she says. "It's weird to me how I still feel like I'm in my twenties myself…until I hear my knees cracking or find myself complaining about the small print on recipes!" Still, she's enjoying this new phase of life. "Now that the children are doing their own thing (or perhaps I should say, 'now that they've managed to pry themselves from my grasp'!), my husband and I spend more time doing things together. It's wonderful to share life with my sweetheart."

 **Dr. Adam Ruiz**, a native of San Antonio, currently serves as a chaplain with Norton Healthcare in Louisville, Kentucky. An avid writer, his journal entries from the early days of the Covid-19 pandemic are included in an e-book, *In Their Own Words: Stories of Chaplains' Courage, Creativity, and Compassion During the Early Pandemic*, published by Transforming Chaplaincy, Inc., in 2022. Dr. Ruiz finds this year's *Walking in Grace* theme, "Called to Peace," especially meaningful in the light of our current world situation—as he was working on this edition, the eyes of the world were on the war in Ukraine, and a school shooting in Uvalde, Texas, was only one of many violent events that sparked public mourning. At a recent presentation, Dr. Ruiz shared with the attendees how God is calling him to a deeper spiritual practice of "blessing the power of Good." He disclosed that this new spiritual discipline gives him greater clarity and strength in his daily life. He

invites all Guideposts readers to prayerfully and intentionally join him in "blessing the power of Good" in their lives.

"My wife, Kate, and I continue to be thankful to see our children grow into such responsible adults, whose lifestyles and values build up others and reflect the best values," says **Kenneth Sampson**. "Receiving spiritual direction, a first for me, from Brother Randy of Holy Cross Monastery keeps me tethered to a monastic community of saints. I've lost a dear mentor this past year—high school coach, English teacher, and lifelong friend Will Byker. The August collapse of Afghanistan, where I served as chaplain in 2002 and 2003 to 2004, was especially difficult. We took one of our first post-pandemic trips to Hawaii, where with gratitude I officiated at the wedding of niece Kimberly and new husband, Edison. The 'mahalo' (appreciation, admiration) experience was dear. We remain thankful for God's peace in all the ups and downs of this past year."

Great-grandson Samuel August was born to **Daniel Schantz's** oldest grandchild, Hannah, in 2021. She and husband, John, live in Columbia, Missouri, which is just thirty-eight miles south of Moberly, where Dan and Sharon reside, so they often get to see the little "wonder boy." The Schantzes find peace and pleasure in their leisurely day trips, like the one to The Crazy Redhead Quilt Shop in Newton, Iowa. On the way, they stopped at rummage sales and Amish candy stores and enjoyed ice cream cones at Elena's in Bloomfield, Iowa. While Sharon shopped for fabric, Dan visited a tree nursery, where he bought a Montmorency cherry tree, which was a little too large for their Ford Escape, but Sharon is used to traveling with tree leaves in her hair. The best part of day trips is sleeping in their own bed at night.

Last year, **Gail Thorell Schilling** of Concord, New Hampshire, felt called to offer spiritual writing classes in addition to regular memoir. "Affirming writers' most profound experiences and giving them a safe place to share their stories is more of a gift than I expected. Remote connection makes gathering easier than ever." Gail is eager to meet her new granddaughter in Los Angeles and hopes to visit her grandson, who has lived in Singapore for two years. In the meantime, she feels blessed to enjoy weekly play dates with her grand-daughter twenty-five minutes away, at least until she starts kindergarten. "When we make fairy villages with acorns and moss, God seems very near." Follow Gail on gailthorellschilling.com.

 "The peace of Christ is my close companion as I've learned to be content living alone," writes **Penney Schwab** of Copeland, Kansas. "I kept my late husband, Don's, gorgeous flower beds up for a year but have now transitioned them to perennials—my favorite is blue flax—for easier maintenance. While I wouldn't say I enjoy doing house and yard work, I'm thankful to have the physical strength to do most things and family, friends, and neighbors to do tractor mowing, cleaning the round-top barn, and other tasks I can't. My dog, Pepper, is a challenge. We're still working on 'Don't knock me down!' and 'Stop chewing everything!' but she is also a joyful companion. Our small but active church is a blessing. I help with afterschool Joy Club most Wednesdays and often teach children's Sunday school. I love to read, enjoy playing bridge occasionally, and am on the Copeland Community Foundation Board. I am especially thankful to have been part of the Guideposts family since 1979 and grateful for the editors, other writers, and readers for their help and support."

Buck Storm didn't exactly tell the truth on the Los Angeles apartment application when he and his wife married in 1989. He listed his profession as "writer." He figured it wasn't much of a stretch—after all, he wrote songs and would get to books eventually. But life often sidetracks. Those songs wound up taking him and Michelle around the globe. It took twenty-five years and a lot of miles for Buck to become a novelist but, several books in now, he finally made good on that application. Buck spends his days writing and spending time with Michelle, his grown children, and two granddaughters. His nights are often out playing music with popular Northwest band The Buckley Storms, a songwriting collaboration project with his son, Ransom. God's mercies are new every morning, and Buck is blessed beyond words. "Thank You, Jesus," prays Buck often. "I feel Your arm around my shoulder. You are good. And the best part is knowing the journey will never end!" Buck is an award-winning literary fiction author, musician, and traveler. His books and songs have made friends around the world.

Jolynda Strandberg serves as a director of religious education who has spent twenty-five years as a civilian with the military. She and her family currently reside in Clarksville, Tennessee. She is also a proud wife and mom to three children, ages twenty-nine, twelve, and eight. It has been a busy year of traveling to horse shows as a family.

Jon M. Sweeney lives in Milwaukee with his wife, daughter, and the two cats they adopted as kittens during the pandemic who now expect too much attention. During the last year, they moved from the suburbs into the city and now live on a busy street, and closer to some of the city's problems. Jon has recently published a book of Franciscan spirituality, *Feed the Wolf*, and edited a collection of anecdotes about one of his heroes, Thomas Merton, called *Awake and Alive*.

This year's *Walking in Grace* theme, "Called to Peace" is close to **Stephanie Thompson's** heart since her daughter, Micah, went to college in the fall, leaving Stephanie and her husband all alone as empty nesters. "Our house is much more peaceful without a busy teen around," confided Stephanie. Not only has their only child moved out, but also there are no more weekly soccer games or school or church activities for them to attend together as a family. "It was relatively easy for me to get used to a quiet house, but it's another type of peace that God is teaching me about," she explained. "Micah is an outspoken and opinionated young adult. For the sake of our relationship, God is directing me to listen more and talk less to preserve the peace." Stephanie and her husband, Michael, live in an Oklahoma City suburb with a schweenie (shih tzu/dachshund mix) named Missy and two fun felines: Mr. Whiskers, a congenial tuxedo cat who appeared on the driveway one cold December day in 2013, and Ron, a playful orange tabby who came to live with them during the first year of the pandemic.

"I often pray for peace when I have deadlines or troubling situations to deal with. If I didn't, the stress would undo me. Thank God for the peace He gives me when I need it." In addition to writing devotions, **Marilyn Turk** writes historical and contemporary fiction seasoned with suspense and romance. She and her husband are lighthouse enthusiasts and have visited over one hundred lighthouses, as well as serving as volunteer lighthouse caretakers on an island off the coast of Maine, so expect to find a lighthouse in each of her books. When not writing or visiting lighthouses, Marilyn enjoys walking, boating, fishing, gardening, tennis, and playing with her grandkids and her golden retriever, Dolly. She is a member of American Christian Fiction Writers; Faith, Hope and Love Christian Writers; Advanced Writers and Speakers Association; Word Weavers International; and the United States Lighthouse Society. She'd love to connect with you on social media or her website, pathwayheart.com.

"It's a season of change and milestones," says **Karen Valentin** of New York, New York. "My oldest son will be going to high school, my parents are living with me as they grow older and need more help, and I'm nearing my fiftieth birthday. My life, which once marked the beginning of new chapters, is now marking its end— the end of childhood for my boys, the end my own youth, the last years of life for my mom and dad. And while I wrestle with my emotions of what these changes will bring, the one thing that keeps coming up is gratitude. As scary as it can be, I find peace in remembering all the blessings, experiences, and moments of love that led us to the season we are in today."

This has been a busy year for **Scott Walker** and his wife, Beth. It seems they suddenly have four grandchildren—two boys and two girls between the ages one and ten! They are discovering that being grandparents is the wonderful thing that everyone promised it would be. Much "easier" than being parents! And the future is so bright. Scott is retired from teaching and directing the Institute of Life Purpose at Mercer University. Much to his surprise, he has discovered that he really does like this new chapter of life. He is in the midst of finishing a biography of the chancellor of Mercer University, Dr. Kirby Godsey, and will soon be starting work on another book manuscript. He also continues to enjoy writing for the Guideposts family, which has brought him so much pleasure through the years. Beth has also retired from working with international students at Mercer University. Now she works just as hard relating to international students through the ministry of their church. So, Scott and Beth have not really "retired"! They have just re-engaged in the work and ministry that they love.

Jacqueline F. Wheelock saw her wanderlust diminished somewhat during the pandemic, but recently the need to see her granddaughter, Selah, in Florida—along with the turquoise beaches that just happen to come with the package—has caused her to brave the fourteen hours of interstate driving. With the promised crocheted "kitty-kat" on the back seat and God's abundant grace steadying her hand at the wheel, Jacqueline managed to arrive having spent only one night on the road. (Incidentally, her eight-year-old granddaughter never concerns herself about the mileage covered. Only the promises kept.) Lately, however, Jacqueline's love for travel is pointing toward the opposite direction. She's looking forward to exploring parts of America's West and, in so doing, perhaps avoid, for once, the severe seasonal allergies in her own state. New scenery, different cultural nuances, and an enriched understanding of history—all while capturing proof with her cell phone camera—never disappoint. "And, as with most every other part of the world I've seen," she says, "God's presence is likely to push me toward pen and paper while I'm there."

 **Gayle T. Williams** is a native New Yorker, now living in the city's suburbs with her husband and her rescue cat, Solomon. She has two adult sons and is a faithful member of New York Covenant Church in New Rochelle, New York. She is a full-time editor and writer who has worked for

local and regional newspapers, a national magazine, and an academic medical center, but it's her work for Guideposts that truly feeds her soul. Still a news junkie, she enjoys a good crossword puzzle, all kinds of games that expand her vocabulary, and public radio programming. She is honored to be able to share God's blessings upon her life with the dedicated readers of Guideposts, and loves hearing from them.

SCRIPTURE REFERENCE INDEX

AUTHORS, TITLES, AND SUBJECTS INDEX

A NOTE FROM THE EDITORS

We hope you enjoyed *Walking in Grace,* published by Guideposts. For over seventy-five years, Guideposts, a nonprofit organization, has been driven by a vision of a world filled with hope. We aspire to be the voice of a trusted friend, a friend who makes you feel more hopeful and connected.

By making a purchase from Guideposts, you join our community in touching millions of lives, inspiring them to believe that all things are possible through faith, hope, and prayer. Your continued support allows us to provide uplifting resources to those in need. Whether through our communities, websites, apps, or publications, we inspire our audiences, bring them together, and comfort, uplift, entertain, and guide them. Visit us at guideposts.org to learn more.

We would love to hear from you. Write us at Guideposts, P.O. Box 5815, Harlan, Iowa 51593 or call us at (800) 932-2145. Did you love *Walking in Grace?* Leave a review for this product on guideposts.org/shop. Your feedback helps others in our community find relevant products.

Find inspiration, find faith, find Guideposts.

Shop our best sellers and favorites at
guideposts.org/shop
Or scan the QR code to go directly to our Shop